SENSUAL EXCESS

SEXUAL CULTURES

General Editors: Ann Pellegrini, Tavia Nyong'o, and Joshua Chambers-Letson

Founding Editors: José Esteban Muñoz and Ann Pellegrini

Titles in the series include:

Times Square Red, Times Square Blue
Samuel R. Delany

Private Affairs: Critical Ventures in the Culture of Social Relations
Phillip Brian Harper

In Your Face: 9 Sexual Studies
Many Merck

Tropics of Desire: Interventions from Queer Latino America
José A. Quiroga

Murdering Masculinities: Fantasies of Gender and Violence in the American Crime Novel
Gregory Forter

Our Monica, Ourselves: The Clinton Affair and the National Interest
Edited by Lauren Berlant and Lisa A. Duggan

Black Gay Man: Essays
Robert F. Reid-Pharr

Passing: Identity and Interpretation in Sexuality, Race, and Religion
Edited by Maria C. Sanchez and Linda Schlossberg

The Explanation for Everything: Essays on Sexual Subjectivity
Paul Morrison

The Queerest Art: Essays on Lesbian and Gay Theater
Edited by Alisa Solomon and Framji Minwalla

Queer Globalizations: Citizenship and the Afterlife of Colonialism
Edited by Arnaldo Cruz Malavé and Martin F. Manalansan IV

Queer Latinidad: Identity Practices, Discursive Spaces
Juana María Rodríguez

Love the Sin: Sexual Regulation and the Limits of Religious Tolerance
Janet R. Jakobsen and Ann Pellegrini

Boricua Pop: Puerto Ricans and the Latinization of American Culture
Frances Négron-Muntaner

Manning the Race: Reforming Black Men in the Jim Crow Era
Marlon Ross

In a Queer Time and Place: Transgender Bodies, Subcultural Lives
J. Jack Halberstam

Why I Hate Abercrombie and Fitch: Essays on Race and Sexuality
Dwight A. McBride

God Hates Fags: The Rhetorics of Religious Violence
Michael Cobb

Once You Go Black: Choice, Desire, and the Black American Intellectual
Robert Reid-Pharr

The Latino Body: Crisis Identities in American Literary and Cultural Memory
Lázaro Lima

Arranging Grief: Sacred Time and the Body in Nineteenth-Century America
Dana Luciano

Cruising Utopia: The Then and There of Queer Futurity
José Esteban Muñoz

Another Country: Queer Anti-Urbanism
Scott Herring

Extravagant Abjection: Blackness, Power, and Sexuality in the African American Literary Imagination
Darieck Scott

Relocations: Queer Suburban Imaginaries
Karen Tongson

Beyond the Nation: Diasporic Filipino Literature and Queer Reading
Martin Joseph Ponce

Single: Arguments for the Uncoupled
Michael Cobb

Brown Boys and Rice Queens: Spellbinding Performance in the Asias
Eng-Beng Lim

Transforming Citizenships: Transgender Articulations of the Law
Isaac West

The Delectable Negro: Human Consumption and Homoeroticism within US Slave Culture
Vincent Woodard, Edited by Justin A. Joyce and Dwight A. McBride

Sexual Futures, Queer Gestures and Other Latina Longings
Juana María Rodríguez

Sensational Flesh: Race, Power, and Masochism
Amber Jamilla Musser

The Exquisite Corpse of Asian America: Biopolitics, Biosociality, and Posthuman Ecologies
Rachel C. Lee

Not Gay: Sex between Straight White Men
Jane Ward

Embodied Avatars: Genealogies of Black Feminist Art and Performance
Uri McMillan

A Taste for Brown Bodies: Gay Modernity and Cosmopolitan Desire
Hiram Pérez

Wedlocked: The Perils of Marriage Equality
Katherine Franke

The Color of Kink: Black Women, BDSM, and Pornography
Ariane Cruz

Archives of Flesh: African America, Spain, and Post-Humanist Critique
Robert F. Reid-Pharr

Black Performance on the Outskirts of the Left: A History of the Impossible
Malik Gaines

A Body, Undone: Living on After Great Pain
Christina Crosby

The Life and Death of Latisha King: A Critical Phenomenlogy of Transphobia
Gayle Salamon

Queer Nuns: Religion, Activism, and Serious Parody
Melissa M. Wilcox

After the Party: A Manifesto for Queer of Color Life
Joshua Chambers-Letson

Sensual Excess: Queer Femininity and Brown Jouissance
Amber Jamilla Musser

For a complete list of books in the series, see www.nyupress.org

Sensual Excess

Queer Femininity and Brown Jouissance

Amber Jamilla Musser

NEW YORK UNIVERSITY PRESS
New York

NEW YORK UNIVERSITY PRESS
New York
www.nyupress.org

© 2018 by New York University
All rights reserved

References to Internet websites (URLs) were accurate at the time of writing. Neither the author nor New York University Press is responsible for URLs that may have expired or changed since the manuscript was prepared.

Library of Congress Cataloging-in-Publication Data
Names: Musser, Amber Jamilla, author.
Title: Sensual excess : queer femininity and brown jouissance / Amber Jamilla Musser.
Description: New York : New York University, [2018] | Series: Sexual cultures | Includes bibliographical references and index.
Identifiers: LCCN 2018011913 | ISBN 9781479807031 (cl : alk. paper) | ISBN 9781479830954 (pb : alk. paper)
Subjects: LCSH: Lesbianism. | Sexual excitement.
Classification: LCC HQ75.5 .M87 2018 | DDC 306.76/63—dc23
LC record available at https://lccn.loc.gov/2018011913

New York University Press books are printed on acid-free paper, and their binding materials are chosen for strength and durability. We strive to use environmentally responsible suppliers and materials to the greatest extent possible in publishing our books.

Manufactured in the United States of America

10 9 8 7 6 5 4 3 2 1

Also available as an ebook

This book is dedicated to dialogue, plurality, being-with, and most especially, MA.

CONTENTS

Introduction: Brown Jouissance and Inhabitations
of the Pornotrope — 1

1. Eating Out: The Labial, Consumption, and the Scalar — 27

2. Surface Play: Flash, Friction, and Self-Reflection — 46

3. Deep Listening, Belonging, and the Pleasures
of Brown Jouissance — 69

4. Performing Witness: Voice, Interiority, and Diaspora — 95

5. Weeping Machines: Automaticity, Looping, and the
Possibilities of Perversion — 119

6. Femme Aggression and the Value of Labor — 144

Coda: Elsewhere, Is the Mother a Place? — 167

Acknowledgments — 181

Notes — 185

Bibliography — 205

Index — 221

About the Author — 237

Lyle Ashton Harris, *Billie #21*, 2002.

Introduction

Brown Jouissance and Inhabitations of the Pornotrope

On the cover of this book and the facing page we see what appears to be a gesture of abandonment—head tilted back, lips, eyes, and collarbone gleaming. This is a posture that belongs to the ecstatic. The closed eyes are signs of a private reverie while the open mouth suggests excess. These are pleasures that cannot be contained; their expression exceeds the frame. Yet, these pleasures are also inscrutable. This is a photograph in media res; we see only this moment; we have no way of discerning or deciphering the source of this pleasure. We can imagine that she is singing for herself even as the light in the distance suggests an unseen crowd. The fur's fuzz, the sharpness of the teeth, the low haze in the background, and the mouth sighing open all point us toward mystery.

This is *Billie #21* (2002), a photograph by Lyle Ashton Harris. It is meant to conjure Billie Holiday, and this changes things. We might, for example, begin to imagine that we understand some of these private pleasures because we know facts about Holiday and her life. We might ask if this is the Holiday of Emerson's Bar and Grill—high and drunk, stumbling and slurring words and emotions as she remembers a history in the limelight and the various betrayals, arrests, and addictions that altered her relationship to stardom. Is this the Holiday of Carnegie Hall—wounded and rambling and so eager for a comeback that she accidentally punctured her head with a hatpin attached to gardenias? Is this a younger Holiday, just beginning to sing in jazz clubs after a youth spent in brothels? Holiday is iconic. Her voice famously layers pain and yearning; it is seductive in its excesses. In his description of Holiday's singing, Fred Moten argues that she brings something new to the fore, something extra-linguistic, something that is not about communication, but something that he describes as the "repetition of suffocated desire and lost object, of transference and drive, that would tell the audience what they want to hear and what they already know."[1] This is to say, as Farah Jasmine Griffin reminds us, that the lure of Holiday's voice and even our attachment to Holiday herself tells us much more about how Holiday circulates as a public figure than anything about Holiday. In particular, Holiday is expected to index—in a formation that Moten describes as what the audience "want[s] to hear and what they already know"—something about the relationship between black women and pain and pleasure.[2] *Billie #21* elicits these histories of woundedness even as it allows us to imagine an inhabitation that exists in excess of them—an excess in Holiday's voice, an excess of selfhood that cannot be fully subsumed by her iconicity and public self.

However, Holiday's voice can never emerge from this photograph—not because of a failure of imagination, but because the self on display is Harris, not Holiday. Even as it recalls one of Holiday's more iconic images, it is Harris who performs this homage to the famous jazz singer. It is Harris who evokes Holiday's mid-century style by wearing light flowers pinned to one side over closely cropped hair, a single strand of pearls, and a white fur nestled around his shoulders. It is Harris's head that tilts back. Through posture, make-up, and props, Harris allows us to conjure Holiday as a mode of dual embodiment, a citation, if you will. The photograph's foregrounding of gloss—the shimmering accents indicating the fullness of lips, the edges of teeth, the tip of a nose, the crease of an eyelid, and the sheen of pearls—aids in the summoning of Holiday's iconicity even as this shininess undercuts straightforward notions of authenticity or transparency. This performative self-portrait tells us a lot about the strategic possibilities of selfhood.

Amelia Jones argues that by "exaggerating their performances of themselves, [performative self-portraits] explore the capacity of the self-portrait photograph to foreground the 'I' as other to itself."[3] What Jones means by this is that these versions of self-portraiture go beyond mere representation and mark creative forms of expressivity that reveal forms of self that exceed capture. In this way the photograph becomes what Jones describes as a *"technology of embodiment*, and yet one that paradoxically points to our tenuousness and incoherence as living embodied subjects."[4] The force of *Billie #21*, then, emerges in our recognition that the photograph is explicitly not revealing Harris's interiority, but that it instead illuminates the possibility of reading Harris as a plural self both in relation to Holiday through his performance of citation *and* in relation to the otherness of himself that he summons. These forms of otherness—excess forms of embodiment—are central to what I call *brown jouissance*. In contrast to an ecstasy that imagines transcending corporeality, brown jouissance is a reveling in fleshiness, its sensuous materiality that brings together pleasure and pain.[5]

Importantly, to dwell in the territory of the flesh is also to grapple with a complex matrix of gender, race, and sexuality. When we situate *Billie #21* within the context of Harris's series of self-portraits, *Billie, Boxers, and Better Days*, we see an array of citations. In addition to Holiday, Harris includes photographs of himself in the guise of Josephine Baker, a bloodied boxer, and other early twentieth-century images of blackness that Anna Deavere Smith describes as "an improvisation. As jazz."[6] Deavere Smith argues that this play with gender is central to Harris's narrative of self: "If you know Lyle, you know that he says a lot of words very quickly. One such string of words was, 'A sissy by five, a faggot by seven, a bitch by twelve, a cunt by eighteen. These were all called to me.'"[7] Though we might understand Harris's particular movement toward black femininity as a form of what Gilles Deleuze and Félix Guattari describe as becoming-woman, Harris is performing something else.[8] His explicit invocation of black femininity and its fleshiness challenges the assumed (and impossible) gendered and raced neutrality upon which becoming-woman relies in addition to illustrating the particular affects that cohere around black femininity.[9] This is why it is important that Harris's transformation exists on the surface—enacted through gloss, make-up, and surgical tape. This is not a performance of becoming. Harris does not become-Holiday; he cites her—positioning his body alongside hers so that we might read the image to understand their mutual investment in black femininity. While becoming-woman seeks to displace traditional humanism through the disruption of patriarchy and the embrace of the disempowered, it does little to think about the transformations of self that can take place in and through fleshiness. In Harris's explicit manipulation of his body, we see that pleasure and pain emerge from the history of black female fleshiness. This is summoned by the citation of Holiday, as well as the pleasures, pains, and possibilities that lie within his own body. It is these multiple dimensions of fleshiness that shape the possibilities that we can imagine and those that we cannot. Fleshiness is inseparable from processes of objectification *and* the production of selfhood.

Citing Holiday gives Harris a way to illustrate the particular parameters of race, gender, and sexuality that make his body and his mode of inhabiting the world legible while also providing him with a blueprint for exploring what exceeds this frame. In her description of *Billie #21*, Deavere Smith focuses on the motivations behind Harris's citation of Holiday. She frames Harris's project as a series of experimental inhabitations that center addiction and sacrifice. She writes, "That which entrances him and haunts him about Billie Holiday is that which he longs for: the sacrifice. He is interested in her addictions. He is interested in how far Billie went. He would like to go that far."[10] She concludes: "I know what I think Lyle would have to risk. He would have to risk touching the loss in black life. It's hard to touch the loss. But Lyle is trying to touch it."[11] Deavere Smith foregrounds Harris's investment in Holiday's pain as part of the precarity that surrounds black life. This renders Harris's act of citation one of exposition—it aims to tell us something about black life, black being. This is a citation that dwells upon Holiday's meaning for others, Holiday's position as signifier, and it is an exploration of what addiction and loss mean for thinking about what it is to be black. It shows us the way that the image traffics in woundedness and hovers around the territory of abjection.

If we read for fleshiness, for surface, not depth, however, we come toward thinking about the parameters of selfhood in the image. By positioning himself alongside Holiday, by drawing on her complex history of loss and pain, and putting it in relation to his own, Harris illustrates the ways that citation can alter the boundaries of the self. This does not negate Deavere Smith's analysis, but it allows us to think about the work that Harris performs in a different light. Instead of asking whether or not this is a commentary on addiction, loss, and blackness, I want to read the parted lips as invoking a self that hungers. In theorizing hunger, Alex Weheliye poses a set of questions asking how we might use the concept to imagine otherwise: "How might we read the scripture of the flesh, which abides among us 'in every single approach to things,' but too often lingers in the passing quicksands of indecipherability, otherwise? What does hunger outside the world of Man feel like? Is it a different hunger, or just the same as the famines created by racializing assemblages that render the human isomorphic with Man? How do we describe the sweetness that reclines in the hunger for survival?"[12]

What Weheliye's questions reveal is the way hunger combines multiple incoherent states—insatiability, joy, and freedom. Hunger, for Weheliye, is not about the possibility of fulfillment or nurturance; there are no objects, just cravings, and this act of craving is part of survival. We might profitably connect this version of hunger with the forms of lateral agency that Lauren Berlant proposes in *Cruel Optimism*, where she argues for a "recasting of sovereignty [that] provides an alternative way of talking about phrases like 'self-medication,' which we use to imagine what someone is doing when they are becoming dissipated, and not acting in a life-building way. . . . Agency can be an activity of maintenance, not making; fantasy, without grandiosity; sentience without full intentionality; inconsistency, without shattering; and embodying, alongside embodiment."[13] This form of hunger, I argue, is constitutive of a type of selfhood that coalesces—even as it gnaws at the edges—in this state of openness and insatiability. The self that Harris presents, the self who hungers, cannot be understood through the matrix of sovereign subjectivity. This is a self created in and through relationality with Holiday. It is a plural self; it is not Harris performing as Holiday, but Harris using a citation of Holiday to move toward an embodiment of hunger. This, in turn, transforms the photograph into one in which pleasure mingles with want—or, rather, joy and selfhood come together in feeling the limitlessness of insatiability. This tells us nothing of Holiday or Harris, but it reveals a sensuality or mode of being and relating that prioritizes openness, vulnerability, and a willingness to ingest without necessarily choosing what one is taking in. This is not the desire born of subjectivity in which subject wishes to possess object, but an embodied hunger that takes joy and pain in this gesture of radical openness toward otherness. This, this fleshy mixture of self-production, insatiability, joy, and pain, is brown jouissance.

Sexuality and the Pornotrope

Historically, flesh is the territory of the marginalized. It is the side of the Cartesian dualism connected to the body; it traffics in objectification, abjection, and mindlessness. Hortense Spillers describes the transformation of black bodies into flesh as one of the artifacts of the transatlantic slave trade. Spillers writes, "Before the 'body' there is the 'flesh,' that zero degree of social conceptualization that does not escape concealment under the brush of discourse, or the reflexes of iconography.... Even though the European hegemonies stole bodies ... we regard this human and social irreparability as high crimes against the *flesh*, as the person of African females and African males registered the wounding."[14] Since becoming flesh depersonalizes and removes subjectivity, we can understand the production of flesh as one of white supremacy's tactics of domination. Pornotroping, that which objectifies people in accordance with hierarchized systems of racialization, is one important way that bodies have become flesh. Spillers describes the process of pornotroping thus:

> (1) the captive body becomes the source of an irresistible, destructive sensuality; (2) at the same time—in stunning contradiction—the captive body is reduced to a thing, becoming *being for* the captor; (3) in this absence *from* a subject position, the captured sexualities provide a physical and biological expression of "otherness"; (4) as a category of "otherness," the captive body translates into a potential for pornotroping and embodies sheer physical powerlessness that slides into a more general "powerlessness."[15]

For Spillers, pornotroping is a process of objectification that violently reduces people into commodities while simultaneously rendering them sexually available. Pornotroping does not just illustrate the materiality of the body, then. Through its discourse of fleshiness it emphasizes the ways that power and projection produce certain bodies as other, thereby granting them a mysterious quality of desirability, which is always already undergirded by violence and the assumption of possession. Drawing on Spillers (and others), a strain of black studies—Afropessimism—has argued that blackness is the foreclosed other to the concept of the sovereign subject and human, thereby revealing the impossibility of grappling with blackness in tandem with gender and agency (among other things).[16] These conversations have been useful and rich in their illumination of the implicit universalization of whiteness and the multiple violences that subtend the idea of the subject.

Writing adjacent to Afropessimism, in *Habeaus Viscus* Weheliye links the processes of pornotropic enfleshment to the mechanism of desire. Both render some subjects and others objects. Bringing the geopolitical to bear on the intimate, he asks, "How does the historical question of violent political domination activate a surplus and excess of sexuality that simultaneously sustains and disfigures said brutality?"[17] For Weheliye, the kinship between the processes that underlie the pornotrope—projection and objectification—and those that underlie sexuality—those of possession and desire—illustrate the violence embedded in the concept of sexuality itself. This continuity becomes particularly visible when examining rapture or ecstasy because these states position the abdication of subjectivity as the height of desire. Desire consolidates the subject, even as it privileges its momentary dissolve. However, this investment in subjectivity (even as prison) forgets that there are some for whom subjectivity has never been granted and that these restrictions on the category of the subject are violently produced; for them desiring is not a possible action. In making us explicitly relate the pornotrope to desire, Weheliye brings these contradictions together: "My argument is not about erotics per se but dwells in the juxtaposition of violence as the antithesis of the human(e) (bondage) and 'normal' sexuality (rapture) as the apposite property of this figure."[18] Often, the framework of rapture or ecstasy imagines that these moments exist in opposition to harm, that they are personal and occur privately; however, the pornotrope allows us to see that violence toward black and brown people is inextricable from theorizations of sexuality. The violence and projection that produce the pornotrope require at their core a subject who desires and who thereby objectifies and possesses others through this desire.

In this book, I explore the underside of these desires as manifest through various inhabitations of the pornotrope, thereby expanding its parameters beyond blackness to think about the way that the category that we understand as people of color is produced through late capitalism, colonialism, and globalization. This move to link blackness and brownness understands race and gender as produced through affective and sensational exchanges. Although the particulars of inhabiting the pornotrope vary, it always involves labor that occurs in relation to heteronormative whiteness. As Roderick Ferguson reminds us, "Nonwhite populations were racialized such that gender and sexual transgressions were not incidental to the production of nonwhite labor, but constitutive of it."[19] Further, he argues, the residue of this fleshiness is the charge of perversion and the disavowal of this racialized labor: "As capital solicited Mexican, Asian, Asian American, and African American labor, it provided the material conditions that would ultimately disrupt the gender and sexual ideals upon which citizenship depended. The racialization of Mexican, Asian, Asian American, and African American labor as contrary to gender and sexual normativity positioned such labor outside the image of the American citizen."[20] At the heart of this sexual normativity is whiteness which is also connected to settler colonialism. As Scott Morgenson writes, "In the United States, the sexual colonization of Native peoples produced modern sexuality as 'settler sexuality': a white and national heteronormativity formed by regulating Native sexuality and gender while appearing to supplant them with the sexual modernity of settlers."[21] Although this project does not explore this relationship explicitly, I want to acknowledge that it serves as the backdrop for understanding that blackness and brownness are produced in encounters with white supremacy. In this I gesture toward Spillers's explicit inclusion of the category of the Native in regard to the harms of the New World order: "That order, with its human sequence written in blood, *represents* for its African and indigenous peoples a scene of *actual* mutilation, dismemberment, and exile," as well as to Tiffany Lethabo King's expansive work, which shows "how slavery and white-settler colonialism fundamentally gave one another their structure, form, shape, and even momentum."[22]

This expansion of the pornotrope is important for several reasons. First, it moves away from theorizing blackness as the space of negation by positioning it in relation to multiple forms of brownness. This is not a move to de-exceptionalize slavery, but to point to continuities in the forms of violence exerted by white supremacy. Further, this amplification of the parameters of the pornotrope allows us to broaden understandings of what constitutes technologies of sexuality and white supremacy. While we are most familiar with the violences of slavery, colonialism, capitalism, and globalization, this project also includes sexology, photography, and psychoanalytic exaltations of the Oedipus complex as technologies of domination because they have functioned to produce and reify imaginaries of sexualized black and brown others.

To think with pornotroping is to acknowledge that some people circulate as highly charged affective objects, while simultaneously being positioned outside of the parameters of normative sexuality and subjectivity. We see this acutely in the ways that black women are posited as the "fleshy limit of theory."[23] Brown jouissance, I argue, gives us ways to think about the possibilities of resignifying that affective fleshiness, by showing us that which is not encumbered by discourses of sexuality, but that which traffics in sensuality, that amorphous quality of fleshiness that Spillers argues was assigned to "the captive body." In thinking with the possibilities of the pornotrope, I position my work as occupying the space of *yes, and* in relation to Afropessimism. I ask what it might be to take the violence of the pornotrope and the accompanying impossibility of sovereign subjectivity seriously while dwelling in the selfhoods, intimacies, and knowledge systems that emerge from thinking with the flesh. For me, the pornotrope offers insight into the affective areas of racialization. In understanding race through the affective and sensational circuits of power and performance, we see that the pornotrope not only names the fleshiness of black and brown people, but also helps us to unpack these relationships to signification, enabling us to read otherwise. As Weheliye argues, turning to the violence of the pornotrope allows us to see the radical potential of excess without flattening the violence at its core. He observes that "alternative modes of life [exist] alongside the violence, subjection, exploitation, and racialization that define the modern human."[24]

Harris's citation of Holiday illustrates both the affective labors of the pornotrope and its excesses. That Holiday's fleshiness as a black woman mobilizes histories of addiction, sex work, and woundedness *and* that this is what audiences want to see when they approach Holiday speak to the appeal of black suffering. In donning Holiday's trademark gardenias, Harris shows us the types of erotic and affective labor that this fleshiness performs while also harnessing it to inhabit something else—a form of radical openness that I describe as hunger. Conceptually, excess disrupts already articulated forms of thought by revealing what cannot begin to be conceived. It is what violence produces and cannot incorporate. This is the *yes, and* to which I refer. Focusing on excess circumnavigates questions of sovereign subjectivity and desire to show us epistemologies rooted in opacity and sensuality.

Epistemologies of Fleshiness and Opacity

In this book, "opacity" refers to many things. On the one hand, it offers a bulwark against the mandate of transparency foisted on minoritarian performers who are imagined to be without subjectivity or interiority. This is the type of opacity that Nicole Fleetwood argues is operationalized in the strategic deployment of "excess flesh" in black female music video performance. As a concept, "excess flesh" emphasizes the faulty notions of a "visual truth" of blackness by representing excess and fantasy.[25] Further, Fleetwood argues that this excess is "an enactment of visibility that seizes upon the scopic desires to discipline the black female body through a normative gaze that anticipates its rehearsed performance of abjection."[26] This use of flesh "refus[es] the binary of negative and positive" and operates as *a performative that doubles visibility: to see the codes of visuality operating on the (hyper)visible body that is its object.*[27] This is to say that excess flesh actually hides in plain sight—opacity is found in the inability to take it all in and produce coherence. This version of opacity is at work in the title of Farrah Jasmine Griffin's treatment of Holiday's appeal, *If You Can't Be Free, Be a Mystery*. In both of these examples we see that opacity functions as a minoritarian strategy because it disrupts the assumption that visuality is equivalent to transparency by alluding to something else, a different set of norms or even an interiority inaccessible to others. In this way opacity exists in relation to José Esteban Muñoz's theorization of "brown feeling," which "chronicles a certain ethics of the self that is utilized and deployed by people of color and other minoritarian subjects who don't feel quite right within the protocols of normative affect and comportment."[28] These brown feelings are Muñoz's mode of describing "the ways in which minoritarian affect is always, no matter what its register, partially illegible in relation to the normative affect performed by normative citizen subjects."[29] When Muñoz argues that these performances "offer comment on a complicated choreography of introjection and projection," one of the things he is talking about is this play with intimacy and opacity.[30] The opacity that Muñoz theorizes is always precarious because it necessitates a willingness to go beyond the over-determined personage produced by projection, which I have been describing as the violent enfleshment of the pornotrope. This precarity can be evidenced, for example, in Christina León's analysis of the failure of some audiences to register Xandra Ibarra's performances as camp because they are unable to interpret her work outside the genre of transparent racialized spectacle.[31] To think opacity, then, means always and insistently thinking with the *possibility*, however momentary, of illegibility rather than a stabilized notion of resistance.

Yet, the quality of impermanence does not negate the re-orderings of knowledge that emerge from the opacity of the pornotrope. This knowledge—what I call *epistemologies of fleshiness* in order to insist on naming fleshiness as a space where ontology and epistemology come together—consists of selfhoods, intimacies, and interactions that are arranged multiply. My insistence on conjoining flesh and knowledge emphasizes theorizing as a fleshy activity, both because theory emerges from flesh—positionality matters—and because theory is enacted by bodies; thought can be located outside of the linguistic, in and through the body and its movements. This rescripting of what counts as knowledge is both a rebuke to the demands of fixity and transparency that have come to characterize various technologies of knowledge and an invitation for us to rethink what counts as minoritarian knowledge production.[32]

Because this project is focused on the knowledge that emerges in and through the excesses and opacities of the pornotrope, it works around discourses of sexuality and desire to think with epistemologies of sensuality. In this positioning of the body as a site of knowledge-making that stands aslant to conventional understandings of sexuality and desire, I join LaMonda Horton-Stallings who offers, instead, an erotics of funk. She writes, "We can glean funk as a philosophy about kinesthetics and being that critiques capitalism and the pathology of Western morality . . . while also possessing the wisdom to know and understand that the two are linked. Because funk sees the two as linked, it provides innovative strategies about work and sexuality that need to be highlighted."[33] According to Horton-Stallings, funk "produces alternate orders of knowledge about the body and imagination that originate in a sensorium predating empires of knowledge."[34] These epistemologies of funk produce a new imagination of eroticism that, importantly, does away with a mind-body dualism. Referring to Michel Foucault's differentiation between the sensual eroticism of *ars erotica* and the impulse toward categorization of *scientia sexualis*, Horton-Stallings asks, "How do we ignore Foucault's privileging of Cartesian dualisms and ways of being, in addition to specific social classes, in his proclamation about ars erotica/scientia sexualis as it relates to the history of sexuality?"[35] Underlying Horton-Stallings's ire at Foucault is that this division elides the presence of sex work, which is the term that she assigns to all labors related to the flesh, and that it implies that these labors of the flesh are separable from the labors of the mind. She continues: "Foucault's refusal to acknowledge other sites of knowledge—fiction, the surreal, and the imagination—maintains a divide between work and labor and leisure and pleasure that we should not accept as fact for societies and cultures that might foster an understanding that truth, pleasure, and knowledge are not mutually exclusive or in opposition to each other."[36] Horton-Stallings works to produce a holistic conceptualization of the erotic that reconnects the mind and body and does away with other dualisms such as work and leisure and truth, knowledge, and pleasure. This is an erotics that confounds categories and prioritizes pleasure.

Like Horton-Stallings's work, this book seeks to do away with a mind/body division by showing the different orderings of knowledge that emerge when we emphasize flesh and fleshiness. To think with the flesh and to inhabit the pornotrope is to hold violence and possibility in the same frame. It is also, importantly, to reclaim and remake selfhood. While I have already mentioned that this re-thinking the self is part of the opacity and excess of the pornotrope, here, I argue that this claiming of selfhood is necessary and urgent because it allows us to think about brown jouissance as political. In asserting that selfhood—though not a sovereign subject—exists in relation to minoritarian knowledge production and epistemologies of sensuality, we are able to see that flesh becomes something else, a space of possibility, interiority, and creativity. Rather than merely abdicating subjectivity, these reclamations of selfhoods provide a scaffolding for imagining and prioritizing ways of being that center coexisting, caring, and sensuality.

Thinking with the reorientations that brown jouissance enables, then, allows us to return to Jacques Lacan and his formulation of jouissance in order to think more precisely around the politics that surround the sensations of being a body. This sensation of pure embodiment, which I locate alongside the pornotropic production of fleshiness, is central to Lacan's understanding of jouissance. Néstor Braunstein, elaborating and clarifying Lacan's versions of jouissance, describes it as "positivity, it is a 'something' lived by a body when pleasure stops being pleasure. It is a plus, a sensation that is beyond pleasure."[37] Jouissance, then, can be understood as excess sensation. Often, however, jouissance, especially phallic jouissance, is understood as something that, however, inadvertently, reifies the idea of sovereign subjectivity through an insistence on dwelling in its space of shattering, thereby emphasizing the dichotomy between subject and Thing. In his own description of jouissance, Lacan positions it in relation to Thingness: "jouissance is on the side of the Thing."[38] In explaining why Lacan uses the term "Thing" instead of "object," Braunstein argues that the Thing is related to jouissance because it possesses a direction separate from the subject, which is to say it is a space of impossibility and illegibility.[39] While focusing on Thingness calls attention to the agency inherent in being material, it neglects to grapple with the way that this materiality circulates within the social world. This is to say, it travels separately from discourses of race, ethnicity, and even gender.

In contrast, brown jouissance emphasizes the production of selfhood in relation to the social. While the self-Other relation underlies all formulations of jouissance, the Other is often neglected, which, in turn, removes the social from the scene of jouissance. Foregrounding relations with the Other brings objectification, race, and gender into the mix. The Other, as Denise Ferreira da Silva reminds us, occupies the space of projection and opacity. The subject is assumed to occupy "the stage of interiority, where universal reason plays its sovereign role as *universal poesis*," while the Other is assigned to the realm of the external as an "affectable I."[40] This means that the properties of the Other are determined from the outside and are therefore deeply constrained and unknowable. To emphasize the Other in theorizing jouissance, then, is to think with the pornotrope and emphasize the simultaneous projections of racialization and gendering that occur through its particular modes of objectification. Brown jouissance emphasizes the social relations at work in enfleshment and suggests that the pornotropic network of projection and objectification can coexist with Thingness and its opacity. Brown jouissance, I argue, occurs in the moments when Thing, Other, and object converge to form selfhood.

By tethering brown jouissance to the oscillations that occur between Thing, Other, and object, we are no longer within the realm of subjectivity, but in the murkiness of flesh, self, and sense. If brown jouissance is a reveling in fleshiness and its attendant web of meanings and possibilities, it brings us very directly to consider the opacity of the self and the set of relationalities and sensualities that emerges from there. Following Édouard Glissant, I see this opacity as forming the basis of ethical relations because it allows for the possibility of existing with difference without mandating transparency. This ethical opacity undergirds the minoritarian knowledge productions and epistemologies of sensuality that I argue constitute brown jouissance. Glissant writes, "For the time being, perhaps, give up this old obsession with discovering what lies at the bottom of natures. There would be something great and noble about initiating such a movement, referring not to Humanity but to the exultant divergence of humanities. Thought of self and thought of other here become obsolete in their duality."[41] Glissant's argument that lingering in opacity offers a way around the cleavage between self and Other because it refuses a prioritization of either and forces a reckoning with unknowability is central to the stakes that underlie brown jouissance.

Brown jouissance offers a critical rejoinder to attempts to imagine that theorizations of selfhood can exist without paying heed to fleshiness and its destabilization of subjectivity. Making pornotroping central to the oscillations between Thing, Other, and object also suggests that sensuality's alternate epistemologies can be found in these movements between abjection and self-creation. This mobility of the flesh and the flesh's ability to signify multiply is a mark of what I term *liquidity*. Liquidity indexes flesh's mutability and asks us to look toward verbs rather than nouns for rewriting sensuality. In making this theoretical shift toward epistemologies that prioritize the instability of the flesh, I position this project alongside recent work in queer theory and new materialisms, which aims to articulate the specificities of fleshiness in terms of race and gender and to find ways to work with difference without falling back into the difficulties of inclusion and wounded subjectivity. Here, I suggest we think Mel Chen's use of animacy, Uri McMillan's theorization of avatars, and Kyla Wazana Tompkins' analytics of eating as pointing us toward incorporating movement into thinking the flesh.[42] The series of verbs and adjectives that these theorists offer brings us toward the particular forms of being-with, sensuality, and disruption that brown jouissance allows us to probe. Instead of focusing on ontology, this is a theory that emphasizes the dynamics of the encounter and the ever-shifting possibilities for generating knowledge through diffuse strategies of embodiment.

When we read for movement, which is what permits the oscillations between Thing, Other, object, and self, we see the Thingness of Harris's flesh, the objectification and Otherness that hovers around Holiday and Harris, and the dual self that emerges from this movement. In his simultaneous movement toward Holiday and his refusal of transparency, Harris highlights the importance of thinking about the production of opacity and rewrites our imaginaries of sensuality. The self that Harris presents—the self who hungers—cannot be understood through the matrix of sovereign subjectivity. This is selfhood created in and through relationality with Holiday. It is a dual self; it is not Harris performing as Holiday, but Harris using a citation of Holiday to move toward an embodiment of hunger. This tells us nothing of Holiday or Harris, but it reveals a sensuality or mode of being and relating that prioritizes an openness, a vulnerability, and a willingness to ingest without necessarily choosing what one is taking in. This is not the desire born of subject wanting to possess object, but an embodied hunger that takes joy and pain in this gesture of radical openness toward otherness. Citation, then, is Harris's mode of producing brown jouissance.

Aesthetics, Sensuality, and Performative Methodology

Thus far, I have focused on the political and epistemological reorientations that brown jouissance offers through its rescripting of selfhood and fleshiness, but here I pause to dwell on the question of the aesthetic and its relationship to brown jouissance. While brown jouissance is not entirely contained by the aesthetic, in this book, I have chosen to analyze its emergence in works of art produced by minoritarian subjects. In many ways I draw on an esoteric aesthetic archive. I analyze and juxtapose singular works of art produced by artists who fall primarily under the category of "people of color," but I am not invested in positioning the particular works of art within the artists' larger oeuvre nor am I interested in figuring out what the artist means to say or how the artist diverges or emerges from conversations within various artistic milieu. Instead, I use these works of art to show us moments of brown jouissance. On the one hand, these works of art provide concrete objects for us to think with; we can analyze them in order to register the ways in which they illuminate particular epistemologies of fleshiness, formations of selfhood, and modes of relating. To this end, I have chosen works of art whose politics and epistemologies of selfhood and sensuality compel me, in that they show us how we might acknowledge violence and still think otherwise. However, I have also chosen to think with art because the category of the aesthetic calls upon us to bring our own fleshiness to the table in order to produce knowledge. This is to say that it solicits performative and relational methodologies of meaning-making, which, in keeping with this book's emphasis on fleshiness, opacity, and sensuality, works to underscore the politics of minoritarian knowledge production that lie at the heart of brown jouissance.

This turn to sensuality prioritizes relationality, feeling, and embodiment. The sensual is the space of excess, as Sharon Patricia Holland, Marcía Ochoa, and Kyla Wazana Tompkins argue in the introduction to *On the Visceral*, writing that viscera forces one to attend to waste, "the materiality of what must be cast out, and . . . the space of the nonproductive."[43] Rizvana Bradley argues that approaching the aesthetic through the sensual reveals important knowledge not only about these objects but about our social world: "Consider how touching, folding, fingering, or tracing the texture of an object, offer themselves as techniques of knowing in art and performance . . . expand[ing] the critical parameters of what the haptic can mean not simply in diverse contexts of art and art making, but more specifically at the crucial edges of performance and social practice."[44] Further, as Kadji Amin, Roy Pérez, and I argue in our introduction to *Queer Form*, foregrounding questions of relation and sensuality leads to new modes of critique, "expand[ing] our conceptions of often unacknowledged norms without necessarily staking a claim for the anti-normative."[45] Hence, the circuits of sensuality—how one connects to the aesthetic—are my way of understanding the epistemologies that emerge from these disparate instances of brown jouissance. Just as David Getsy's and Jennifer Doyle's arguments that the relationships between artist, work of art, and viewer are sensuous—filled with what Doyle terms the erotic and treats "as a language or a set of affects animating and inhabiting this kind of work, but also as a mode of knowing (or even being known by) the object," and with what Getsy often describes through the language of tactility—I take this emphasis on embodiment and sensuality to bring forth the question of method since attempts to read the aesthetic without attending to the sensual foreclose moments of embodied connection and meaning-making.[46]

In turning toward sensuality as method, I return to the analytic practice of empathetic reading that I developed in *Sensational Flesh*. Empathetic reading works to highlight the work of sensation and empathy within the practice of reading: "Empathetic Reading is a reading practice, a critical hermeneutic, and a methodology. . . . [As] a critical hermeneutic and methodology . . . it highlights how we can discern the structure of sensation in various texts/performances and it works to give those sensations meaning, which in turn allows us to read difference in a sensational mode."[47] In *Sensational Flesh*, I suggested that readers use empathy to position their body alongside theorists in order to render theory corporeal. Empathy, I argue, could be harnessed to imagine the way that sensation structures thought. In this way, empathetic reading is useful for articulating the felt ways that structures of power impinge on the body and, in turn, how those sensations contour theorizing.

My project in *Sensual Excess: Queer Femininity and Brown Jouissance* is different. Here, I turn toward sensation in order to imagine epistemologies that emerge from excess. The expressiveness of excess flesh—the aesthetic—makes theory, I argue. Instead of dwelling primarily on the ways that epistemologies shape expressivity, I use empathetic reading to discern the reorderings that brown jouissance enables. This is a performative methodology, and there are, admittedly, ways that this mode of reading itself produces a form of plural selfhood, one that sits alongside the forms of selfhood that I argue are central to brown jouissance. This performativity, however, works to underline the political stakes of brown jouissance and its move away from a subject/object binary. There is no way to parse the distinction between theorist and theory or reader and text or spectator and art object. These epistemologies can be fully discerned only through the experiential. Because it is a methodology rooted in the sensual, I use empathetic reading to probe the contours of the aesthetic, so as to register *how* (form and content) these oscillations of brown jouissance are produced and *what* (epistemology) versions of selfhood and relationality emerge.

Billie #21, I argue, shows us brown jouissance in several ways. As I have already discussed, we see brown jouissance in Harris's/Holiday's inhabitation of hungering; we also see it in the ghost of Holiday's performances; and in Harris's inhabitation of the space alongside Holiday. The citational self that Harris conjures is explicitly produced in relation to Holiday and his use of her iconicity. Citation is Harris's particular mode of relating to Holiday. Through citation, he links his body to hers in a way that emphasizes gesture as a mode of knowledge transmission and allows us to ponder what exactly one inhabits when one borrows from Holiday—what comes from Harris and what comes from Holiday and what do we do with this trans-temporal merging of corporeality? Importantly, however, we also experience *Billie #21* as a material manifestation of brown jouissance itself in that its presence as an art object, as a Polaroid, gives us its own entry point into the relationship between aesthetics and brown jouissance. Thinking with the aesthetic in this case highlights brown jouissance's refusal of transparency and *Billie #21*'s particular relationship to the fleshiness of the instant.

When one takes a Polaroid, chemicals wash over paper and the image reveals itself after several minutes (or seconds—depending on the actual camera used). In this way, the Polaroid, like many other technologies of photography, offers a material instantiation of the instant, bringing the instant's fleshiness to the surface. The Polaroid cannot promise to represent depth; it only skims the surface of the world, making visible through its capture of the instant the infinite uncaptured possibilities of movement and image. This illumination of potential through limitation is what Kaja Silverman describes as a fundamental aspect of photography, which works through analogy, or representation that reveals the abundant materiality of the world.[48] More specifically, the Polaroid image, Peter Buse argues, rearranges the relationship between subject and object because it requires proximity, which, in turn, reveals the intimacy of the relationship between photographer and image-subject. Buse writes, "Intimacy in the Bataillean sense, is an impossible immanence, a conjunction of immediacy and proximity. This is what the Polaroid often promises, when it is asked to signify."[49] Buse's enthusiasm for the

Polaroid's intimacy is important because it emphasizes the specific material dimensions of the form. One must be close to the image-subject, at least briefly.

That this citation of Holiday is articulated through the form of a Polaroid draws our attention to the fleshiness of time. This is to say that we experience time as material in a particular way that allows us to understand it as an infinite set of layers or surfaces. In this way, citationality is an explicit manipulation of the layering of different moments of temporality. The Polaroid, after all, captures just the surface of fleshiness, and citation produces a nonlinear path through these temporalities. Through citation, time becomes legible as surface, material, and flesh. By positioning his fleshiness alongside Holiday's, by drawing on her complex history of loss and pain, and by attaching himself to it, Harris moves toward the way that citation alters how we understand selfhood. Citation produces plural selfhood in this reference to the past while also illuminating the multiplicity of the present. To be in time, to inhabit a moment, is to be made legible through that which came before.

Billie #21 is a snapshot of a moment; it can never be recreated, but it also exists as an object with its own unstable relationship to temporality in that it is also an artifact. This is to say that in addition to recording a particular intimacy, it is also a unique material object, whose contours are particular to Harris's manipulation of the Polaroid camera's process of surface development. We see this manipulation in the black bar that occupies the lower portion of the photograph. Moreover, the same chemicals that enable specificity are also those that produce the Polaroid as an image that it always edging toward fading. To argue, then, that hunger is a form of brown jouissance at work in the sensual excess of the photograph is also to suture the citational self and the Polaroid's materialization of temporality to insatiability and vulnerability. It enables us to ask whether the oscillations between Thing, object, and Other that speak to hunger and its vulnerability are also structured by impermanence, layered temporality, and the plural, porous self of citation. That the aesthetic allows us to ask these questions and draw these ideas together signals its importance in making sense of the epistemological and political questions that emerge from brown jouissance.

From Here to Elsewhere: The Sensual Spaces of Brown Jouissance

This book, then, offers multiple inroads into thinking with and through brown jouissance and the pornotrope. Each chapter draws our attention to particular aspects of pornotropic capture that black and brown people must negotiate. These technologies differ according to the nature of the encounters with white supremacy, but together, they add to our understanding of the ways that structures of domination produce violence and work to contain bodies and pleasures within certain legible parameters. In relation to parsing the modes and mechanics of objectification, I also identify and analyze moments of brown jouissance that exceed these constraints. These are spaces where I locate epistemologies of selfhood and sensuality that can sit alongside those of white hegemonic normativity and are in conversation with other scholarship by those who also think otherwise in fields such as black feminism, queer studies, queer of color critique, and Asian American, Black, and Latinx studies. Finally, I also make arguments in relation to the possibilities opened by my understanding of each artwork's particular entanglement with the sensual. This move outward offers a way to think with the ways that aesthetic forms might rearrange knowledge by engaging differently with fleshiness and how we apprehend it. This three-pronged approach is designed to help us understand brown jouissance as robust, political, and fleshy. In addition to containing critiques of normativity and proffering epistemologies of sensuality against those of sexuality, this project of minoritarian knowledge production is designed to enable one to sit with opacity and uncertainty. This is not a project of mastery, but one of sensing and imagining otherwise, wherever and whatever that might be.

The first two chapters, "Eating Out: The Labial, Consumption, and the Scalar" and "Surface Play: Flash, Friction, and Self-Reflection," theorize forms of brown jouissance that offer sensual reorientations of what it is to be in relation by focusing on representations of the black vulva and the epistemologies we can conjure from its materiality. Recent feminist scholarship has been working through the difficult terrain of agency, violation, and pleasure by attempting to recuperate black female sexuality from its persistent association with pain to read other affects such as pleasure, ecstasy, and indulgence into our frameworks for thinking about representations of black women and their sexuality. Yet, they are also wary of imagining an understanding of black female sexuality completely untethered from these histories of pain.[50] These are important modes of resisting dominant narratives that render black women voiceless and without agency, but these strategies still pivot around agency (fugitive though it may be). Clearly, we need new frameworks for imagining intimacies and sensuality under duress. These chapters work toward that project by eschewing sexuality's emphasis on desire, subjectivity, and agency to dwell, instead, on the materiality of the vulva and the production of intimacies premised on spatiality. These intimacies ask us to rethink the relation between sex and the self in addition to redrawing the boundaries between self and other.

"Eating Out," focuses on the sculpted vulvas of Judy Chicago's *The Dinner Party* (1979) and Kara Walker's *A Subtlety* (2014) in order to draw out some of the issues that underlie the representational politics that surround the black vulva. Although these installations diverge in many ways, I argue that they enable a meditation on the possibility of permeable, dialogic selfhood—selves that illustrate the impossibility of a border between self and Other—rendering porosity and the labial as important for an ethics of mutual vulnerability. Yet, I caution against forgetting asymmetries of power. Reading across the installations and the controversy over Walker's installation in particular forces us to acknowledge that the differences between pleasure in vulnerability and the sensation of racial violation are related to the differences between the structures of our epistemologies of gender and race. Dwelling on the sensuality that inheres in *A Subtlety*, however, offers a way to reorient porosity by thinking with the dimension of smell as one site of the installation's excess. The scalar, in turn, allows us to imagine formulations of brown jouissance in relation to fleshiness that exceeds the individual in multiple directions.

"Surface Play" delves more deeply into the matter of the black vulva in arguing for a revaluation of narcissism, friction, and superficiality by dwelling on Mickalene Thomas's use of rhinestones as excessive decorations in *Origin of the Universe 1* (2012). Thomas's work is a reimagining of Gustave Courbet's infamous headless, nude portrait of a woman, *The Origin of the World* (1866), in which Thomas positions her rhinestone-embellished genitals in the center of the frame. I argue that

Thomas's painting offers a meditation on Audre Lorde's matrilineal womanism while also allowing us to think with the idea of surface within the medium of painting. This calling forth of both 1970s and 1980s black lesbian feminism and the textures of the surface bring forth friction as a form of relationality and narcissism as a necessary form of self-creation. Brown jouissance, I argue, inheres in the excesses of surface that the painting presents.

The third chapter, "Deep Listening, Belonging, and the Pleasures of Brown Jouissance," delves into the specific pleasures that brown jouissance produces by comparing it to feminine jouissance, which differs from the self-shattering of phallic jouissance, and to abjection. The pleasures that emerge from feminine jouissance and abjection are those that come from rethinking psychoanalytic modes of belonging, which I do through an analysis of Cheryl Dunye's pornographic romantic comedy *Mommy Is Coming* (2012). Brown jouissance's pleasures, I argue, emerge in the admixtures of feminine jouissance and abjection, a combination that I analyze in Amber Hawk Swanson and Xandra Ibarra's collaboration *Untitled Fucking* (2013) by focusing on the strap-on and latex gloves as aspects of Ibarra's performance of spic-ness. These elements show us topping as deep listening, which itself is an investment in the opacity of the other's pleasure, while also illuminating dimensions of racialized abjection and care.

This chapter's insistence on working through psychoanalysis should be read as an intervention into psychoanalysis's treatment of race. In its early twentieth-century incarnations, its grappling with racial difference was spotty at best. Freud confined racial difference to the atavistic and primitive in *Civilization and its Discontents*. Following Freud, other early twentieth-century analysts tended to ignore underlying racial dynamics at work in their theories, which created an assumption of whiteness even as they have since allowed a rich body of contemporary critical work excavating these tensions and explicating normative fantasies about race and racism.[51] When the minoritarian subject is addressed, in a lineage that we might trace from Frantz Fanon and Albert Memmi to David Eng and Anne Anlin Cheng, we find an emphasis on the trauma and melancholy of racialization, colonialism, and assimilation.[52] In both of these threads, we see that psychoanalysis registers the centrality of the Oedipus complex as one of pornotroping's technologies of domination in that it reifies particular norms around the family, family dynamics, and the formation of subjectivity and desire. Race cannot help but act as a distending force because of the violent familial ruptures produced by enfleshment and the difficulty of accommodating familial formations that differ from the norm. However, as Spillers also points out, to work with psychoanalysis is to interrogate intersubjectivity and one's place in the symbolic order, situations that must be thought through a minoritarian position because it impacts our understanding of belonging. Furthermore, this chapter works to rethink what constitutes familial dynamics—even and especially in fantasized-about form—as they are shaped by racialization in order to see where brown jouissance might fit within larger narratives about belonging.

The fourth and fifth chapters show us how looking for brown jouissance might allow us to read against narratives of meaning-making that might see only woundedness and pain. We do not necessarily come toward pleasure, but we come to something else. Although these chapters are still concerned with formations of relational selfhood, they dwell less on the intimacies that these selves produce and more on the possibilities of expressivity. In these readings brown jouissance gains more texture as an aesthetic intervention in relation to both the spectators and the artists.

In this way, I read Carrie Mae Weems's *From Here I Saw What Happened and I Cried* (1995–1996), Nao Bustamante's *Neapolitan* (2003), and Patty Chang's *In Love* (2001) as working in and against discourses of woundedness and the affective regulations that swirl around race and sexuality. Race, I argue, is a social phenomenon of power, sentiment, and spectatorship. The specter of the black body in pain mobilizes affect, especially grief, which offers another node for thinking about the process of pornotroping. Following Dana Luciano's argument that affect be thought as part of Foucault's theorization of sexuality, we can see that grief produces a hierarchy of appropriate expressiveness, which Luciano argues "should be comprehended within the framework of bodily hygiene."[53] In articulating the work that discourses on grief perform in their disciplining of the modern subject's relationship to sentiment and bodily comportment, Luciano makes an important case for thinking modern sexuality as a mode of affective regulation, and not merely as genitally or reproductively based. Thinking grief in relation to discourses of racialization brings questions of respectability, empathy, and sympathy to the fore. These chapters ask us not only to read for woundedness, however, but to read alongside these affects to find what else is being generated.

The fourth chapter, "Performing Witness: Voice, Interiority, and Diaspora" analyzes Weems's photographic installation *From Here I Saw What Happened and I Cried* as a performance of witnessing in which Weems restores voice to the archive of portraits that she reprints. While Weems's installation has been read as trafficking in woundedness, I argue that thinking photography as a technology of reproduction allows us to see her work as enlarging concepts of diaspora and mothering while also insisting on the opacity of interiority. Here, the concept of brown jouissance allows us to reimagine the work that is going on in this piece of art. It enables us to theorize witnessing and photography as fleshy enactments of spiritual resistance and to reimagine possibilities of black gendering.

Chapter 5, "Weeping Machines: Automaticity, Looping, and the Possibilities of Perversion," juxtaposes Bustamante's and Chang's video installations, both of which depict weeping as performances of theatrical excess. Here, brown jouissance opens us toward reading with modes of affective unruliness, so that we can understand the non-normativity of brown feminine domesticity and emotionality in order to locate its productive excesses. *Neapolitan*, which shows Bustamante crying at the final scene of *Fresa y Chocolate*, and *In Love*, which shows Chang passionately kissing her parents while crying, both rely on divergent models of automatic behavior. Bustamante offers a theatrical version of the hysterical Latina, while Chang performs the mechanical coldness that Asian Americans are imagined to inhabit. By toying with these expectations, both Bustamante and Chang veer into the territory of perversion, enabling us to see both the racialized norms of affective comportment and their possibility for subversion via the technology of the loop, which shows us brown jouissance as the multiplication of the present. In this chapter the charge of automaticity becomes fodder for alternate experiences of reality.

The final chapter, "Femme Aggression and the Value of Labor," makes the question of affective labor explicit as it works through Maureen Catbagan's video series *Crush* (2010–2012), which features a woman in high heels crushing plastic toys. Catbagan's decision to feature a white woman in their critique of domestic labor brings to light the pervasiveness of discourses of white feminine misery and the nature of fetishism while also asking viewers to read for race and sensuality in other modes. Catbagan's Filipinoness can be discerned through elements of framing and the videos' mobilization of aggression. This affective labor illuminates the workings of brown jouissance in relation to mimesis and virality, which, in turn, upend questions of value, commodification, and representation.

Catbagan's work is also important because it gives us a way to ask what it means to think about race without trying to locate racial difference explicitly within the frame. In this way, I see *Crush* as resisting the pornotropic demands of minoritarian representation even as it illuminates the fetishization and objectification that surrounds white femininity. In this rejection of the norms of representation, *Crush* activates brown jouissance in its refusal to display the processes that commodify people of color in the name of spectacle (or diversity). This is to say that minority subjects are valued for their difference because visible difference, in our current climate, reflects well on the institution—signaling a particular commitment to "social good." Roderick Ferguson voices deep criticism of this turn toward diversity because it incorporates difference into existing systems of power. Ferguson writes, "Whereas modes of power once disciplined difference in the universalizing names of canonicity, nationality, or economy, other operations of power were emerging that would discipline through a seemingly alternative regard for difference and through a revision of the canon, national identity, and the market."[54] In becoming something that institutions prize, diversity works as a tool to discipline subjects—making them more aware, as Ferguson argues, of their place within the particular economies of minority difference and making that difference matter in ways that do not disrupt the prevailing system. He further observes: "This new interdisciplinary biopower placed social differences in the realm of calculation and recalibrated power/knowledge as an agent of social life. For the American academy, the American state, and an Americanized capital in the sixties and seventies, the question would then become one of incorporating difference for the good rather than disruption of hegemony."[55] This is to say that the presence of minorities signals a particular investment in the project of diversity even as representation is not equivalent to an actual epistemological shift.[56] Race as representation is its own form of affective labor, which Catbagan subverts by displacing their own body from the frame and mobilizing the power of invisibility.

I end the book with a meditation on the brown and black mother and her role in producing brown jouissance. Rather than a working through of any particular work of art, "Elsewhere, Is the Mother a Place?" is a theoretical meditation on her estrangement from the familial. While this distention might (and does) result in mourning, we might also locate non-Oedipal possibilities for relationality that center a queer (and black and brown) femininity. This orientation around the mother and her economies of care, coexistence, and possibility is the elsewhere promised throughout the text.

1

Eating Out

The Labial, Consumption, and the Scalar

The black vulva is mired in a complex representational conundrum. On the one hand, its absence, which we see most clearly and poignantly in Judy Chicago's installation *The Dinner Party* (1979), illuminates the problematic erasure of black women from schemas of sexuality. On the other hand, its presence—as looming and sugar-coated—in Kara Walker's *A Sublety* (2014), has generated its own set of anxieties. This chapter asks how we might begin to think the black vulva by focusing not only on the intimacies and selfhoods produced by the labial, but on the ways that thinking with race and fleshiness through a discourse on proprioception forces us to attend to power asymmetries.

The Dinner Party asks us to dwell on consumption. On permanent display in the Brooklyn Museum, Chicago's installation imagines a dinner party between important women in history. Each woman has an embroidered runner, gold chalice, utensil, and china-painted porcelain plate. Chicago's display has earned a prominent place within feminist art; it is noteworthy for recognizing women's varied contributions to society and for drawing on an intensely collaborative practice—many people worked together on the installation to conduct research, craft the materials, and get the piece displayed again after it stopped being shown in museums in the early 1980s.[1] On the one hand, the installation enables us to consume information about these women so that we create a new tapestry of history. On the other, it allows viewers to imagine these women as consumers through its explicit centering of eating.

These alimentary aspects are often subsumed by the plates' suggestion of the vulval, which Chicago achieves through color and ceramic folds—rendering vaginal lips abstractly enough to reference the individuality of each woman and literally enough so that visitors understand that they also reference vulvas. The installation's fusion of consumption and genitalia provides an opportunity to meditate on the erotic charge of the labia. Arguing that "eating functions as a metalanguage for genital pleasure itself," Kyla Wazana Tompkins calls for *queer alimentarity* to "signal the alignment between oral pleasure and other forms of nonnormative desire."[2] Further, Tompkins encourages us to privilege consumption, which is the work that the mouth performs, so that we can "theorize a flexible and circular relation between the self and the social world in order to imagine a dialogic in which we—reader and text, self and other, animal and human—recognize our bodies as vulnerable to each other in ways that are terrible—that is full of terror—and, at other times, politically productive."[3] The consumptive pleasures that *The Dinner Party* brings forth—that of a vulva that eats, eating a vulva, or having one's vulva eaten—require that we pay attention to the porous relation between self and other that consumption produces. Specifically, it requires that we pay heed to the labia and its role in producing a porous boundary between interior and exterior and self and other. Instead of possession, an economy of the labial speaks to mutuality, receptivity, and vulnerability.

Most explicitly, this labial economy invites us to think with Luce Irigaray's feminist language of lips, which act as an ambiguous beacon for a nonphallocentric position. "When Our Lips Speak Together," a stream-of-conscious dialogue between lips, waivers between the you/ I/ we positions in order to produce a discourse (perhaps an ethics) on receptivity and mutual vulnerability. One of the main themes of the essay is the impossibility of the singular subject: "Between our lips, yours and mine, several voices, several ways of speaking resound endlessly, back and forth. One is never separable from the other. You/I: we are always several at once."[4] This plurality—what I call *permeable selfhood*—in turn, enables pleasure and mobility through its valorization of porosity: "We shall pass imperceptibly through every barrier, unharmed, to find each other. . . . For a long time now they have appreciated what our suppleness is worth for their own embraces and impressions. Why not enjoy it ourselves?"[5] As Annemarie Jagose notes, Irigaray's essay waivers between "an autoeroticism, a pre-Oedipal, and therefore precultural and prediscursive, undifferentiation from the mother, and, finally, a female homosexuality."[6] I suggest that we interpret Irigaray's essay as a performance of the refusal of fixity, a performance of dialogism in excess.[7] In the ambiguity that Irigaray announces we can see the possibility of jouissance in the way that the labia mobilize oscillations between interiority and exteriority and subject and object. This is to say that the labia function as a marker of flesh's liquidity—formulated here through conversational excess—because they call attention to the movement and materiality of the body while also evacuating a stable "I." Lynne Huffer argues that this refusal of stability offers the basis for an ethics: "The catachrestic lips . . . articulate an ethics of relation that differentiates them from the pure negativity of queer antisociality. For it is in their catachrestic, heterotopian attempt to speak otherwise that the lips are simultaneously here and elsewhere, now and not now: not a pinned-down figure of the Other of the Same, but a hovering, catachrestic Other's Other."[8] What Huffer stresses is that the lips exist only and always as relation. In and of themselves, they do not index anything particular, but they stand for the Other, its opacity, and the importance of this difference in thinking ethics and pleasure. Irigaray, Huffer argues, inscribes alterity as "a nonprocreative, sensible transcendental ethics of eros."[9] Read through Huffer, Irigaray gives us a way to think about the labial as a relationship of sensuality, vulnerability, difference, and indifference—since the permeable self makes it impossible to truly separate self and Other.

However, there is more to the labial than dialogical excess, vulnerability, and relation; there is also materiality. While the labial is something that exists in the space *between* bodies, this labial economy emphasizes a dialogic formation of self that operates in and through proprioception. Proprioception, the feeling of being oriented in space, brings together Sara Ahmed's discussion of orientation as a turn *toward* something with a spatial mode of thinking fleshiness.[10] It allows us to ask what it means to mobilize the oscillation between touching/not touching in conjunction with categories of social difference. Emphasizing the labial in relation to proprioception means thinking with the array of sensations that embed the lips within social dynamics. When we configure this in relation to Irigaray's lips touching, the swell and heat of arousal, a turn *toward* perhaps, might amplify certain forms of touch while making others painful. Likewise, a turning away might reduce the space between lips, impacting porosity. This is to say that these questions of psyche, which I will discuss in relation to appetite rather than desire, have material consequences. They illustrate that not all conversations are the same, nor do they take place on equal footing. To truly consider the dialogic self, one must attend to the asymmetries of appetite and power. Here, turning to one of the failures of Chicago's *The Dinner Party* is instructive because we can see what happens when proprioception is left out of the picture.

While Chicago's installation helps us grapple with the concept of relation and mutual vulnerability, it has surprisingly little to say about differing access to consumption and the fleshiness of turning toward consumption. In part this is because despite its emphasis on the formal dimensions of eating, we must extrapolate appetite from absent mouths. But, much of this, I think, has to do with the installation's difficulty grappling with race. It is telling, I think, that Chicago's installation elides the representational conundrum of black female sexuality. The only black woman at the table, Sojourner Truth, is represented by one of only two plates without vulval imagery. In a now defunct FAQ section of her website, Chicago describes the plates: "'Sojourner Truth' . . . is based upon African masks to honor her African-American heritage and 'Ethel Smyth' . . . is a piano whose lid threatens to compress the form."[11] Importantly, Chicago uses the existence of these plates to argue that *The Dinner Party* does not collapse every woman it features into a vulva. In historicizing Chicago's choice, Jane Gerhard writes, "Chicago's (naïve) assertion is, nonetheless, her heartfelt attempt to bridge differences among women by emphasizing the discrimination they face because of their shared female bodies. This reading of history, however, depends on viewers not seeing the reality of Truth's racialized body. Given the symbolism of the vulva as representing unity among women, Truth's lack of a central core image translates poorly. If central cores represent real selves, what or where is the truth of Truth?"[12] Gerhard's assertion that *The Dinner Party* uses vulval imagery to suture a feminist relation between self, sexuality, and agency allows us to see how Chicago's choice of alternate imagery for Sojourner Truth's plate is a manifestation of the lack of discourse, feminist and otherwise, around black woman as sexual agents—the continued relevance of Truth's plaintive declaration "Ain't I a Woman" is poignantly on display here. By being left out of the vulval representational schema, Truth becomes a public self, a representative of her race rather than a body in possession of appetites and pleasures. We cannot even begin to imagine how Truth might orient herself, what she might hunger for, or what might bring her pleasure. Hortense Spillers takes Chicago's omission as symptomatic of mis-seen and unvoiced black women, writing, "By effacing the genitals, Chicago not only abrogates the disturbing sexuality of her subject, but also hopes to suggest that her sexual being did not exist to be denied in the first place."[13] This absence is symptomatic of the paucity of frameworks for grappling with black female sexuality, and it highlights the importance of thinking about the multiple hierarchies at work within the concept of relation and the permeable self. As we see in Chicago's failure to incorporate Truth's vulva into *The Dinner Party*, race—blackness in this case—becomes an unassimilable fleshy difference that disrupts the fantasy of a labial order of egalitarian pleasure, consumption, and mutuality.

The reception of Kara Walker's 2014 installation, *At the behest of Creative Time Kara E. Walker has confected: A Subtlety, or the Marvelous Sugar Baby, an Homage to the unpaid and overworked Artisans who have refined our Sweet tastes from the cane fields to the Kitchens of the New World on the Occasion of the demolition of the Domino Sugar Refining Plant*, offers another case study to think about the fraught relationship between blackness and sexuality. Here, the presence of the black vulva disrupts because it illustrates the difficulty of seeing black women outside the realm of the consumable. Walker was commissioned by Creative Time studio to produce a piece to commemorate the July 2014 demolition of the Domino Sugar factory in Williamsburg, Brooklyn. Her installation had two main components: the "Sugar Baby," a thirty-five-foot tall woman-sphinx made out of sugar-coated Styrofoam, positioned at one end of the factory, and her attendants, thirteen five-foot tall boys "confected" from molten sugar, which dotted the factory floor. Walker erected these figures to illuminate the complicated imbrications of sugar, race, and American capitalism. The Domino factory itself has a particularly fraught history in relation to different phases of capitalism. It was built in 1882, refined 50 percent of the sugar in the United States in the 1890s, and was the site of one of the longest labor disputes in New York City in the 2000s.[14] The Sugar Baby and her attendants offer a reminder of the black and brown lives lost in the service of making sugar while simultaneously evoking other histories of exploited labor—including the specter of Egyptian slave labor. These bodies and histories circulate through the exhibit, but the controversy focused on the Sugar Baby or Sphinx, whom Walker styled, using a headscarf, as a mammy.

Generally regarded as ideological construct rather than actual historical personage, the mammy has been cast as a loyal worker whose domestic care for the plantation family is symptomatic of a cozy interraciality that erases (or cannot incorporate) racist violence against slaves and other blacks in favor of imagining that her black motherly care brings racial harmony.[15] Micki McElya argues that the idea of the mammy's fidelity to the family that owned her served as a balm against the reality of tense relations between black and white Americans.[16] The mammy's particular role was to be accommodating, affectionate, and servile in order to facilitate white domestic idyll, thereby erasing her role as slave in favor of remembering her as quasi-kin.[17] As a maternal surrogate and slave, much of the mammy's work required tending intimately to the bodies of others.[18] As keeper of the hearth and the domestic warmth that it implied, the mammy offered her physical labor in the service of food to produce home.[19] This set of crossings registers the reliance of white comfort on black affective labor and the particular commodification of the black body into something edible. In revealing that the white appetite for black sweetness, labor, and sex underlies the production of domesticity, the mammy's smile cloaks a destructive history. It is this subversive edge that has made the mammy ripe territory for radical reappropriation by Walker and others.[20]

In keeping with the mammy's ability to soothe, white critics interpreted Walker's Sugar Baby as a triumphant model of black womanhood. Kara Rooney hints at this narrative of redemption when she draws connections between the Sugar Baby and black feminism. She asks Walker, "Does this New World sphinx—what sounds like a veritable femme-fatale—relate in any way to the black feminist literature that emerged in the '70s, initiated by Alice Walker, for example, or is it something more visceral and personal?"[21] Behind Rooney's question is the suggestion that the Sugar Baby may be a mammy, but she behaves as a queen—commanding respect because she appears to channel the pharaohic energy of the Egyptian sphinxes. Writing in the *New York Times*, Blake Gopnik registers important differences between Walker's earlier work and the Sugar Baby: "One set of silhouettes is easy to confuse with another, whereas the 'Marvelous Sugar Baby' is unlike any of them."[22] Elaborating on this observation, he writes, "With her earlier work, even her supporters conceded that the recurring antihero of Ms.

Walker's work—known as "the Negress"—had never had true control of her fate. But with Ms. Walker's Negress-as-sphinx, that underdog may have at last become the unbeatable overcat.... The figure may be wearing a mammie's kerchief, but she'll never be beaten into submission."[23] Roberta Smith's review of the installation, also for the *New York Times*, takes similar pleasure in describing the Sugar Baby as agential, especially in relation to the redemptive narrative of the black mother as originary, powerful, and wise.[24]

This was not the universal narrative, however. When the exhibit opened to the public, some patrons felt that the mammy figure served to represent the violence of consumption and mirrored their own unpleasant experiences of racialized commodification within the installation. Many visitors criticized the work (and the public response to it) as disrespectful and problematic because of Walker's decision to show the Sugar Baby's vulva, which, in turn, brought up the specter of violated, which is to say penetrated, blackness.[25] Throughout the course of the installation, patrons narrated offense and anger at other patrons' behavior online. Nicholas Powers's essay, "Why I Yelled at the Kara Walker Exhibit," describes feeling "rage" at the commodification of black pain. He writes: "So here it was, an artwork about how Black people's pain was transformed into money was a tourist attraction for them. A few weeks ago, I had gone to the 9/11 museum and no one, absolutely no one, posed for smiling pictures in front of the wreckage."[26] Stephanye Watts also describes feeling enraged by other people's responses when her mourning is interrupted: "I obviously didn't expect to start crying, but it happened and I let those tears run free. I was snapped out of my sob by a white guy yelling, 'This is boring!' Tears for my ancestors turned into hot, angry tears. It took everything in me to not walk over and clobber him to death."[27] Watts and Powers both use rage as a framework for unpacking their responses to other people's behavior in the installation. Having come to the installation expecting to recall the long history of anti-blackness, they understood the installation as a space to commemorate various forms of black pain. Responses to the Sugar Baby that were not intelligible as commemoration were upsetting and seemed to signal a lack of respect, thereby repeating anti-black violence. In voicing their disdain at other patrons' behavior, those visitors imply that there are appropriate and inappropriate sets of behaviors in the installation.

Inappropriate behavior—specifically taking selfies in front of the Sugar Baby in a way that suggested a sexual interaction with her—was read as a violation, a sign of disrespect to the legacy of slavery and an assault on the black people viewing the exhibit. Other black patrons felt as though they were being watched for their emotional responses to the piece, which felt like a different form of violation. Gloria Malone, for example, writes, "And so I ask: How could those spectators visit an exhibit and pose in a sexually suggestive manner with artwork paying homage to women who are exploited and often working in the shadows of society and show little regard for the artwork and the other women in the room, especially the Black women, some of whom were moved to tears because of the emotional impact the installation had on them?"[28] In arguing that patrons are violating the Sugar Baby by taking photographs of her in sexually compromised positions, Malone points to the way that the wound of black women's long history of being unable to consent is displayed. Yesha Callahan at the *Root* writes, "History has shown us time and time again how a black woman's body was (and sometimes still is) objectified. From the days of the slave trade to even having black butts on display in music videos, the black woman's body seems to easily garner laughs and mockery, even if it's made out of sugar."[29] Even as the Sugar Baby can be read as a monument that speaks to these historic violations, some viewers experience the imagined repetition of violation through photography as new, not just for the Sugar Baby, but for all black women.

In some ways this sexualized version of violation is one of the most expected responses to the Sugar Baby because it is in keeping with seeing black women as always already violated and always already available for consumption. What is more difficult to parse, though it also belongs to the realm of consent, is the feeling of emotional abuse, of experiencing suffering while others laugh. In this experience, which provokes rage in Watts and Powers, what is at issue is not a corporeal violation (though we might argue that its ghost remains), but an affective one. We might link this feeling of violation to Audre Lorde's description of abuse in "Uses of the Erotic:" "To share the power of each other's feeling is different from using another's feelings as we would use a Kleenex. When we look the other way from our experience, erotic or otherwise, we use rather than share the feelings of those others who participate in the experience with us. And use without consent of the used is abuse."³⁰ The violation that these patrons experience is that of becoming a spectacle, of being made consumable, without having consented to that. Malik Thompson gives voice to this feeling in his description of visiting the installation:

> In the muted light of the sugar factory, her very blue-eyes glowed as they searched my very pained face; they glowed with a mixture of pity, guilt, and confusion—perhaps these are the components of the ever toxic sentimentality? *Then, at that moment, I became uncomfortable, realized that even though this was obviously a cemetery, a place of remembrance and mourning for how Blackness has been distorted and destroyed throughout history, the pain I felt would always take a backseat to the comfort white people seek in lies. In that moment, I began remembering what violation felt like.*³¹

The becoming-spectacle that Thompson narrates is inextricable from race. His response becomes more visible to other patrons because he is read as black. In registering this difference, other patrons might also imagine that his response to the piece would be different from their own and watch him in order to come into contact with a "black" experience of viewing the piece. The visibility of Thompson's affective response is also in keeping with discourses that suture animatedness with blackness and blackness with pain.³²

The specter of the black body in pain is related to the violations that patrons might imagine have been visited on the Sugar Baby (or her flesh and blood counterparts), but it belongs to its own genre of racialized violence. Importantly, the specter of the black body in pain subtends discourses on liberal subjectivity through analogy. The feelings that these black bodies generate lead to guilt, which is a problem of not acting when one had the opportunity. While black bodies in pain might generate sympathy or empathy, these feelings ultimately become guilt and passivity, which manifest in performances of laughter, discomfort, and a certain type of willed ignorance. In describing the affective labor that the specter of the suffering black body performs, I argue that white innocence "is constructed through a focus on the suffering that guilt produces, which, in turn, manifests itself as empathy and analogizes the white body's current guilt to the black body's past (and present) trauma.

Through empathy, the substitution of the white body for the black body, current guilt or suffering distracts from the choice of inaction and produces color blindness."[33] In other words, while patrons might imagine that they are extending sympathy or empathizing with Thompson and the collective suffering of black people, what is really at stake is the potential to erase the specificity of black pain and the black body. Where black emotions function to privilege white pain or guilt, black bodies are again used without consent and are thereby further distanced from the parameters of sovereign subjectivity.

What links these patrons' experiences is not simply violation, but the danger of consumption. Each anecdote illuminates the powerful recoil at the idea that black (or brown) bodies are performing for white bodies. These performances are sexual or affective, but they all illustrate the difficulty of being perceived as a consumable commodity. As Hiram Pérez writes when exploring the dynamic of brown people performing for whites, the brown body acts "as a repository for the disowned, projected desires of a cosmopolitan subject, it is alternately (or simultaneously) primitive, exotic, savage, pansexual, and abject."[34] Vincent Woodward centralizes and literalizes consumption in *The Delectable Negro*, his history of cannibalism and homoeroticism in slave culture in the United States. Woodward argues that consumption was often hidden behind a rhetoric of objectification and abjection, but it worked to solidify the bonds of whiteness as it cloaked desire for blackness: "For white men, sex with and sexual attraction to black men was a natural by-product of their physical, emotional, and spiritual hunger for the same."[35] Further, Woodward positions this desire for black men as the basis for the existential question of what it is to be black: "Long before the poignant questions of the color line and the Negro problem registered in the black imagination, it seems that a more pressing problematic confronted the black citizen. In the form of a question, it might have registered as: 'How does it feel to be an edible, consumed object?' In other words, how does it feel to be an energy source and foodstuff, to be consumed on the levels of body, sex, psyche, and soul?"[36]

What Walker's installation makes clear is the importance of thinking about appetite as the manifestation of one's location within multiple circuits of power. Appetite belongs to the realm of the proprioceptive because it shows how power orients desire. The Sugar Baby and her fraught reception bring our attention to the powerlessness that can be experienced in being consumed. Walker's installation allows us to ask what it feels like to be constituted not only as desirable, but also consumable—a process akin to Irigaray's dialogic conversation in that it disassembles subject and object, but which is often experienced as loss, rather than pleasure. This sensation is one of being overwhelmed, taken in by the Other, regardless of whether one wants to participate in this dynamic or not. As we see in these descriptions of their experiences at *A Subtlety*, these participants felt violation rather than a pleasurable indistinguishability from the Other. Despite these difficult experiences, I do want to think what it might mean for us to stay with the proprioceptive and imagine pleasure in a permeable selfhood despite structural inequalities. In moving toward this possibility, we must reorient ourselves so that we remain attentive to the fact that the Sugar Baby acts as a reminder of the violent nature of the desire for sugar, for sweetness, for disposable ("free") labor, for forgiveness, for brown women, for accessible vulvas, but also remember that she is still a participant in her own economy of sensuality and appetite. Being overwhelmed does not mean that she has been annihilated, even as we may have to move beyond the individual and toward other registers of agency in order to see the ways that she activates a pleasurable porosity.

* * *

Working through the differences between the feeling of violation in Walker's installation and the pleasures of vulnerability in Irigaray's language of lips touching means thinking further with proprioception because it engages with the body's fleshiness and its relationship to the world (that is, how it touches and is touched). The challenge of thinking economies of racial violation in conjunction with those of gendered vulnerability is emblematic of several key issues. First, there is the difficulty scholars have had in imagining black female sexuality outside of a framework of violation, which stems not only from the historic atrocities of slavery, but also from the still tenuous relationship between blackness and agency. When sexuality is kept tethered to agency and sovereign subjectivity, it becomes easy to see that its organization flows hierarchically, so that some subjects are perpetually given tenuous (at best) sexual citizenship. Second, despite the discourse of intersectionality, gender and race are still often imagined separately, so that Irigaray's reorientation of the phallic economy does not always register as a critique of whiteness, and the problem of the animated, black consumable body is not framed as being applicable to the problem of phallocentrism. The difficulty reading these issues together is not a matter of compiling different identities, however. It is a question of epistemology and translation—how can we make these critiques of white phallocentrism speak to each other?

With regard to the issue of language and translation, one of the main difficulties has to do with the primacy of the visual, which assigns differential levels of agency to race, gender, and sexuality. In "Maiden Voyage" Dana Takagi argues that the assumption that race is always visible poses particular difficulties for thinking about the intersections of racial identity and sexual identity. Takagi writes, "There are numerous ways that being 'gay' is not like being 'Asian.' . . . There is a quality of voluntarism in being gay/lesbian that is usually not possible as an Asian American. One has the option to present oneself as 'gay' or 'lesbian,' or alternatively, to attempt to 'pass,' or to stay in 'the closet,' that is, to hide one's sexual preference. However, these same options are not available to most racial minorities in face-to-face interactions with others."[37] Whereas making one's sexuality visible is assumed to be a matter of agency, one's racial identity is understood as a matter of external perception. Jasbir Puar argues that understanding race through visuality is emblematic of the discourse's embeddedness within disciplinary society. Moving toward a new theory of race, she argues, entails paying attention to geopolitics, space, and becoming. She writes:

> Resuturing the foundational function of race within biopolitics to the production of ontologically irreducible entities in control societies, the geopolitics of racial ontology marks the manifestation of different spatializing regimes of the body, and its particles, such that the biological caesura that demarcates the cut of or for racism is now not just a question of visible racial difference or of the taxonomic and eugenic science of phrenology and the scientific racism of the eighteenth through early twentieth centuries. . . . The emphasis on geopolitics amends what might otherwise be a location-less notion of ontology, an unmarked locational investment of recent work on ontology, much of it neither accounting

for the productive force of geopolitics within its scholarly purview nor acknowledging the geopolitical forces that enable theorizing.[38]

Puar's turn to a geopolitical ontology resonates with my focus on the proprioceptive dimensions of the labial. Both projects require us to think about the specifics of flesh's location in space as a way to understand how intimacies embedded in asymmetrical relations of power might work. Specifically, race orients by emphasizing the danger that exists in being consumed while also offering the possibility of thinking with the pleasures of consumption. When thinking with race, relation must be thought in conjunction with the perils and possibilities that inhere in inequality.

In order to imagine the Sugar Baby's orbit of sensuality, then, we must bring critiques of whiteness into conversation with critiques of phallocentrism in order to move toward a more embodied understanding of racial difference. It is not that differences should not matter, but they should be understood in a register separate from the sovereign subject and its possession of agency. An over-focus on agency as the pivot point for who constitutes a subject is the logic that undergirds the denigration of the feminine that Irigaray critiques and the racialized hierarchies that render blackness the edge of what it means to be a human.[39] In Irigaray's disruption of this logic of choice and agency, we see receptivity and relation, but we need to expand our understanding of what these heterotopias might consist.

Treva B. Lindsey and Jessica Marie Johnson write toward this form of heterotopia in their analysis of the possibility of theorizing pleasure during slavery. Walker's Sugar Baby, they suggest, "compels the viewer to encounter the black female body as subject and object, as laborer, desired, and commodified; as desiring, erotic, and violated; as visible but illegible; as mysterious, unknowable but knowing; as ambivalent and as powerful. The virility of the Sugar Sphinx is palpable, but her desires and intimate longings remain mysterious, though not unknowable or unspeakable."[40] Further, they write, "If we approach the history of enslavement as though orgasms, wetness, and writhing, pulsating, aroused bodies existed, our understanding of enslaved and free women of color's lives will begin to defy slaveowners' conceptions of black sexuality. Instead of depicting enslaved and free women of color as once again becoming the property of someone else, scholars must challenge themselves to write fully actualized, *erotic*, historical subjects."[41]

In a similar vein, Alex Weheliye argues that desire be re-thought through the matrix of hunger. By bringing together a longing for freedom and the experience of captive bodies, hunger is crucial for thinking about pleasure and enfleshment: "Partaking of the flesh, albeit the habeaus viscus kind rather than the pure abjection varietal tenders flavors and textures found in lives of imprisoned freedom, desires for survival, and viscous dreams of life that awaken future anterior humanities, which exceed Man's inesculent culinary laws."[42] Reading with Lindsey and Johnson's plea to imagine black women as desiring, even under conditions of duress, as well as with Weheliye's argument that hunger is vital to the possibility of freedom, gives us a way to approach the question of relation anew. In particular it announces spatiality and orientation as aspects of fleshiness, which operate on multiple scales and which produce differing intimacies as a result.

When we think beyond the individual, we can grasp the fleshiness, sensuality, and pleasure of *A Subtlety* on multiple registers. First, we can position the installation in relation to a critique of global capitalism. Nato Thompson, the head curator of Creative Time, describes Walker's intervention in his curatorial statement:

> Walker's gigantic temporary sugar-sculpture speaks of power, race, bodies, women, sexuality, slavery, sugar refining, sugar consumption, wealth inequity, and industrial might that uses the human body to get what it needs no matter the cost to life and limb. Looming over a plant whose entire history was one of sweetening tastes and aggregating wealth, of refining sweetness from dark to white, she stands mute, a riddle so wrapped up in the history of power and its sensual appeal that one can only stare stupefied, unable to answer.[43]

Further, Walker's use of sugar, itself a commodity central to the establishment of capitalism per Sidney Mintz's argument, centralizes the role of appetite as a driving force in colonialism.[44] Indeed, Walker's installation plays with the imbrication of capitalism, labor, and race in ways that are not only representational but also site-specific. Tavia Nyong'o notes that the project was financed by the owners of the Domino Sugar factory who, in addition to exploiting brown and black workers, profited from closing the factory and selling the land to condo developers as part of Williamburg's gentrification. Nyong'o writes:

> The combined and uneven development of global capitalism was rarely more clearly on view than here, in a public art project that worked simultaneously as reputation laundering for the Fanjul brothers, corporate barons whose blood money (extracted from the cane fields in the Dominican Republic, where Haitian migrants labor in post-slavery conditions) bankrolled the exhibit. The piece cannot begin to make sense without accounting for the manner in which Fanjul Corp., owners of Domino Sugar, stand to profit off the deindustrialization of their former factory, and the reimagining of its extended footprint as a further extension of their creative capital.[45]

From this perspective we might argue that the decision to create public art at the site of the Domino Factory is an attempt to negate the violence that occurred (or, is occurring via gentrification) in this space. However, Walker's Sugar Baby consolidates these appetites onto one figure and thereby becomes a memorial to exploitation. Reading Walker in relation to Lisa Lowe's emphasis on reinvigorating the relations between "the emergence of European liberalism, settler colonialism in the Americas, the transatlantic African slave trade, and the East Indies and China trades in the late eighteenth and early nineteenth centuries" reveals the complex global intimacies that are attached to these forces and desires.[46] In *The Intimacies of Four Continents*, Lowe argues for moving intimacy away from its conventional mooring to the framework of sovereign subjectivity toward a broader perspective that privileges relation. In place of the subject, interiority, and personal property, Lowe prioritizes "a 'political economy' of intimacies, by which I mean a particular calculus governing the production, distribution, and possession of intimacy."[47] For Lowe, intimacy is about a set of relations occurring on the global stage, which gives some subjects access to personhood and keeps others in the shadows. By revealing the shadow processes, people, and geographies that produce subjectivity and sexuality, Lowe displaces the sovereign subject and the subject/object binary. This is another mode of thinking with the dialogic self. Lowe's work expands our critique of white phallocentrism and moves us toward a reconceptualization of the sensorial registers by which we should apprehend intimacy.

In displacing the primacy of subjectivity, we move toward the space around the individual—and, incidentally, around the vulval. This space includes both those forces that exceed the subject such as capitalism and colonialism, which Lowe's analysis describes, and those forces that occur "before the individual," which Kyla Schuller positions in relation to Tompkins's analysis of eating.[48] Power, Schuller writes, "materializes in the form of force that circulates and aggregates below and before the level of the individual. Power transpires through a field of the consumable, penetrant, dispersible, and absorbable, coordinating life well beyond the human, beyond the nominally alive, even as it forms the shifting parameters of embodied difference."[49] This is to say that the smaller, ingestible, molecular aspects of the consumable also reorient appetite. I locate this reorientation within the parameters of the labial, however, because the molecular also relies on porosity and produces permeable selfhood—even if the chief organ for this is not necessarily the vulva or the mouth. We see this mobilization of the molecular in the grains of sugar and Styrofoam that make up the Sugar Baby as well as in the smells that waft from the installation courtesy of the melting five-foot tall boys that dotted the factory floor. Through the course of the installation these figures become molecular, filling visitors' nostrils with an increasingly pungent smell.

Though less controversial than the Sugar Baby, these youthful attendants are ripe for our analytic gaze. Confecting them from a mixture of molten sugar and covered with molasses, Walker modeled these boys on plastic trinkets depicting blackamoors, which she purchased online.[50] Throughout the installation the heat in the factory caused the figures to melt into the floor. Some lost limbs; others became coated with brown sugar. Most began to smell after a few weeks. Unlike the Sugar Baby, whose Styrofoam base ensures that she will remain erect, the attendants visibly suffer the ravages of time and show the costs of laboring.

These servants, already part of racist iconography, are perpetually at work; they carry empty baskets or bunches of bananas. Their efforts are part of multiple circuits of history and migration. As early modern sculptural objects, the blackamoors served as bejeweled decorations for rich European households, offering reminders of the wealth and power amassed by conquests in Africa. In this way, they provide a glimpse of the colonial consumption of black servant bodies. Walker, however, encounters these objects not in museums, but as plastic trinkets made in China. This contemporary locus touches on the globalization of an appetite for black performance while also indexing the exploitation of Chinese workers and an economy that privileges plastic's disposable pleasures—exempting, of course, its endurance as waste.

As monuments in Walker's installation, the blackamoors bring together disparate histories of labor, but they also resist commodification through the act of melting. Melting not only signals these objects' ephemerality—even as many of them circulate after the installation as preserved museum objects—but also illuminates the power of becoming-molecular. As molecules they permeate the atmosphere, becoming unassimilable to an economy of racialized consumption in which their bodies give other people pleasure. They cease to become recognizable bodies, and their molecularization means that they permeate the viewer intensely and perhaps more intimately. In Lowe's reframing of intimacy she offers disintegration and decay as possible sites of theorization, naming them "those processes that are forgotten, cast as failed or irrelevant because they do not produce 'value' legible within modern classifications."[51] Melting also functions as a manifestation of liquidity, which offers an escape from the totalizing grasp of consumption and brings the blackamoor (or rather the puddle that was part of the blackamoor) into a separate economy of sensuality and appetite. In the blackamoors' becoming-molecular, they show us the alternate ecologies at play in the installation. Nyong'o describes their performance as one of disintegration:

> The fragile sugar sculptures (each baby constructed according to a different method of assembling sugar crystal, molasses and wire) retained their shape if only for a particular duration before melting and falling apart at different rates.... And the child sticking eager hands in pools of red goo on the final day of their installation was but the most direct evidence of the manner in which mass audience affected the material objects: on at least some days the collective temperature, respiration and perspiration of the audience would have subtly interacted with the state of the molas-

ses sculpture, accelerating their decay into liquid pools without even a physical touching.[52]

As Nyong'o notes, porosity is part of the point. The fragility of these objects illuminates the influence of humans, vermin, and weather on the processes of consumption. Most saliently, these forces are part of how audiences perceived the installation through the sense of smell. This is because we register this spectacle of decay on the level of the olfactory. Becoming-molecular, in this case, is becoming pungent.

As the boys melted and the temperatures inside the warehouse soared, the molasses on the walls and on the boys began to smell. Blake Gopnik writes, "The smell hits you first: sweet but with an acrid edge like a thousand burned marshmallows."[53] Leigh Silver describes it as "the smell of rot. It's the smell of decay."[54] Into this landscape, we gain another way to think about the ways that bodies might mingle outside of subject/object binaries—through the floating particles of smell and through the intimacy of the nose. Smell in Walker's installation offers a reminder of what the factory used to do, but it also offers a connection to the diasporic in Martin Manalasan's argument that "olfaction is a marker of the marginal stranger/foreigner and the ways that such sensorial markers become part of grids that speak to issues of hygiene, disgust, and aspirations."[55] Here, we see the way that smell speaks to the molecular component of appetite. Attraction and repulsion are propelled by these chemical interactions. LaMonda Horton-Stallings frames the alternate epistemology of smell—particularly that of the malodorous variety—within a genealogy of black funk. She writes, "The etymology of *black funk* emphasizes that funk is a rewriting of smell and scene away from a nineteenth-century ordering and socialization of corporeal power that represses what stinks, but that does not mean it does mean it lacks intelligence or spirituality; rather, it provides other paradigms of intellect and spirit."[56] When we keep the stench of *A Subtlety* with us, not only does it offer a chance to experience the repulsive side of appetite, it changes the scale of relationality and receptivity. Smell is, after all, insistently spatial. It offers a way to orient to another without necessarily working through the visual. This form of becoming-molecular shows us the porosity of the individual and the fleshiness of chemistry; bonds form and break in the service of intimate sensuality. Here, we might also think about the

Sugar Baby's granularity, which breaks apart at the touch, as also enacting its own form of molecular mixing.

Through the lens of proprioception, we see that appetite operates "beyond" the individual and the sovereign subject such that it inheres in either the global or the chemical. Both scalar shifts allow us to see how thinking with the movement *toward* eclipses the question of agency. Instead, relations emerge from everywhere—dynamics within the nostril and forces of global capital. The field of the labial is expansive because everything is porous; but we must think simultaneously with the pleasures and dangers of fleshiness—that space of brown jouissance—in order to understand the stakes of inhabiting a dialogic, permeable self.

2

Surface Play

Flash, Friction, and Self-Reflection

In her painting of a rhinestone-encrusted black vulva, Mickalene Thomas challenges our understanding of black women's relationship to knowledge and self-production. She explores and rejects the conventional objectifying discourses of *scientia sexualis*—an expansive set of logics that includes the exploitation of black women's bodies within gynecological experimentation and a pornographic gaze that seeks to fix the truth of race or gender within black women's splayed legs. Instead of trafficking in this legacy of anonymous pain, Thomas illuminates the pleasures of tactility and opacity offered by excess surface.

Most overtly, Thomas's *Origin of the Universe 1* (2012) revises Gustave Courbet's *The Origin of the World* (1866), a painting that created a minor scandal when it was unveiled because it dared to bring the pornographic into the milieu of fine art.[1] In contrast to other nudes of the era, Courbet's elision of the rest of the naked figure directed viewers' gazes to that which had circulated mainly in private spaces—the vulva. We can also read his decision to absent the model's head, legs, and arms as emblematic of a sexological discourse that sutures female sexuality to the genital, while his deployment of a realist aesthetic allows us to see how this painting furthered pornography's argument that sexuality is visually knowable. As such, *The Origin of the World* was imagined to transmit truths not only about genitalia, but also about sexuality as a whole. That the painting purported to illuminate "the origin of the world" further amplified this aura of truthfulness. This knowledge was, however, understood to be private, since Courbet assumed that whoever possessed the painting would want to conceal it because of its provocative nature—indeed, Jacques Lacan, who owned the painting for many years, kept it hidden behind a screen in his house in Guitrancourt.[2] However, as Linda Williams reminds us, the practices of visibility and categorization

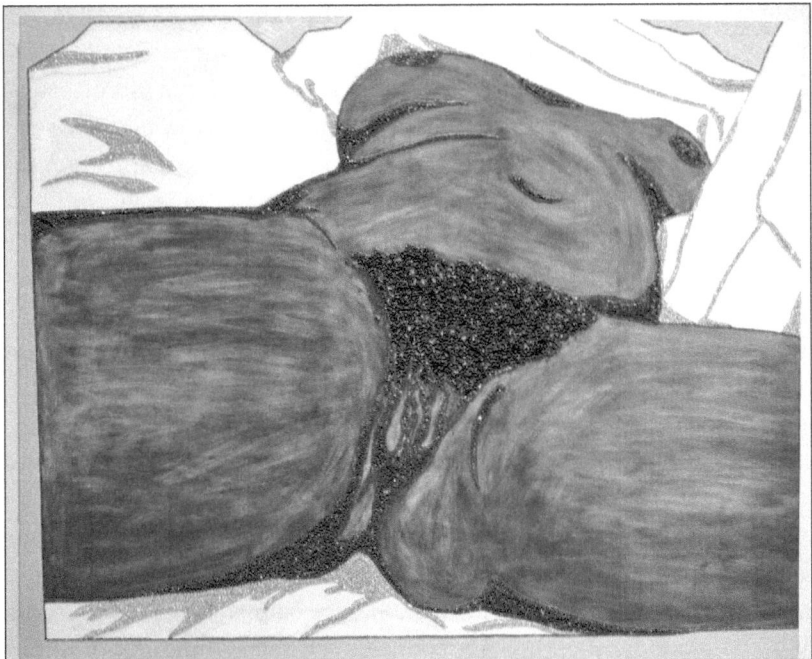

Figure 2.1. Mickalene Thomas, *Origin of the Universe 1*, 2012. Image and original data provided by Larry Qualls; Photographer: Larry Qualls; © 2012 Artists Rights Society (ARS), New York.

that underlie pornography and sexology also reify the notion of invisible female pleasure and enigmatic female sexuality: "This maximum visibility proves elusive in the parallel confession of female sexual pleasure."[3]

While Thomas takes her cue from *The Origin of the World*, she draws on this representational conundrum to present queer pleasures, making a spectacle of their unknowability by bringing our attention to the surface and the importance of opacity. We can understand Thomas's reworking of Courbet as part of a larger project to portray black and brown women as more than merely objectified. In her framing of Thomas's work, art critic Roberta Smith writes that her "quotations are notable for going beyond mere one-liner mimicry or conceptual appropriation; they radically de-Europeanize and contemporize their sources."[4] The de-Europeanization that Smith refers to is not just a matter of Thomas's drawing on black and brown models, but of her doing so in a way that moves them away from the space of pornographic objectification and positions them as selves with their own erotic pleasures. It is notable, for example, that in contrast to Courbet's anonymous model, the genitals that Thomas paints are her own. This fact positions her as both subject and object of her own creation, signaling her agency and her self-awareness of her objectification within an economy of *scientia sexualis*, and it locates the painting within the realm of brown jouissance.

Thomas produces this portrait of agency, pleasure, and objectification by employing surface as a formal strategy of producing opacity. This activation of a surface aesthetic serves as a rejection of the mandate of transparency, while also enabling alternate modes of apprehending pleasure and selfhood. There are several layers to thinking Thomas's relation to surface. First, there is the question of size. *Origin of the Universe 1* is a large painting (sixty by forty-eight inches), which invites the contemplation of surface as a spectacle. In this way, I understand spectacle to be operating in opposition to the pornographic or scientific gaze in that through its excess, it disrupts the possibility of contained knowledge. Additionally, the nature of spectacle invites us into the specific realm of black hypervisuality through Thomas's use of the rhinestone and the reflective dimensions of their shine. Instead of vagina as void, the rhinestones emphasize the ways that this vulva's materiality lies at the center of two epistemologies of intimacy—friction and narcissism.

Rhinestones, Surface, and the Pleasures of Commodification

Origin of the Universe 1 insistently traffics in a spectacle of excess surface and surface excess. In grappling with excess surface, I have already mentioned its large size, but when we think with the rhinestone, we can also see how this form of excess relates to tactility and cover. Surface excess, meanwhile, can be understood to lie in the rhinestone's relationship to shine and decorativeness. Both concepts help us refine what is at stake in thinking with the surface.

Anne Anlin Cheng argues that the fascination with the idea of the surface emerged from a twentieth-century fetishization of transparency and "the mysteries of the visible."[5] In other words, surface functions as the underside of a scientific and pornographic drive toward locating knowledge in an "objective" image. However, in contradistinction to this ideology of objectivity and transparency, flirting with the surface can,

Cheng asserts, lead to "profound engagements with and reimaginings of the relationship between interiority and exteriority, between essence and covering."[6] This means that surface offers the possibility of doubleness, troubling transparency and the idea of authenticity. In this way, surface complicates categorization because it confounds ideas of what knowledge is, where it lies, and how we can apprehend it. Cheng writes that the problem of the modern surface is "distinguishing decoration as surplus from what is 'proper' to the thing."[7] In *Origin of the Universe 1*, what we want to ask, then, is whether surface is about nakedness and being stripped down or about shine and glamor. Reading with surface emphasizes multiple strategies for producing opacity.

In *Origin of the Universe 1* Thomas places rhinestones where we might expect to see shadows. They appear in the creases of sheets, to mark the contours of flesh, to demarcate nipples, pubic hair, and labial folds. They disrupt the flat planes of color with their raised and sparkling presence. Instead of peeking inward, we are distracted by surface and ornamentation. Rhinestones offer Thomas a palette beyond oils; they provide a way to expand the surface of her paintings and to gesture toward epistemologies not captured by realism. Meghan Dailey describes the impact that working with rhinestones has had on Thomas's work:

> The rhinestones, some are Swarovski crystal, are what define her paintings. She sets them like jewels in already bold floral and animal prints, creating a dazzling optical intensity and adding, through their sparkle, a sense of movement. She also uses them to outline the contours of the women's bodies and emphasize their most sensual features—lips, eyes—and parts that are usually concealed: nipples, the lines on the soles of their bare feet. "Oil painting was never satisfying to me," Thomas explains. "I always felt like I had to put something on it or it was never finished."[8]

We might also, however, understand this decorative excess as providing a type of cover, which preserves the opacity of interiority. In this way, Thomas halts the gaze at the surface. In lieu of satisfying the scientific/pornographic gaze's desire for visual knowledge as "truth," Thomas presents an excess of ornamentation and cover. Here, we see that in refusing the edicts of interiority, hewing to the surface becomes a radical act in its privileging of opacity. In this, we can read the rhinestone in relation to

Krista Thompson's analysis of the ways that black diasporic artists have deployed shine as distraction in order to produce an "un-visibility," so that blackness is spectacular, but not knowable.[9]

We can also read Thomas's replacement of flesh with rhinestones as a comment on the history of the commodification of brown bodies. This follows from Thompson's analysis that shine signals "a distinct aesthetic of material excess . . . a 'bling-bling' aesthetic—'bling' being a word that in its doubling highlights the spectacular display of material surplus."[10] This attachment to materiality acts as a reminder of the long association between black people and the commodity, while at the same time offering an opportunity to take on this objectification as a mode of producing opacity *and* as emphasizing what happens when we think with the commodity. In other words, shine makes it difficult to separate the fleshiness of black bodies from the materiality of the decorative. This calls into question the separateness of the categories of person and thing without embracing any of the negative affects of commodification. Shine plays joyfully with the idea of the body as body while rejecting the demand to present anything other than surface. Thompson writes, "In many respects, we might see the fascination with adorning and picturing the body's surface in jewels, the taking-on of the shame of things, as a type of screen."[11] Thomas's use of rhinestones, then, is also about the inability to separate the flesh of the body from the manmade commodity of the rhinestone.[12]

We might ask, then, what it means that rhinestones are *not* precious gems, but relatively inexpensive and disposable. This quality of rhinestones is part and parcel of their resonance with funk, the musical/dance genre that emerged in the mid-1960s from blues, soul, and jazz and gained widespread cultural visibility in the 1970s with acts such as George Clinton, Sly and the Family Stone, and Betty Davis. These musicians melded together rhythmic beats, sexually suggestive vocals, and movement into big, loud performances. Funk is excess surface, something that LaMonda Horton-Stallings argues offers a black radical "rejection of the Western will to truth, or the quest to produce a truth about sexuality, and underscores such truth as a con and joke. In lieu of singular truths about eroticism or sexuality, [these artists] offer multiple fictions of sex to slip the yoke of sexual terrorism, violence, and colonization."[13] The "funky erotixxx" that Horton-Stallings seeks to cultivate "is unknowable and immeasurable, with transgenerational, affective, and psychic modalities that problematize the erotic and what it means to be human."[14] Indeed, from this perspective we can see Thomas's use of rhinestones as a rejection of the will to truth and an embrace of the possibility of pleasure in all of surface's excesses.

Thomas's use of rhinestones also speaks to one of the undersides of reading with surface—the production of part objects. This happens when the surface is mistaken for the whole. Cheng argues that this occurs especially in the fetishization of surface in relation to ideas of race as a surface phenomenon of difference. Seeing racial difference as surface can prevent one from registering the wholeness of those deemed racially Other. She traces this through the fantasy of "remaking one's self in the skin of the other," which works both for imagining whiteness as a form of escape and for thinking about brownness as a space of the exotic.[15] This fantasy of the surface cannot even begin to imagine interiority because it is so taken with fragmentation. Along these lines, she writes, "The crystallization of 'surface' as an aesthetic ideal at the birth of the twentieth century holds profound philosophic and material connections to (not just disavowals of) the violent and dysphoric history of racialized, ruptured skin."[16] This is to say that the maintenance of the integrity of one surface may be dependent on the breaking up of another. In addition to rendering her pleasures opaque through distraction and cover, then, Thomas's use of rhinestones can also be read within the framework of fragmentation. By bedazzling the painting of her vulva, Thomas produces herself as a set of part objects, so that the final product is whole, but the fragments remain. On the one hand, this breaking apart prevents us from imagining that we are seeing *all* of Thomas; on the contrary, it highlights her opacity, even as she has made a portrait of her vulva available to us. On the other hand, in her existence as part object—especially vulval part object—we see the possibility of the objectifying gaze that registers her as consumable.

While I use the rhinestone and its aesthetics of surface excess as an example of brown jouissance's strategic fleshiness, in this inability to exist untethered from racist and sexist imaginaries we see the perils of strategies of the flesh. This oscillation between opacity and vulnerability is one of the difficulties of trying to sever surface from depth, and it invites us to think about this manifestation of brown jouissance as excess surface in relation to tactility. Since the duality of self-making and objectification become encoded on the surface of the painting through the rhinestone, touch is another way to think about the work that brown jouissance accomplishes. This zone, where the depth of interiority becomes perceptible on the surface, is what Rizvana Bradley names the *haptic*. She writes, "The haptic can be understood as the viscera that ruptures [sic] the apparent surface of any work, or the material surplus that remains the condition of possibility for performance."[17] Further, this physically tangible surface excess allows us to see touch as a form of penetration. In this, I follow Kathryn Bond Stockton, who in her critique of surface reading—a movement within literary studies that favors the descriptive—argues that words penetrate their readers in order to gain meaning.[18] Stockton compares reading to kissing: "Think of all that happens when you kiss a text (if I can use these terms). Penetration's in the kiss. A dizzy array: kissing with your eyes (since you don't lick a text) becomes in an instant a penetration of you; from this penetration, there's immediate birth."[19] Kissing's tactility is put on display as a mode of coming toward an understanding of interiority. In this analogy, Stockton argues that it is impossible for something to remain "only" on the surface. The act of perception (in this case reading) is objectifying. In another essay on the same topic, kissing becomes barebacking, which Stockton codes as "lesbian": "Gay male barebacking is like dildoing is like kissing is like reading: it's *a fetishizing of a sign and surface* that must get inside us, where a sign-and-surface birth and cause some death."[20] In a cheeky reading of surface, Stockton arrives at the lesbian by reading an attachment to surface as its own form of penetration because of the impossibility of grappling with surface *without* coming toward penetration. In Stockton's writing, the word "sign" is what comes to signify surface, but signs cannot be thought without activating individual and cultural understandings of these concepts, which can be described as penetrations of the word. This is better understood when she elaborates on the term "lesbian":

> We have been dildoed by the sign "lesbian." We've been pleasured by it, as it's come inside us—I've had to try to take it like a man—but we've also split from each other at the very point of our contact with the sign. Somewhere where denotation births connotation, we start feeling erotic

rips and tears. Ours is truly a fractured sameness in several directions. We are like the figure of two lips touching, touching *through* their gapping, that Luce Irigaray offered and explored in the 1970s as a figure for (self-)caressing through (self-)splitting (lips I wrote about in the 1990s as a figure for a sexual self-estrangement). Through our contact with the sign "lesbian," my lover and I, so profoundly different, touch upon the nearness Irigaray conceptualized through the touching lips, deriving pleasure "from what is so near that [we] cannot have it, nor have [ourselves]." Some self-fracturing, breaking sameness, is to be found in a "lesbian" kiss.[21]

This gap between the sign/surface and experience is where Stockton locates attachment, pleasure, and meaning-making. This is also the space between Thomas and the histories of black femininity that she references in *Origin of the Universe 1*. While Thomas uses her self-portrait as an expansive and ornamented surface, she cannot help but be penetrated by the sign of black woman. In summoning her own agency, she cannot escape her objectification, but she does have tools for augmenting the space between sign and surface—queerness and rhinestones—and, in this production of the gap, black femininity penetrates the viewer differently. I register the painting's penetrations as moments of brown jouissance in which Thomas's fleshiness claws back at objectification.

Sister Outsider: Surface Residue and Generational Friction

That Thomas's rhinestones evoke a 1970s aesthetic is not incidental; they serve as a marker of her attachment to 1970s womanism, which she describes in an interview with Sean Landers as "formed in large part by Audre Lorde's discussion of a Sister Outsider, of being a part of feminism but still being outside and under recognized." As Kara Walker does, we might read this attachment as a form of nostalgia: "Thomas's paintings signal nostalgia for that transitional moment when desire, individuation, and upward mobility press against Blaxploitation."[22] However, Thomas herself pushes against this framing to argue that her attention to the 1970s is part of a "recontextualizing process" designed to show the complexity of who she is: "I try to incorporate all these aspects of myself in my work: what I grew up with, what I'm inspired by—textiles, African photography, Yoruban art, Cubism, Matisse. How can I take the ingredients of who I am and put them into a painting? What does that look like? What does that feel like? What's the residue of that?"[23] Through Thomas's emphasis on residue, we see what happens when one brings womanism, which I read as a politics that draws attention to the frictions within feminism, to the surface.[24]

This turn to womanism renders Thomas's choice to use the word "universe" instead of "world" (as Courbet did) significant. It indicates an epistemology in which queer black sexuality is the point of origin. In some ways this is literal. Though she passed away in 2012, Sandra Bush, Thomas's mother, was not only a mother, but also a muse:

> As an artist I have always been astonished not only by my mother's strength and tenacity but also by her sustained elegance and charisma in spite of harsh obstacles. Although she was not able to attain the adulation she desired from the fashion industry, her flair as a model and entertainer was perpetually self-evident. Sandra became the model for my own photographic investigations. We worked together in a productive artist-and-muse relationship, ultimately generating a series of photographs and paintings known as "Mama Bush."[25]

Their collaboration also helped to heal a rift caused by Bush's drug use while Thomas was a teenager. In an interview with the *New York Times*, Thomas frames these sessions as "a kind of therapy. I began to look at her as a person and accept her weaknesses, her failures."[26] Thomas portrays her mother in numerous guises: "Mama Bush, as her mother is known, has stood in for everything from a 1970s diva to a nude odalisque in some of Thomas's exuberant, rhinestone-encrusted collage-paintings; in the 2009 video piece 'Ain't I a Woman (Sandra),' Bush vamps to Eartha Kitt in a bold red-and-black sweater with big shoulder pads."[27] But, through an elastic reading of generationality, I prefer to think about the ways that her mother also stands in for her. We see this most poignantly when Sean Landers asks her whom she sees in the mirror and Thomas answers, "It's always me. Sometimes it's also my mother, my grandmother, or my great-grandmother."[28] In this imagination of an expansive matrilineal selfhood, Thomas echoes words from the prologue of Lorde's biomythography, *Zami: A New Spelling of My Name*: "I have felt the age-old triangle of mother father child, with the 'I' at its eternal core, elongate and flatten out into the elegantly strong triad of grandmother mother daughter, with the 'I' moving back and forth flowing in either or both directions as needed."[29] I read this as a way to think queer black sexuality through the expansive self that is created by thinking with the maternal. In this, I argue not only for a consideration of Thomas as mother or child, but for a more capacious understanding of the maternal as a form of multigenerational selfhood.

Thomas's insistence on having this expansive self and its sensuality, desire, and woman-loving politics meet as "residue" reminds us of surface's connection to touch and the fleshiness of the surface. The residue that Thomas invokes does not remain in the past, however; it frames our current perception of the black female body. By insisting on a language of maternity and sex, she brings the residue of Lorde and womanism into the future. This is the origin of a new universe, attentive to the radical insights of Lorde's feminism while open to the surface possibilities of friction. In this resignification of the past, I see Thomas's emphasis on residue operating as a sign of temporal drag, to use Elizabeth Freeman's term. According to Freeman, temporal drag looks like "corporeal and sartorial recalcitrance" and is associated with "retrogression, delay, and the pull of the past on the present."[30] It offers insight, however, into the potential excesses of history, in which drag functions "as a *productive* obstacle to progress, a usefully distorting pull backward, and a necessary pressure on the present tense."[31] In this formulation, the residue that Thomas describes functions as a marker of the presence of 1970s black lesbian feminist politics and lesbian feminism in general *within* contemporary iterations of black female queerness.

This insistence on 1970s black lesbian politics is especially radical because these politics, especially in their entanglement with the larger sphere of lesbian feminism, is usually positioned as essentialist and monolithic, antithetical to a queer sensibility that is imagined to be capacious and fluid. Though Lorde has been incorporated into a queer canon of sorts, her lesbian feminism has not been.[32] This is the case even as womanism is explicit about its relation to lesbian feminism, which we can see in Alice Walker's definition of the term: "Womanist . . . A woman who loves other women, sexually and/or nonsexually . . . [and is] committed to survival and wholeness of entire people, male *and* female."[33] Instead, its attention to racism and racial inequality is often (retrospectively) viewed as a source of friction within lesbian feminism.

Lesbian feminism is often positioned as what needed to be surpassed in order to arrive at the present. The 1970s is, therefore, as Clare Hemmings argues, "consistently marked as thoroughly unified in its aims, unreflexive in its theorizations, yet bold in its ambitions."[34] Further, in these characterizations of the 1970s, as Linda Garber notes, it is the figure of the lesbian feminist that bears the brunt of negative political representation. This is where the friction/residue of race comes in. Clare Hemmings writes that the lesbian feminist is stereotyped as "the flannel shirt androgyne, close minded, antisex puritan humourless racist and classist ignoramous essentialist utopian; [the lesbian feminist] often stands as a symbol for the limits of cross-class and cross-race alliances in second wave feminism."[35] In this scripting of the 1970s as passé, the presumption of whiteness and the charge of racism emerge as symbols of this out-of-time-ness. Being passé, however, also carries with it the implication that lesbian feminism was not interested in the sexual and, in fact, demonized most expressions of sexuality. In part, this perception is due to lesbian feminists' focus on depathologizing lesbianism and moving it out of the realm of the sexological toward the territory of the everyday, attaching it to feminism, femininity, and family. Unfortunately, this emphasis on female homosociality was often coupled with a condemnation of pornography and S&M as antifeminist and harmful to women.

While Lorde's focus on the erotic as a feminine resource is exemplary of this broadening of feminine desire—she highlights the nurturing and egalitarian aspects of femininity and argues that pornography emphasizes anti-sociality and inauthentic feelings—this charge of passéness enables people to assign some of Lorde's ideas (about pornography, for example) to the realm of a disavowable lesbian feminism even as Lorde herself is often figured as a proto-queer theorist. However, this whitewashing of lesbian feminism neglects to take into account the potential value of Lorde's (and other women of color feminists') critiques. Rather than simply registering them as part of a moralistic anti-sex panic, we might see them as moving toward an intersectional analysis of sexuality in which the objectification of black women carries with it particular histories that complexify (or add friction to) any straightforward cultural condemnation or embrace of a sexual practice. Writing in this vein, Sharon Holland argues that "absenting *these* somewhat conservative black feminist opinions from the women of color intellectual project performs damaging work" by removing the specificities of race from discourses of sexuality.[36] By drawing our attention to Lorde's black maternal universe, Thomas leads us to consider the possibilities of generational friction anew, and friction, in turn, allows us to contemplate less discussed sensual intimacies.

By this, I mean that the residual and frictional come together most pointedly in Thomas's emphasis on the clitoris. While Courbet's *The Origin of the World* eschews any representation of the clitoris in favor of portraying the vagina as void, Thomas's depiction of her clitoris is at once more anatomically correct and excessive in that it gestures toward the possibility of pleasure that is activated through friction rather than by penetration. Further, the clitoris's designation as vestigial (or residual) organ—it is understood within evolutionary biology as developmentally homologous with the penis, but vestigial because scientists cannot specify an adaptive purpose—speaks to its inability to be contained within a universe of scientific objectivity.[37]

Thomas's emphasis on the clitoris is in many ways emblematic of the 1970s feminist reclamation of the organ. Following William Masters and Virginia Johnson's findings that the clitoris played a role in both clitoral and vaginal orgasms, feminists argued for a clitorally-based rather than vaginally-based sexuality. In an expanded version of her 1968 article, "Myth of the Vaginal Orgasm," Anne Koedt wrote that disseminating physiological data would combat the previous misinformation about sexuality: "Rather than starting with what women *ought* to feel, it would seem logical to start out with the anatomical facts regarding the clitoris and vagina."[38] She celebrated Masters and Johnson's findings of a universal clitoral orgasm and its promise for feminism. Sexual autonomy, specifically the image of an orgasmic woman, was a vital component of second-wave feminism. As Jane Gerhard writes, "A new generation of feminists envisioned sexual pleasure as empowering, as helping men become more human, and as a route out of patriarchal repression of the body. While pleasure did not mean the same thing to every woman, it nonetheless became synonymous, briefly, with liberation."[39] The centrality of sexuality to a particular radical feminist re-visioning of woman is evident in Koedt's passionate disavowal of the vaginal orgasm. In 1968, she called upon women to take control of their sexuality: "What we must do is redefine our sexuality. We must discard the 'normal' concepts of sex and create new guidelines."[40] Koedt equated the vaginal orgasm with patriarchy because it catered to male ego, sexual pleasure, and sense of superiority while neglecting women's desires. Insistence on vaginal orgasm was emblematic of the structural inequality between men and women; the clitoral orgasm illuminated the potential for equality and offered a way to conceive of women as autonomous in both sexual and nonsexual ways. Reframing orgasm around the clitoris allowed feminists, as Gerhard argues, "to claim a uniquely female form of sexuality that had the potential to transcend the narrow and pathologizing classifications of male experts."[41]

The emphasis on the clitoral orgasm was especially important for lesbian feminists, some of whom argued that lesbianism was a form of uncorrupted femininity *and* that lesbians were not part of an economy of "female" sexuality. According to this logic, female sexuality was the province of women who engaged in sex with men and were part of a different sphere of desire and practice. As Monique Wittig writes in "The Straight Mind" in 1978, "It would be incorrect to say that lesbians associate, make love, live with women, for 'woman' has meaning only in heterosexual systems of thought and heterosexual economic systems. Lesbians are not women."[42] In arguing that a relationship to the phallus separates women from lesbians, Wittig articulates an important difference between lesbian sexuality and female sexuality. Alice Walker voices a similar logic when she narrates the experiences of an African American heterosexual woman who turns to the words of Lorde to teach her husband to stop objectifying her and to retrain his erotic impulses.[43] Though these discourses differ in relation to the possible role for men and masculinity, all understand the clitoral orgasm as the foundation for a sexual practice that is not oriented toward penetration but that relies on surface stimulation of the clitoris.

Some of Thomas's embrace of the clitoris indexes this feminist residue of self-determination. However, we cannot think about the clitoris without also acknowledging a sexological history that has scrutinized black female genitalia for signs of racial difference. This allows us to register anew what it means for Thomas to reject the aesthetics of the pornographic and sexological, which have historically turned to anatomy to naturalize black female difference. Jennifer Nash argues that these two discourses rely on "'the desire to know and possess,' to 'know' by possessing and possess by knowing. . . . Ethnography and pornography share a desire to know the 'truth' of other/Other's bodies and a commitment to crafting a representational universe which contains the Other."[44] While Thomas's painting refuses this will to knowledge through its aesthetics of surface, her emphasis on the clitoris cannot help but gesture toward racialized conceptions of sexual difference.

This is because among various sites where difference has been imagined to reside on the body, the clitoris has its own special place in the crossings of race, gender, and sexuality. In these schemas, black female bodies are situated as repositories of the less evolved, imagined as closer to nature, and rendered pornographic (which is to say eroticized and objectified). We are most familiar with this story as it has been narrated from the perspective of Cuvier's fixation on the buttocks of Saartjie Baartman and the production of the myth of the Venus Hottentot, but late nineteenth-century anxieties about black female homosexuality and the myth of the black enlarged clitoris are also part of this pattern of ascribing physiological difference to blackness and mapping high libidos and indiscriminate sexual desires onto physiology.[45] In the early twentieth century, describing a clitoris as enlarged was an announcement of sexual deviance. This means that doctors imagined that black women, poor women, and lesbians possessed especially large clitorises and that finding a large clitoris would foretell deviance to come.[46] Siobhan Somerville describes the prevalence of this trend:

> In an early account of racial differences between white and African-American women, one gynecologist had also focused on the size and visibility of the clitoris; in his examinations, he had perceived a distinction between the "free" clitoris of "negresses" and the "imprisonment" of the clitoris of the "Aryan American woman." In constructing these oppositions, these characterizations literalized the sexual and racial ideologies of the nineteenth century "Cult of True Womanhood," which explicitly privileged white women's sexual "purity," while it implicitly suggested African-American women's sexual accessibility.[47]

Linking lesbian and black anatomies with deviance marked them as simultaneously "less sexually differentiated than the norm . . . [and] as anomalous 'throwbacks' within a scheme of cultural and anatomical progress."[48] It is important that we understand these intersections as part of the larger narrative of the un-gendering of blackness because it makes the black clitoris into a different sort of object altogether. Specifically, it makes the black clitoris both perverse and corrupting; it becomes an organ that seeks out other clitorises and vaginas for pleasure, and it detaches the black clitoris from the sphere of womanhood. We can register the meaning of this transformation when we see the ways that eroticism was projected into interracial scenes of homosociality, thereby promoting segregation as a means of guarding against the possibility of perversion.[49] This narrative imagines that black clitorises are imbued with overt masculine sexuality—visualizable through the specter of enlargement, which went hand and hand with the sexological imagination of the black clitoris as an organ used in penetration.[50]

Thinking with the clitoris, however, also brings us toward tribbing, a sex act comprised of friction. While tribbing has a long history, some of which Valerie Traub positions contra to hetero/homo binaries, Jack Halberstam locates the practice within an economy of female masculinity.[51] He writes, "Tribadism, because it seemed to resemble intercourse in either its motion or its simulation of penetrative sex, was often linked to female masculinity and to particularly pernicious (because successful?) forms of sexual perversion."[52] Although this masculinization of the practice might allow us to think about tribbing as a racialized act, here, I am interested in its contemporary association with the 1970s and 1980s, as Linda Williams reminds us when she describes its aesthetics: "the often decorative, nonpenetrative nature of much lesbian sex in heterosexual pornography has long been reviled by contemporary lesbians who deem themselves more 'authentic' than previous generations. Hence the vehemence toward scissoring and reverse cowgirl, though I would point out that these were once quite popular, even idealized, positions in 'explicit' lesbian pornography made by and for lesbians in the mid-1980s."[53] Because it is outside the logic of penetration, tribbing exceeds many understandings of what constitutes sex and therefore stands outside of it. Historically, this means queer women looking to reclaim lesbian sex and eroticism from this lacuna of homosociality emphasized the eroticism of penetration with dildos, fists, and tongues, and distanced themselves and their practices from the surface economy of tribbing, which registered as passé and inauthentically—which is to say, anachronistically—queer.

Tribbing, then, is a practice that shows us the generative possibilities of friction—both through the reclamation of the passé-ness of lesbian feminism and by working with the clitoris as residual and racialized organ. In reading *Origin of the Universe 1* in relation to tribbing, I argue for understanding a queer present for the practice and a way to reread its relation to friction. The reluctance to claim tribbing as part of a contemporary queer set of sexual practices while simultaneously deploying its symbol as a sign of queerness (I am thinking here of the popularity of the scissors icon as a shorthand for queer sex) speaks to a difficulty in understanding the role of surface and friction in thinking about sexuality. In historical terms we see this in the apprehension that surrounds 1970s and 1980s black lesbian feminist and womanist discourses on sex—especially since they emphasize the vulnerability of bodies within racist and patriarchal hierarchies. But in hinting at tribbing and the pleasures of friction, we also return to a theorization of the clitoral orgasm and the frictional pleasures of mutual vulval contact. Thinking about sexual relations as a matter of two surfaces coming together is both a matter of friction activating nerves and leading to orgasm *and* a subversion of the objectifying regime of the visual in favor of that of the tactile. This is because there isn't much to see. Both surfaces are laboring frictionally toward a visually unmarked end. In many ways this activation of the surface further reifies an economy of opacity in relation to sexual pleasure. Instead of figuring vagina as void, however, what becomes more mysterious is the connection between surfaces and pleasures. Perhaps this is why these tribbing scenes have become popular among heterosexual men: they represent (or at least allude to) the pleasures of the surface, which do not translate visually.

This is part of the excess of tactility that surfaces generate. Tribbing negates histories of objectification through excess, often to the point of orgasm. In *Origin of the Universe 1*, I locate this frictional excess as something that threads through the rhinestone and the clitoris by way of a resignification of the 1970s. Thomas activates this 1970s residue by engaging with womanism and its emphasis on thinking about multiple forms of marginalization in order to disrupt simplistic ideas of pleasure and power. These critiques, in turn, mobilize the possibilities of opacity that inhere in the unrepresentability of tribbing. This is territory that brings us back to Lorde, who, Sarah Chinn writes, "reimagines and represents lesbian sexuality in ways that profoundly challenge her readers, as something situated on the surfaces and in the crannies of the body, as floating up into nostrils and ears, as myrrh: a fragrant, viscous scent absorbed into the skin."[54] With this statement, we suddenly find ourselves in the excesses of surface sensation that tribbing offers; we are in its sweat, surface, and funk. This is the other side of 1970s; it offers brown jouissance in a whiff of the "bodies and pleasures" about which Foucault waxed rhapsodically. Here, we remember that one of the lures of the surface is that it offers a space to think toward brown jouissance and its alternate choreography of pleasures, relationality, and self-making.

Self-Love, Masturbation, and Impersonal Narcissism

To think the surface, however, is also to traffic in the superficial and narcissistic, which are the categories that we typically use for thinking about surface in relation to selfhood. However, I do not see the operations of self-making that Thomas displays as registering within the realm of solipsim. Thomas's mobilization of rhinestones destabilizes the idea of a coherent, knowable self through fragmentation and cover. Likewise, her positioning of women of color as the origin of the universe produces a plural self attentive to the frictional temporalities of generational time and the possibilities of resignification. Here, I theorize these relationships to surface and self as a way to understand *Origin of the Universe 1* as presenting the self-portrait as a vehicle for self-love, which, in turn, is an alternate framing of narcissism and superficiality as political practice.

While Thomas veers away from authenticity, interiority, and even individuality, her insistence on presenting—nay, flashing—a self that is objectified and relational speaks to brown jouissance's mobilization of flesh's liquidity. It also, importantly, speaks to the pleasure that liquidity might index. Here, I interpret the rhinestones as a record of a practice of self-love. In reading the rhinestone as a material remainder of Thomas's pleasure, I argue that they remind us of physical aspects of Thomas's sexual excitement in addition to illuminating a version of self-care that is tethered to pleasure. While Courbet's model's pleasure is rendered mysterious, Thomas uses the rhinestone to show us how we might consider her pleasure as present and material even as it remains opaque. Hence, I see the rhinestone as part of a formulation of liquidity in that they gesture toward interiority and agency while refusing that the flesh settle into subject or object. Thinking the rhinestone as a trace or residue of Thomas's wetness and excitement allows us to hold violence, excess, and possibility in the same frame. Even as the source is ambiguous, the idea that rhinestones might offer a record of pleasure—pleasure that is firmly constituted in and of the flesh—shows us a form of self-possession. This self is not outside of objectification, but its embellishment and insistence on the trace of excitement speaks to the centrality of pleasure in theorizations of self-love.

Within the register of black queer pleasure, this concept of self-love finds an echo in Lorde's theory of the erotic. Lorde describes the erotic as "a measure between the beginnings of our sense of self and the chaos of our strongest feelings" and as "an assertion of the lifeforce of women; of that creative energy empowered."[55] The erotic is both something that belongs to individuals and something that cannot be contained by them. In this way, Lorde's version of the erotic can be understood as a particular response to the trauma of racism and discrimination, which prevents the formation of community among African American women. Racism produces self-hatred and anger and must be met with self-love. In "Eye to Eye" Lorde writes, "It is empowerment—our strengthening in the service of ourselves and each other, in the service of our work and our future—that will be the result of this pursuit. . . . I have to learn to love myself before I can love you or accept your loving."[56] The erotic, for Lorde, is a call for self-care and community to repair the damage done by patriarchy and racism and to formulate ways of moving beyond those systems. Reading Thomas's investment in pleasure and desire as a version of Lorde's erotic allows us to dwell on the importance of self-love as a politics.

In her analysis of black feminism's relationship to the politics of love, Jennifer Nash argues that the specificity of love within black feminist thought in the 1970s and 1980s has to do with the centrality of the self.[57] Nash writes that this form of self-love is a departure from love as "simply a practice of self-valuation" and that it is, instead, "a significant call for ordering the self and transcending the self, a strategy for remaking the self and for moving beyond the limitations of selfhood."[58] In describing womanism's conception of self-love, in particular, Nash emphasizes that this reorganization of self is where politics emerge. To use the terms that I have been using in this chapter, self-love is what produces the possibilities of frictional engagement. Nash writes:

> Walker's womanist subject "loves herself. *Regardless.*" The italicized "regardless" reveals that self-love is absolutely essential, that it persists in spite of everything else. Although Walker's call to self-love is certainly an "artful advocacy of unconditional love that starts with our acceptance of ourselves as divinely and humanly lovable," it is also far more. With "regardless" modifying "loves herself," Walker suggests that self-love stands at the heart of the womanist project, and functions as a prerequisite for other kinds of humanistic, sensual, erotic, and spiritual loves that the womanist embodies. Self-love, it seems, is the only love that must *always* exist; it is the love that enables the other loves Walker's womanist embodies, engenders, and relishes.[59]

Nash's reading of Walker positions self-love as something necessary for politics and something that takes *work*. Self-love is not necessarily restricted to pleasure; it requires "ethical management of the self," "pushing the self to be configured in new ways that might be challenging or difficult."[60]

This prioritizing of self-love for the production of politics and the simultaneous eschewing of the romantic leads us to a consideration of the masturbatory for several reasons. First, it reinforces the link between pleasure and the political practice of self-love by emphasizing the importance of relating to the self. Second, it brings us back to tactility's role within the practice of self-love. In particular, this tactility highlights the role of embodied knowledge production. Knowing how to manipulate one's body to produce pleasure was considered an important feminist step in understanding the capacity of the body and in freeing oneself from the tyranny of the medical establishment. We especially see this connection in *Our Bodies, Ourselves*, a collaborative project started in 1971 by members of the Boston Women's Health Book Collective. The collective urged women to touch themselves to gain a better understanding of their bodies and to find freedom from patriarchal norms. Women were encouraged to explore the surfaces of their body in addition to examining themselves in mirrors: "We emphasize that you take a mirror and examine yourself. Touch yourself, smell yourself, even taste your own secretions. After all, you are your body and you are not obscene."[61] This project of sensual knowledge production reemphasizes the dimensions of knowledge that the visual occludes. To touch oneself—to understand how to use touch to bring pleasure to the self—is an important political act. This is yet another way of reading Thomas's use of the rhinestone: After all, why separate orgasmic pleasure from pleasure in the decorative, and why give it priority? From this perspective, I read *Origin of the Universe 1* as a continuation of feminist projects to use tactile explorations of one's body as a technology for subverting the scientific/pornographic gaze's will to know and empowering the self. This, in turn, allows us to read Thomas in relation to Lorde's description of masturbation as a healing practice. In *The Cancer Journals*, Lorde chronicles her use of masturbation as a way to find a connection to herself and others:

> November 2, 1978 How do you spend your time, she said. Reading, mostly, I said. I couldn't tell her that mostly I sat staring at blank walls, or getting stoned into my heart, and then, one day when I found I could finally masturbate again, making love to myself for hours at a time. The flame was dim and flickering, but it was a welcome relief to the long coldness.[62]

Masturbation is a practice of radical self-love. It brings Lorde closer to the erotic and the political.

In fusing radical self-love with the masturbatory, we can also begin to see how the erotic might allow us to rethink narcissism as political. Here, I put Lorde and Thomas in conversation with Leo Bersani and Adam Phillips, who conceptualize ethical relation as a form of impersonal narcissism.[63] Impersonal narcissism is built upon the finding of sameness rather than difference—though we might question whether all dimensions of difference are given equal weight in this schema. They write, "The self the subject sees reflected in the other is not the unique personality vital to modern notions of individualism."[64] When individuality is less important than commonalities, difference registers as supplemental, and relation relies on narcissism. Bersani writes, "The experience of belonging to a family of singularity without national, ethnic, racial, or gendered borders might make us sensitive to the ontological status of difference itself as what I called the nonthreatening supplement of sameness."[65] What Bersani and Phillips suggest is that if we attach to sameness through narcissism, we are free to lose ourselves in the Other because we do not see our individuality at stake. This, in turn, opens toward an alternate formation of ethics. While Bersani and Phillips do not describe this narcissism as a form of radical self-love, it has much in common with Lorde's version of the erotic in that it begins with the self and extends that self outward. While Lorde emphasizes the importance of starting with individual selfhood, her version of the erotic is, above all, a mode of bringing people together—despite their differences. Specifically, Lorde emphasizes the importance of individual empowerment for collectivity on a multigenerational scale: "The aim of each thing which we do is to make our lives and the lives of our children richer and more possible."[66] The individual is where things begin, but the erotic's politics are tied to the production of an affective community—a community bound together by feeling and politics rather than surface similarities. Lorde writes, "The sharing of joy, whether physical, emotional, psychic, or intellectual, forms a bridge between the sharers which can be the basis for understanding much of what is not shared between them, and lessens the threat of their difference."[67] The erotic, then, is "an assertion of the life force of women; of that creative energy empowered"; it is both something that belongs to individuals and something that cannot be contained by them.[68]

This emphasis on sameness becomes a mode of thinking with others because it invites a contemplation of the self as unbounded and plural. This is a plurality that Thomas invokes in multiple ways. We see it in her response to a query about whom she sees in the mirror: "It's always me. Sometimes it's also my mother, my grandmother, or my great-grandmother," and we see this in her decision to make *Origin of the Universe 1* a diptych.[69] Its pair, *Origin of the Universe 2* (2012), is a portrait of Thomas's then-wife, Carmen McLeod. Thomas describes the paintings as "a sort of call and response, dealing with the nature of sexuality on a different level, romanticizing the nature of relationships and

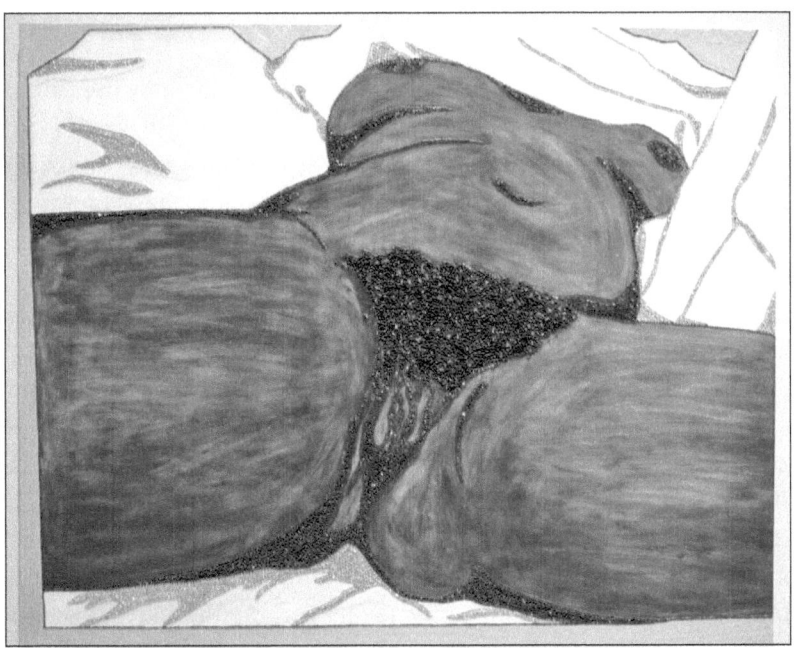

Figures 2.1 and 2.2. Mickalene Thomas, *Origin of the Universe 1* and *Origin of the Universe 2*, 2012. Images and original data provided by Larry Qualls Photographer: Larry Qualls © 2012 Artists Rights Society (ARS), New York.

intimacy—and also having this connection with a black body in relation to a white body."[70] Although Thomas describes the paintings as a form of call and response, reading through the lens of impersonal narcissism and radical self-love we can also see that there is an emphasis on sameness with McLeod: rhinestones, clitoris, spread legs are present in both. The skin tones are different, but thinking about their pairing through the lens of similarity, we can imagine that Thomas has produced a plural self-portrait that begins from the place of self-love.

This search for sameness not only has echoes with Lorde's erotic, but also with Walker's womanism, which supports a love "that embraces everyone for the purposes of healing, change, and liberation."[71] Yet, in thinking with brown jouissance, it is important to remember that this possibility of finding sameness (coalition) begins with locating the self, not only in relation to others, but in relation to violence. Just as Nash reminds us that "womanism's universality is rooted in black women's particular experiences," Thomas's embrace of the possibilities of self-love begin with the centering of the black queer body.[72] This is not about segmenting along lines of identity, but about understanding the ways that particularity is rooted in the politics of knowledge production and is *not* merely a surface structure. Beginning with a black queer female body offers a reorientation of relation and politics, even as it enables an embrace of plurality. It is the origin of the universe, after all, and through this body, we can trace histories of oppression and objectification in addition to refusal, love, and the sensualities of surface.

3

Deep Listening, Belonging, and the Pleasures of Brown Jouissance

Untitled Fucking, a 2013 collaboration between Xandra Ibarra and Amber Hawk Swanson, features Ibarra penetrating Hawk Swanson with a Tapatío bottle secured to a harness. After twelve minutes of rhythmic penetration, Ibarra opens the bottle of hot sauce and jerkily empties its contents onto Hawk Swanson's back in a simulation of ejaculation while she continues to penetrate Hawk Swanson digitally. Throughout the performance, Hawk Swanson repeats the line, "Feminism? That's deep. I think I need a minute to think about that, so . . . I don't know." The utterance connects this collaborative work with Hawk Swanson's *Feminism? Project*, a series of videos in which she recontextualizes interviews on feminism with women in Iowa by using a stylized "valley girl" intonation to repeat lines from the interviews while in the middle of various sex acts. Ibarra's use of the hot sauce strap-on likewise marks a continuity between this performance and her own multifaceted work on Chicana identity as La Chica Boom. In another La Chica Boom project she remakes Tapatío into Tapatía by using her image on the label and describing its particular "spic-y" qualities. Juana María Rodríguez argues that *Untitled Fucking* "capture[s] feminism's ambivalent and decidedly sticky relationship to racialized sexual politics," while Iván Ramos positions it within a form of "gustatory aesthetics."[1]

The "gustatory aesthetics" that Ramos refers to are part of a longer tradition of Chicano/a art practices that use the alimentary to unsettle. Ramos argues that Ibarra's multiple mobilizations of the Tapatío bottle "articulate a visceral anti-assimilationist politics that appropriates and critiques the racist imagery that has defined Latina/o subjects in the United States."[2] In Ramos's reading, Ibarra's use of Tapatío makes the "spiciness" attributed to Chicanas vital to her project: "Spiciness functions as a central metaphor that serves to illuminate not only the fear around immigration but also part of an adjacent, if under analyzed, history in which Mexican *food* has managed to lead the entry of the Mexican *body* into the United States."[3] Spiciness indexes not only the simultaneous fear of and desire for difference on the part of white normative culture, but also Ibarra's rejection of assimilation. Ibarra wields power through this hot sauce. She makes her racialization visible *and* desirable. As Ramos writes, "The desire for the hot Latina that La Chica Boom embodies is returned, but instead she will top the viewer, in her own terms."[4] Further, the gustatory functions as a mode of excess. The viewer cannot help but be reminded of the hot sauce's taste and texture—"For those of us familiar with the taste and texture of the sauce, this faux cum-shot is exceptionally visceral. Upon each viewing, I can sense the smell, the texture, the taste. The sheer excess of it, the whole bottle in fact, creates a crimson mess that seeps into the very sensorial memory of our own encounters with a bottle of Tapatío" in a mode that suggests a "political aesthetic that dissolves the self in favor of sensorial overload."[5]

Rodríguez focuses less on the possibility of excess and more on the feminist conversation that the performance stirs with its centralization of sex and the erotics of race. If one of Hawk Swanson's aims in her *Feminism? Project* is to bring conversations on sex into feminist discourse, this collaboration with Ibarra is important for showing the ways that eroticism and race co-mingle. Rodríguez is particularly interested in what it means that Ibarra tops Hawk Swanson, especially since both women embody forms of conventional femininity—Ibarra "dressed in *cucaracha* pasties, stilettos, and not much else, fucking a bent-over, equally feminine and sultry, Amber," who, as Ramos writes, is "in full femme regalia, wearing black stockings and high heels; her presence reminiscent of a 1950s pinup, a la Betty Page."[6] When Hawk Swanson begins to forget her lines, Ibarra disciplines her by pulling her hair: "Their exchange functions as a peculiar kind of sexualized race play, where the Chicana femme top seems to run the show, even as her polite Midwestern bottom asks for 'another finger please.'"[7] Rodríguez reads this exchange as one in which white liberal feminism is confronted by racial difference, rendered "unable to speak," and opened to the possible pleasures of sex as politics in whatever incarnation they appear: "A Latina power-top with cockroach-covered nipples? Feminism taking it from behind, and loving it? Cross-racial feminine erotics as condiments for our consumption? Or a riotous convergence of the delicious pleasures and fiery politics that feminism still has trouble ingesting?"[8]

We might say, then, that Ibarra and Hawk Swanson's exchange functions as an extension of the 1981 dialogue between Amber Hollibaugh and Cherríe Moraga, "What We're Rolling Around in Bed With," in which the activists discuss feminism's difficulty grappling with power and sexuality. Hollibaugh and Moraga argue that feminism has struggled to make sense of sexuality apart from a structure of oppression, which has resulted in an ideology where "lesbianism (since it exists outside the institution of heterosexuality) came to be seen as the practice of feminism. It set up a 'perfect' vision of egalitarian sexuality, where we could magically leap over our heterosexist conditioning into mutual orgasms, struggle-fee, trouble-free sex."[9] Hollibaugh goes on to argue that not only is this idealization of lesbian sexuality impossible to realize, but it speaks to a repression of people's desires and fantasies: "I think the reason butch/femme stuff got hidden within lesbian-feminism is because people are profoundly afraid of power in bed. And though everybody doesn't play out power the way I do, the question of power affects who and how you eroticize your sexual need. And it is absolutely at the bottom of all sexual inquiry"[10] From there, the conversation evolves into a discussion of the power of butch/femme role play with both women arguing against an ideology in which femininity is equated with passivity. Hollibaugh says, "Femme is active, not passive. It's me saying to my partner, 'Love me enough to let me go where I need to go and take me there. Don't make me think it through. Give me a way to be so in my body that I don't have to think: that you can fantasize for the both of us."[11] Moraga adds that as a butch she tries to find the moment with her partner when "she entrusts me to determine where she'll go sexually. And I honestly feel a power inside me strong enough to heal the deepest wound. . . . My power is that I know how to read her inside of her own passion. I can hear her. It's like a sexual language."[12]

In Hollibaugh and Moraga's desire to find a space for lesbianism where sex can make a body a body, we find an important space for thinking about penetration and its relationship to power. In this formulation of brown jouissance, the racialized hierarchies that mark appetite are brought into explicit conversation with the pleasure of penetrating another. While Hollibaugh and Moraga play out this tension through a summoning of butch/femme role play, a contentious practice in 1981, *Untitled Fucking* invites us to reconsider the conversation through the lens of topping and bottoming. This work invites us to see that topping is made legible through Ibarra's performance of penetration and her guidance of her and Hawk Swanson's sexual choreography while bottoming connotes the receptive, though not passive—as we see in Hawk Swanson's request for "more"—partner. In Hawk Swanson and Ibarra's "conversation" about feminism, power and penetration act as fulcrums for pleasure, and we gain a new language for thinking about brown jouissance. In their artist statement, they emphasize the importance of the "queer sexual vocabulary of topping, bottoming, and 'bottoming out,'" for "stag[ing] the deep and complicated interplay between the performance of white feminism and the feminisms of color that whiteness excludes. . . . Working the erotic interplay between saying and doing, Hawk Swanson and Ibarra rehearse the queer and feminist contradictions that arise when explicit sex and performance collide, directing us toward the untitled and yet to be articulated horizons of political possibility."[13] While the other iterations of brown jouissance that I discuss in this book gesture toward sex—often incorporating fraught histories of sexualized black and brown people—this chapter takes the performance and form of sex itself as a site to analyze brown jouissance, its relationship to queer frames of belonging, and its production of pleasures—both in the self and in others.

Working around Oedipus: Family Dramas and Multiplications of Jouissance

By now, the description of jouissance during sex that Leo Bersani proffers in "Is the Rectum a Grave?" is ubiquitous. Bersani uses it to articulate the pleasures of anal sex at the height of the AIDS emergency, when sex between men was imagined as a death sentence. He uses jouissance to undermine the homophobic imaginary of "the intolerable image of a grown man, legs high in the air, unable to refuse the suicidal ecstasy of being a woman."[14] The peril that Bersani reports is of punctured masculinity in which approaching femininity or "being a woman" signals both submission and being penetrated. In this, Bersani takes his cue from Michel Foucault's historical analysis of Greek and Roman sexuality and Catharine Mackinnon's and Andrea Dworkin's analysis of patriarchy: "*To be penetrated is to abdicate power.*"[15] The tethering together of anatomy and passivity links sexuality to masochism and invites jouissance as a mode of self-shattering into the picture. In the conclusion to the essay, Bersani writes, "Male homosexuality advertises the risk of the sexual itself as the risk of self-dismissal, of *losing sight* of the self, and in so doing it proposes and dangerously represents *jouissance* as a mode of ascesis."[16] Bersani's essay has been much analyzed, so I will not dwell on its many complexities here, but I am interested in complicating this idea of penetration as self-shattering. As others, including myself, have argued, Bersani is writing from the position where one has a self to shatter, which is to say a position of already inhabiting sovereign subjectivity. This is phallic jouissance.

When we expand the frameworks for thinking with jouissance, we see how deep the alignment is between the sovereign subject and the Oedipus complex. According to the Oedipus complex, the child must repudiate his or her initial love for the mother in order to become a subject and gain recognition from the father. As Judith Butler reminds us, this positions desire for the mother as the antecedent to the processes of gendering because the incest taboo and maternal absence from the erotic scene are the conditions that permit the psychic formations of gender and sexuality.[17] The subject is thus constituted by desire and undone by occasional sensations that jar the subject from this matrix. These moments of coming undone constitute phallic jouissance, which is a crisis of self-shattering and the destruction of the imaginary of coherence. For Jacques Lacan, however, there are two other important modes of thinking about jouissance, both of which actually resurrect the mother in some fashion: jouissance of being and feminine jouissance.

Néstor Braunstein describes jouissance of being as something that happens before entry into the symbolic order, when "a mutual fulfillment exists between the *infans* and the Other, the mother. This 'moment' comes prior to lack and desire."[18] Separation from the m/Other launches the subject into the world of desire as s/he longs to fulfill the m/Other's desire and return to this state. This moment before the inauguration of the subject and before desire positions the m/Other-child relationship as unknowable and separate from the imagined coherence of the subject. Julia Kristeva's theorization of a primary pre-Oedipal love for the maternal body is emblematic of jouissance of being. In this stage before subjectivity, love for the mother is all encompassing and provides the basis for the possibility of becoming a self. Kristeva describes this as the space before desire (before the subject/object division) and beyond pleasure. Kristeva names this pre-Oedipal space "the semiotic" because it precedes the subject's entrance into the symbolic. In the space of the semiotic, the subject is unraveled, incoherent, and revels in her corporeality. The semiotic is filled with an alternate language—often poetry. In her reading of Kristeva, Judith Butler writes that "the semiotic, through rhythm, assonance, intonations, sound play and repetition, re-presents or recovers the maternal body in poetic speech. Even the 'first echolalias of infants' and the 'glossalasias in psychotic discourse' are manifestations of the continuity of the mother-infant relation, a hetereogenous field of impulse prior to the separation/ individuation of infant and mother, alike effected by the imposition of the incest taboo."[19] Kristeva's emphasis on the time before the child can distinguish between itself and its mother as the source of eroticism emphasizes dependence and temporal continuity, rather than the temporality of the event that marks Oedipal narratives. Importantly, this positions jouissance of being as occurring before subjectivity and intimately connected to sensations of corporeal co-dependence.

In this formation of jouissance as occurring "before," I understand jouissance of being as indicating that this connection and deep relationality with the mother is what must be foreclosed in order to inaugurate subjectivity, desire, and sexuality. When attention has been specifically given to the role of the mother in theorizations of feminine desire, there have been divided sets of responses. On the one hand, some, like Kaja Silverman, argue that this foreclosed love for the mother is the condition that allows female desire to develop. She writes, "The girls' feelings for her mother classically express themselves through the wish to give her a child, and to receive one in return . . . which sets the wheels of unconscious symbolization in motion and establishes the girl as a full-fledged subject. It is here . . . that female desire begins."[20] On the other hand, for others, the idea that feminine desire can be traced to the mother has been troubling. In addition to the difficulty of thinking through the figuration of incest (despite the relative discursive silence on its mother-daughter formations), there is a fear that articulating a desire for the mother will bleed into theorizations of lesbianism. Teresa de Lauretis, for example, has been more skeptical of this turn toward the maternal as a site of lesbian analytic possibility because it threatens to desexualize lesbianism. De Lauretis writes, "Thus to make desire for, as well as identification with the mother a *sine qua non* condition of feminism continues to blur the already fraught distinction between heterosexual feminism and lesbian feminism, to say nothing of the far more consequential differences between lesbian sexuality or subjectivity and heterosexual female sexuality or subjectivity."[21] Additionally, de Lauretis points to the uproar over Adrienne Rich's essay "Compulsory Heterosexuality and Lesbian Existence," which opened possibilities to read a number of female-female relationships through the lesbian.[22] In some ways, the problem that de Lauretis identifies is that lesbianism is presented as though it enjoys a particular relationship to maternity or desire for the mother that other subjects do not. Further, this form of lesbian exceptionalism threatens to veer toward attaching the lesbian to the specter of the unnatural. In suggesting that we think more broadly about the generative possibilities of queer m/Other love (alongside, but not restricted to the figure of the lesbian), I am interested in its status as excessive relative to the order of sexuality dominated by the phallic and reproductive.

In order to ground this analysis of queer m/Other love in something more tangible, I turn to Cheryl Dunye's 2012 film, *Mommy Is Coming*. "Mommy's coming!" Helen, the titular mother played by Swiss-based sexologist Maggie Tapert, announces cheerily over the telephone. She makes this proclamation to her daughter, Dylan, who has interrupted a taxicab tryst with her girlfriend, Claudia, to take the call. Although Dylan, sex educator and actor Lil Harlow, does actually require romantic counsel—she accuses Claudia of wanting too much from her emotionally while simultaneously accusing her of being withholding because she refuses to be penetrated—mommy's decision to leave their hometown to visit Berlin is occasioned by Dylan's noncommunicativeness, as well as by her boredom in her marriage to Dylan's father and curiosity about Berlin and the potential sexual adventures it offers. From here the film mixes pornography and plot, often situating its actors as talking heads within the movie to explain their characters' motivations for the actions that we see. Dylan and Claudia separate; Claudia, played by black

Boricua genderqueer performer Papi Coxx, dons a mustache, and as Claude, he explores a Berlin sex club, where he finally receives the love and attention that he feels he has been lacking. Helen arrives in Berlin and promptly seduces Claude (not realizing his dual identity as Claudia) in order to have her own Berlin sex adventure. Dylan enjoys a threesome with friends and realizes that she does miss Claudia's affection after all. The hijinks culminate when Claude/ia attempts to have sex with both mother and daughter in adjoining hotel rooms only to produce a situation in which Helen is blindfolded and unknowingly mounted from behind by her daughter. Once mommy has come, the mistaken identity is revealed, and the trio laugh it off. The film ends with Helen dispensing motherly advice to Dylan to "love who is front of [her]" and Dylan and Claudia cooing lovingly on the train platform.

Dunye's cheeky title leads us to anticipate Helen's orgasm, while also giving us a way to understand something of the world of m/Other love and what it is to break the incest taboo. While Kristeva describes the importance of mother love as a psychic formation, she does not grapple with it as a potential physical sex act. In large part this is because of the strength of the incest taboo, which means that a sexual attachment to one's mother opposes normative ideologies of subject formation. *Mommy Is Coming*, however, allows us to think the mother and sexual relations with the mother outside the realm of taboo. The discovery that Dylan has fucked her mother does not result in trauma, only laughter. Although properly speaking the vectors of desire emanate from Claude/ia, which means that this desire could be classified as part of a conglomeration attached to the MILF (Mother I'd Like to Fuck, a term popularized through the 1999 film *American Pie*). The MILF challenges the traditional assumptions about femininity; scholars have argued that within the realm of pornography her appeal stems from "playing against type," that is, asserting herself sexually and professionally.[23] However, more often than not, she isn't actually anyone's mommy.[24] Yet, *Mommy Is Coming* does present us with mother-daughter sex, opening the door toward rethinking sensual modes of connecting with the mother, even as it sidesteps the question of daughterly desire.

In the film, we see mother love actualized in Dylan's penetration of Helen, an act that results in orgasms for both. In showing Helen as penetrated and in pleasure's thrall, Dunye activates a different type of relation between penetration and jouissance. This is not the "suicidal ecstasy" that Bersani designates as womanly. Helen does not shatter; she comes and in the process understands herself and her desires more fully—one of the film's subtexts is Helen's quest for more sexual experience so that she can satisfy herself more expertly. In addition to this, she strengthens her relationship with Dylan—a testament to the intimacies foreclosed by an Oedipal repudiation of the mother. Importantly, all of this action occurs outside the parameters of the paternal: at the film's close, Helen says, "Well, I won't be telling your father about this!" This tells us that this jouissance is about connection and belonging rather than individuation. To be sure, there are links between Helen's orgasmic experiences and the jouissance of self-shattering that Bersani articulates. Just as Bersani's jouissance is a testament to the here and now, in *Mommy Is Coming*, Helen's produces nothing for the future—no baby, only orgasms—but there is no death or shame after its production. What we witness instead is a surplus of pleasure—surplus in that it exceeds the sphere of the reproductive and surplus in that it does not require the paternal. In this way, we can connect the pleasures that Helen experiences to what Maggie Nelson, working through Susan Fraiman, terms *sodomitical maternity*, which "is . . . meant to indicate the mother with a sexuality that's in excess of the procreative capacity."[25] In *The Argonauts*, Nelson sutures sodomitical maternity to her enjoyment of anal sex and her awareness of the swirls of own mother's desires. This suggestion of anality not only reminds us that Dylan might have penetrated Helen anally, but it also allows us to think about the ways that anality in relation to the maternal body is considered as excess. Anality has generally been considered the province of gay men, but, as Eve Sedgwick argues, its relation to jouissance allows us to more deeply ponder a variety of non-Oedpial possibilities.[26] This hole is not a substitute, but rather another space that offers its own deep pleasures and excesses. This anality is about experiencing the body as body in a multitude of ways and permitting connections and sensualities outside the reproductive.

In this tableaux of family intimacy, we see a return to the mother, but this return does not occasion trauma or a denial of the symbolic. Once Claude/ia turns on the lights, both women realize that s/he is not the one with whom they were actually having sex. Helen exclaims, "Claude!" Dylan, unable to see without her glasses, says "Momma?" and their names bounce off each other's tongues as the situation becomes clearer—"Dylan?" "Mommy!" "Helen," "Helen?" "Dylan . . . Helen!"—before being interrupted by Dunye as cab driver, who emerges from the background with the final words of the scene, "Excuse me, I'm just here to return her [points to Dylan] wallet." The film does not end there, however. After an intertitle, "Is this how our fairytale ends?" the film picks up at the train platform with Helen's parting words to Dylan and the trio's laughter. Dylan and Claudia walk off together, and Claudia asks, "Now what? You're sorry? You want to be kind and more loving to me? You figured out that I was the one for you." Dylan says, "Yes. Now can I fuck you?" Claudia asks, "Now can I trust you?" before playfully slapping her behind while saying, "Sometimes it pays to listen to your mamí!"[27] Through these maternal intimacies, then, the film suggests that Dylan now knows how to "have a real life" with Claudia, a life that presumably involves care, sex, and vulnerability—per her earlier conversation with her mother. She is, in other words, deeply invested in co-existence and listening to the Other, a conglomeration that brings us toward feminine joussiance.

Feminine jouissance is related to jouissance of being in that it involves an Other, but it takes place in relation to the unknowability of this Other. It is a jouissance that prioritizes openness regardless of outcome. Braunstein writes: "The Other's jouissance is an ineffable mystery, beyond words, outside the symbolic, beyond the phallus. Its model is surfeit, a surplus, the supplement to phallic jouissance of which many women speak without being able to say exactly what it consists of, like something felt but unexplainable. The jouissance of the Other is therefore assumed as the jouissance of the Other sex, an other than phallic joussiance, in other words feminine jouissance."[28] Feminine jouissance challenges the primacy of self-shattering in relation to jouissance because there is no coherent self to shatter. Instead, this deep entwinement with the Other leads to the adjective "feminine." Feminine jouissance is what Jean Luc Nancy describes as "neither the possession nor appropriation of something, but rather openness to an alterity, since the woman is in the position of what Lacan calls 'the Other,' the big Other."[29] Reading Nancy and Lacan together, I argue that we treat feminine jouissance as a set of sensations that emerge from a deep relationality with opacity. I understand feminine jouissance as the jouissance of listening and being with the Other, a process that includes dwelling in the opacity of Otherness.

Helen's jouissance is literally the jouissance of the m/Other, while Dylan's feminine jouissance is expressed in her ability to produce pleasure for the Other—in this case it is literally her mother, but during the act she imagines it to be Claudia. In their encounter, Dylan enters the dark room wearing Claudia's strap-on and quickly penetrates Helen. The film then goes through the range of visual tropes indicative of a satisfying sexual encounter. There are moans from both parties; Dylan's hands grab Helen's shoulders. Dylan slaps Helen's rear. We see close-ups of Dylan's hands moving rhythmically near the top of Helen's corset, shadows on the bed, Dylan's breasts jiggling, furrowed brows, and finally Helen yelling, "I love you," as Dylan orgasms. After this pronouncement, Claude/ia turns on the lights, and the mix-up is revealed. Aside from the moans, the sex scene does not consist of dialogue until the end, which means that its choreography is one produced through *deep listening*, which, I argue, is what characterizes this form of feminine jouissance. Dylan gets pleasure from attending to the m/Other's body and learning its rhythms. She is open to the Other's alterity. In advance of sneaking into what turns out to be her mother's room, she tells Claudia, "I'm not leaving until I get a piece of you."

In this scene, it is clear that feminine jouissance emerges from a relational structure that locates pleasure in being a body that is oriented toward an Other and her pleasure, opaque though it must be. Dylan marks this opacity as "a piece of you," but when we move away from the logic of property—barring mutilation—the only "piece" of Claudia or any Other that is available can be gained, and only temporarily so, through a process of learning, or what I am calling deep listening. This version of listening is distinct from the idea of listening as a loss of self, which Roshanak Kheshti describes in relation to the phenomenon of third-world music.[30] In that articulation of listening, Kheshti uses Roland Barthes's concept of *significance* to critique the processes of fetishization that occur in relation to difference and produce pleasure through the possibility of knowing and possessing the Other. This type of listening imagines a loss of self through passive receptivity, while Dylan's performance of listening is one of extension. She extends herself to feel what might produce pleasure for Claudia/her m/Other. This version of listening is more in keeping with that articulated by Nancy, who argues that to listen "is to be straining toward or in an approach to the self."[31] This is to not to say that listening is about defining the self, but that the activity allows contemplation of what the limits to the concept of the self are and what it is to be in relation to others. Nancy describes listening as "enter[ing] that spatiality by which, at the same time, [the I] is penetrated, for it opens up in me as well as around me, and from me as well as toward me . . . To be listening is to be *at the same time* outside and inside, to be open *from* without and *from* within, hence from one to the other and from one in the other."[32] In bringing together topping and listening, then, we can see that topping is about projecting oneself into the world. This movement outward belies the instability and deep relationality of the idea of the self. And, in addition to illustrating the fundamental vulnerability of the self, it highlights the self's relation to the space and movements of the Other. Feminine jouissance emphasizes moments of connection with the world; it shows the self as a being-toward someone/where else.

We must also think about what it means that this production of pleasure, this feminine jouissance, occurs via a strap-on, a phallus, which when wielded by Dylan becomes an extension of femininity rather than masculinity. The strap-on, as Lynda Hart reminds us, is "a real thing" in that its use requires that the one who wears it think of it as an extension of the body in order to effectively produce motions both subtle and not. Hart argues that this production of the strap-on as real

> instigate[s] a representational crisis by producing an imaginary in which the fetishistic/hallucinatory "return" of the penis onto a woman's body goes beyond the "transferable or plastic property" of the phallus to other body parts by depicting a phallus that has no reference to the "real" of the penis. . . . Lesbian-dicks are the ultimate simulacra. They occupy the ontological status of the model, appropriate the privilege, and refuse to acknowledge an origin outside their own self-reflexivity. They make claims to the real without submitting to "truth."[33]

This is to say that this lesbian form of extension disrupts the phallic by not being subservient to a masculine order. Instead, it reveals the plurality of extension and penetration. Additionally, Judith Butler argues that the lesbian phallus is threatening because it unsettles the notion of a subservient woman and it illuminates the non-necessity of masculinity within an economy of pleasure. She writes:

> Consider that "having" the phallus can be symbolized by an arm, a tongue, a hand (or two), a knee, a thigh, a pelvic bone, an array of purposefully instrumentalized body-like things. And that this "having" exists in relation to a "being the phallus" which is both part of its own signifying effect (the phallic lesbian is potentially castrating) and that which it encounters in the woman who is desired (as the one who, offering or withdrawing the specular guarantee, wields the power to castrate).[34]

Though the strap-on is one form of bodily extension, there are others—hands, tongues, and so on—that illustrate the multitude of sensualities that exceed the paternal and its economy of singularity.

While mother and daughter imagine that they are having sex with Claude/ia, both have different motivations underlying their desire—Helen, that Claude will penetrate her with something other than his hands, and Dylan, that she will *finally* penetrate Claudia. Although neither of these actions come to fruition, I am interested in what these divergent fantasies about Claude/ia can tell us about the location of blackness in the semiotic. In many ways Helen's wish to be penetrated by Claude hews more closely to the imaginary of hypersexual black masculinity in that she wants to be pleasured with what she thinks will be a black penis. Although she has already orgasmed with Claude in previous encounters, this form of penetration's appeal, I argue, stems from Claude's blackness and Helen's understanding that he possesses a form of sexual mastery. Conversely, Dylan's desire to penetrate Claudia is about stripping her of power and making her vulnerable—a project of emasculation that also has to do with blackness. Indeed, we might see these fantasies as trafficking in multiple important tropes having to do with blackness—that of rape (of both the white and black woman) and that of castration.[35] Each of these dueling fantasies produces different genders and embodiments for Claude/ia, and while Claude/ia doesn't actualize either fantasy, they illustrate the difficulty of thinking blackness outside of a hierarchy of mastery and abjection. While Helen and Dylan's feminine jouissance occurs in a different métier from these hierarchies, Claude/ia's relationship to pleasure cannot be thought separately from his/her racialization.

Here, I turn to Dareick Scott's discussion of abjection, which he articulates as related to the excess that blackness produces vis-à-vis normative family structures. Scott writes: "the break between family (and concomitantly, all that family structures shape, most notably gender positions and sexuality) and nation that characterizes . . . blackness . . .— the break that is made by what conquest, enslavement, and domination has broken . . . of traditional life, and that *is* abjection—restarts sociogenic processes and makes possible new nations, different families, different gender positions and sexualities."[36] Scott emphasizes the potential for alternate sensualities and genders that emerge from blackness's estrangement from white normativity. While I will explore the pleasures in abjection later, here, I am interested in abjection's *difference* from jouissance. As such, I use the phrase "Claude/ia's relationship to pleasure" because it reminds us that Claude/ia ends up outside of this scene's sexual economy with his/her participation occurring at the level of fantasy and through spectatorship. We do not, however, see his/her pleasure. No, instead, we see his/her shock at seeing this moment of mother-daughter sexual contact and horror at being its inadvertent cause. S/he and Dunye (playing the voyeuristic taxi driver) are witnesses, aware of what is happening, but also unable to stop it until they flick on the lights at the last minute. In this way, the exteriority of blackness to the scene works to secure white familial intimacy by acting as a fantastical and real mediator.

The place where we do see Claude/ia approach jouissance (or orgasm at the very least) is during Claude's encounter with two leather daddies at the queer sex club. After taking a tour of the club and the myriad pleasures it provides, Claude allows himself to be bound, suspended, and penetrated by both men. The scene begins with an introduction, "This is my boyfriend, Tory," followed by a question, "Feeling superior?" The couple secure a collar to his neck and tell him that he'll have to "suck both of ours." He complies, is asked to remove his clothing, then the penetration and whipping begins. Throughout, both bark orders at him and he responds by saying "yes, sir." Eventually, both of them fist him simultaneously until he is left exhausted on the floor of the club. They all kiss, and he says, "thank you, sir."

Claude's explicit submissiveness and his willingness to be penetrated is central to his pleasures. When we read for race, it is not incidental that this moment of jouissance, when he experiences himself as a body, occurs in relation to BDSM and its economy of humiliation and pain. In her analysis of this scene, Jennifer Declue describes the significance of Claude/ia's simultaneous embrace of masculinity, penetration, and submission: "Claude's relenting to S/M seduction and his submission to Tory's deep German fist unsettles limiting homonormative gender separation and mixes in the complexity of gender, the corporeal cooperation of woman and man, and the mystification of gender."[37] Race, however, is unremarked upon in the film, but as viewers we cannot help but graft this gender play onto a racialized schema of violence in which being black and being a bottom is to engage in race play. Declue writes, "The erotics of the bottom for Claude are a complex of gender subversion as a top and a foray in unnamed race play that is left up to the viewer to tap into. Through the intensity of moving beyond a resistance to penetration into an oasis of titillation and release, the trauma of historic racial violence is embarked upon and passed through in this scene."[38] Although, Declue argues that this mixture of pleasure and submission might enable ways to read black queer pleasure anew—"Claude's erotic abandon in the queer sex club carries histories of sexual exploitation and the politics of silence into ecstatic pleasure. Claude's sexual agency as well as the experience of pleasure and satisfaction visualized in the scene adds some building blocks of cinematic grammar to the lexicon of black queer sexuality, but not without being routed through trauma"—I am interested in what happens when we stick with the messiness of BDSM.[39] On the one hand, we might relate Claude's performance of submission to *bottomhood*, the term that Nyguen Tan Hoang employs for embracing less valorized sides of multiple sociocultural formations including femininity and being anally penetrated. Hoang argues that receptivity, a key aspect of bottomhood, is "an active engagement that accounts for the senses of vulnerability, intimacy, and shame that one necessarily risks in assuming the bottom position."[40] In another passage, he writes that receptivity "engages openness, vulnerability, and receptivity to others: other looks, bodies, agencies."[41] Hoang rewrites the anus as active and finds power in the act and imaginary of submitting to the other and their desires. This is a complex dance, however. Hoang writes, "I use descriptions of the physical sensations of bottoming to affirm some of the ideological meanings assigned to anal eroticism, for example, feelings of exposure and defenselessness. At other times, I complicate cultural assumptions, for example, the idea that bottoming is necessarily passive and feminizing."[42] While aspects of feminine jouissance are filtered through this lens, especially in relation to the attachment to the desires of the other, there is a key difference—that of being in charge of producing that pleasure. Feminine jouissance registers the feeling of surplus embodiment through the control and incitement of the other's pleasure, while bottomhood offers the joys of submission and abjection. It is notable, however, that Hoang analyzes bottomhood in relation to Asian American masculinity and its stereotyped effeminacy, while Claude has actually moved farther away from femininity, which we see through his stick-on mustache, thereby shifting the charge of submission. What does the perceived violation of masculinity tell us about the types of power relations that are being worked through, especially since Claude's gender play might be read in relation to the status of blackness as external to the social order? And, how do we make meaning from the family that Claude forms with his two leather daddies?

We have several modes of thinking about Claude's desire for family. On the one hand, we can read his attachment to the leather daddies as an attachment to whiteness. As Juana María Rodríguez writes, "Queers love Daddy. The idea of intimate familial power serving as a source of erotic pleasure has wide rhizomatic reach in queer communities."[43] Rodríguez is referring to the outpouring of erotica such as Pat Califia's collection, *Doing It For Daddy*—the vibrant scenes of daddy-boy or daddy-femme play in queer communities where Daddy may not be a biological father (or indeed even identify as a man), but he occupies a particular fantasy space where narratives of "ownership and submission, a belonging to and belonging for another" can comingle with affection, guidance, and support.[44] Importantly, this desire for submission, for paternalism, also functions as racialized desire for the protections of whiteness. Rodríguez argues:

> In the metaphoric collapsing of the state as Daddy who is authorized to dispense "fatherly discipline," the power, privilege, and authority of both roles is unmasked as aligned not just with masculinity but also with

whiteness. In this sense, because economic and social power is so firmly attached to white masculinity, the very ability to *be* Daddy becomes racialized, whether that is imagined as a source of material support and benevolence or as a source of corporeal discipline. And Daddy's citizen-children are regarded and punished in accordance with their proximity to the white masculine ideal of the state.[45]

Through Rodríguez we can see how these fantasies shore up particular ideologies of white masculinity. And, Claude's enthusiastic bottoming for daddies (in juxtaposition with his refusal to be penetrated by Dylan) allows us to see the ways that these forms of masculinity and whiteness produce family through disciplining and protection. In these scenarios, the bosom of the (white) family offers privilege and power. Excluded from intimacy with Dylan, Claude is offered a place in this masculine whiteness—a place, it should be noted, that is as/at the bottom, pleasurable though that may be.

Yet the queerness of these daddies, both in the film and within the queer worlds that Rodríguez analyzes, also undoes some of patriarchy's potency because this ad hoc family formation traffics in fantasy, a space where agency can be grasped in all sorts of positions. Rodríguez argues that fantasy when mobilized in relation to queer daddies can "rewrit[e] these scripts [of white heteronormative national hegemony] through an assertion of [the queer's] own agency, even as that agency is understood as constituted by previous disciplinary formulations."[46] This process of rewriting is one that we might understand in relation to Scott's discussion of the pleasures in abjection, which include the representation of pleasure for the enslaved, whose: "imagination of these scene creates a way for them and their readers to identify with being violated or having been violated—and, in the manner of a willed (as opposed to developmental) identification, to do so from a position of power, relative to the real, historical, or present beings they might refer to, and thus to do so from a position better able to occupy or to utilize those otherwise hidden or overwhelmed powers that reside in the experience of black abjection."[47] Scott and Rodríguez both stress the importance of thinking agency in concert with this space outside of the real. For Rodríguez, in particular, these familial fantasies work to produce an insistence on belonging rather than social exclusion: "for those racialized queers who are written out of nation and often out of family itself, there is an urgency in engaging directly with the cultural taboos that have produced us as abject sexual subjects.... Eroticizing the familial enacts a simultaneous insistence on belonging through imagined familial relations, and not belonging through fantasized abuse and rejection of familial (and national) norms of protection and care."[48] As fantasy, then, we can register Claude's daddy play as giving him a family to belong to. That this family is queer is also important. It sets this family apart from the Oedipal triad by showing us two daddies, both of whom claim the power of the father through performance within the confines of the dungeon where permission is solicited for each act. In this case, Claude's gender play works to solidify his agency within this scenario's familial fantasy.

Scott, by contrast, is less invested in resuturing the family and more interested in accessing the power of thinking with this space of bottoming. In mining abjection for potentiality, Scott argues that humiliation and pain might in themselves be sources of pleasure: "The transformation of the elements of humiliation and pain, and the like, into a form of pleasure, the *taking* of pleasure out of the maw of humiliation and pain, and the utilization of that pain that windows into pleasure and back again for an experience of the self that, though abject, is politically salient, potentially politically effective or powerful."[49] Some of this pleasure is produced through the processes of fantasy and imagination, but other aspects of this pleasure stem from disarticulating pleasure from the concept of the sovereign subject and his or her relationship to desire and sexuality, which are legacies of our Oedipal fixation. This space outside of sovereignty puts us in the territory of jouissance, though like feminine jouissance, this excess is not created from either the shattering of the self or the loss of mastery.

While we can theorize feminine jouissance as occurring in proximity to the Other's opacity, abjection's pleasures emerge from the excess sensations (their own form of sensuous opacity) that come from the violence of objectification and social exclusion. Since abjection is so intimately related to the sensation of being a body, albeit one excluded from the social, I see Kristeva's theorization of jouissance of being as sitting the closest to its pleasures. Kristeva herself notes the kinship between abjection and jouissance, writing in *The Powers of Horror* that jouissance is found "out of such straying on excluded ground."[50] This is to say that jouissance exists in relation to the foreclosed mother, while abjection *itself* is a condition of foreclosure in relation to subjectivity.

Although Kristeva does not present abjection as a racialized term, Scott writes powerfully about the relationship between blackness and abjection. In *Extravagant Abjection*, Scott works to claim a form of black power in abjection. He writes, "I argue that abjection in/of blackness endows its inheritors with a form of counterintuitive *power*. . . . This power (which is also a way of speaking freedom) is found at the point of the apparent erasure of ego-protections, at the point at which the constellation of tropes that we call *identity, body, race, nation* seem to reveal themselves as utterly penetrated and compromised, without defensible boundary."[51] For Scott, abjection offers a space outside of subjectivity and outside of forms of belonging, including the aforementioned identity, body, race, and nation. This nonbelonging is a potentiality because it enables a consideration of blackness's excesses, especially in relation to discourses of sexuality. Much as feminine jouissance and jouissance of being challenge Oedipality, abjection as a form of black power reveals the sensualities that reside outside of blackness's sexualization through the pornotrope. Scott writes, "The twinning of blackness and the sexual—the relentless, repetitive sexualization of black bodies, the blackening of sexualized bodies—also fails always to fully contain the forces that articulation works to control: eruptions occur or can be provoked."[52] The question of abjection haunts that of enfleshment, revealing the ways that abjection sits alongside jouissance's feeling of being a body.

Perhaps a form of brown jouissance can be found in this understanding of the body as object and abject? This version of brown jouissance carries a notably different valence than feminine jouissance, which privileges the pleasure and opacity of the Other. It explores and revels in the affects and opacity that accompany objectification. It is a space without subjectivity (as traditionally defined), but it is a space where there is pleasure in embodiment and the radical possibilities that being an object provides. In *Embodied Avatars*, Uri McMillan uses the term "objecthood" to think through the potential agency within objectification. McMillan argues that

> objecthood provides a means for black subjects to become art objects. Wielding their bodies as pliable matter, the black women performers . . .

Figure 3.1. Xandra Ibarra and Amber Hawk Swanson, still from *Untitled Fucking*. © 2013 Xandra Ibarra and Amber Hawk Swanson.

repeatedly become objects.... Becoming objects, in what follows, proves to be a powerful tool for performing one's body, a "stylized repetition of acts" that rescripts how black female bodies move and are perceived by others. Put differently, performing objecthood becomes an adroit method of circumventing prescribed limitations on black women in the public sphere while staging art and alterity in unforeseen places.[53]

Performing one's objecthood relies on the abjection inherent in being an object, but it manipulates that abjection into agency: "I argue for rescrambling the dichotomy between objectified bodies or embodied subjects by reimagining objecthood as a performance-based method that disrupts presumptive knowledges of black subjectivity," writes McMillan. "What happens, I ask, if we reimagine black objecthood as a way toward agency rather than its antithesis, as a strategy rather than a primal site of injury."[54] It is in this call for embracing objecthood, the agency of the Thing, and the space of the self that we find some of the stakes of brown jouissance. Brown jouissance is about pleasure, abjection, and embracing alterity—either one's own or that of the Other. When we see the ways that brown jouissance is related to both feminine jouissance and abjection, we see that it can reveal modes of pleasure that can attach to experiencing the body as body, to the opacity of self and Other, and toward producing the self as plural rather than singular. These pleasures of brown jouissance inhere in the body's fleshiness and opacity.

"Feminism? That's Deep"

Although *Untitled Fucking* does not foreground familial intimacies, the performance highlights brown jouissance's complexification of belonging and being with the other. Sex, here, is a place where speech may be lost—witness both parties' difficulty with language as the performance goes on—but politics is not. Ibarra's performance is shot through with critiques of racism and US imperialism as she works to top whiteness in some form, and Hawk Swanson's enjoyment in being penetrated and her parroting of white feminist discourse could be imagined as a residual form of white guilt that perpetually seeks punishment for its racist past/present. When we read for brown jouissance, however, we go toward the borderlands where inclusion and exclusion are always in process and always contentious.

The opening shot of *Untitled Fucking* shows Hawk Swanson kneeling before Ibarra's Tapatío strap-on in order to cover it with multiple condoms. Ibarra prepares for their encounter by climbing onto the bed behind Hawk Swanson, donning black latex gloves, and applying lubricant to the bottle. From this point onward, Ibarra's gloved hands might appear to be superfluous, but they are actually in charge of the action. Her left hand rests on Hawk Swanson's rear where it helps to pull their hips together; her right hand guides the Tapatío bottle into Hawk Swanson's vagina. From its position atop a tripod, the camera permits us to see only Hawk Swanson being mounted from behind; penetration must be inferred from the position of hands, the movement of bodies, and Hawk Swanson's moans. As the performance continues and Hawk Swanson lowers herself onto the bed, Ibarra's left hand occasionally grabs her by the hair so that she can face the camera and utter her line again. Once Hawk Swanson tires of penetration, the hands become even more of a focal point. One is used to "ejaculate" the Tapatío sauce, while the other penetrates Hawk Swanson until she cannot orgasm anymore and the video concludes.

Through her performance of topping as responsiveness and anticipation, Ibarra performs the pleasure of listening to Hawk Swanson's words as well as the rhythms of her body. She disciplines and reassures her in order to facilitate her inhabitation of orgasm and in that way becomes body herself. She might be leading, but this is far from a fantasy of absolute domination over the Other or a flattening of the Other into a predetermined decipherable shape. This version of topping is about using her body as an instrument of pleasure. This, too, is being a body, but it is being a body in deep relation to another's body. We can see this performance as a form of sexual exchange, in which, as Rodríguez argues, "attempts to understand bodily signs occur through a sensing of the attitude and mood that hover over movements and words."[55] Ibarra strives not for recognition as an individual, but for an embodied *being with*.

By suturing her labors of pleasure to the Tapatío bottle, Ibarra also shows us the ways that racialization exceeds the parameters of feminine jouissance. This is to say that we must also think about the ways that her own body acts as a racial signifier in relation to scripts of legibility and performance. This residue of racialization is part of the "sexual archives flavored by attachments and memory" that Rodríguez describes.[56] Specifically, Ibarra's performance underscores that she understands that her Latina body is already read as pure body, a situation that doubles its instrumentality and links her to abjection. As Ramos argues, Ibarra "make[s] the audience aware that Latina labor is always already erotic in its abject physicality."[57] This "abject physicality" is more than the objectification that occurs through racialization. It is a product of pornotroping and the specific histories of Mexican labor in the agricultural industry, the increasingly global demand for Tapatío hot sauce, and the imaginary of the hot-tempered and sexually available Latina. Ibarra's performative allusions to the spread of Chicanidad (via the cucaracha pasties and hot sauce) work against the propping up of white state supremacy. This brings the difference between Claude's bottoming and Hawk Swanson's receptivity into sharp relief. Hawk Swanson shows us femme receptivity, which, following Ann Cvetkovich's analysis of Joan Nestle, we can understand as "both an openness to one's own pleasure and a willingness to give someone else pleasure, although the former is foregrounded in femme discourse."[58] Cvetkovich argues that Nestle imagines receptivity as a form of power play rather than self-shattering: "The femme thus both gives and takes in a process of being penetrated that allows her to 'match her [lover's] demanding with my giving, her hand with my insides.' In this act of simultaneous giving and taking, Nestle claims that the butch's 'power' to take gives 'me myself' quite a different conception of power and exchange from that implied by the construction of penetration as an act that destroys the selfhood of the person being penetrated."[59] In Hawk Swanson's performance of bottoming, we see this form of receptivity at work—she takes the Tapatío bottle willingly, all the while communicating her pleasures and needs with Ibarra. Noticeably absent from this is the sense that she is abjected by the action of penetration or that she is threatened by Ibarra's brownness.

Although the Tapatío bottle carries the symbolic weight of Ibarra's racial difference—we may profitably put it in conversation with Nao Bustamante's *Indigurrito* (1992) performance in which she uses a burrito as a strap-on and invites audience members who wish to atone for colonialism to bite from her burrito—Ibarra's use of gloves suggests that she understands her physicality in relation to abjection *and* care.[60] These sheathed hands are the locus of Ibarra's sexual expertise. While she listens with her entire body, it is her hands that provide pleasure: the Tapatío bottle requires a guiding hand and Hawk Swanson's orgasm ultimately arrives as a result of Ibarra's dexterous manipulation. Both strap-on and fingers work as forms of a lesbian phallus in that they gesture toward a sensual economy outside of the penile and Oedipal. As such, this handiwork, I want to suggest, might be construed as belonging to a particularly queer and possibly feminine form of practice and expertise, one that encapsulates brown jouissance in relation to opacity, abjection, and care. While we can interpret the condom as a necessary prophylactic against potential injury from the hot sauce, or more symbolically as a barrier against spiciness, the latex gloves serve a different function. They block Ibarra's hands from coming into direct contact with Hawk Swanson's genitals. On the one hand, this barrier allows viewers to imagine that there might be another possible layer of intimacy—one in which Ibarra's hands would be unsheathed—that we are not privy to, thereby facilitating our understanding of this as a performance. On the other hand, the presence of gloves positions this encounter within a repertoire of safer sex that flourished in the era and aftermath of the AIDS emergency. This double reference to safer sex—through condoms and latex gloves—cannot help but bring the specters of abjection and care to the fore. This happens because we cannot think these items without linking them to the AIDS emergency, but also because their purpose is to prevent contamination. Within the context of intimacies with strangers (or outside the frame of monogamy), we can think about safer sex as an important part of a regime of care.

In this mélange of feminine jouissance, abjection, and care, I see brown jouissance, which, in turn, brings us back to thinking about the conversation that *Untitled Fucking* stages between "white feminism and feminisms of color that whiteness excludes." Ibarra and Hawk Swanson's performance shows us topping and bottoming as a dialogue in which rhythms, movement, and words constitute their own language—something that comes from the crossings of Chicanidad and whiteness, a combination of white feminism and feminisms of color, something that belongs to both. Their performances move beyond the fantasy of queer mother or father love toward a performance of belonging itself as queer. This is a form of belonging that brings us toward to the borderlands—that geography of porosity where inclusion and exclusion cannot be thought as discrete categories. The fear of contamination that Ibarra plays with and Hawk Swanson's openness to penetration speak to the flexibility of the border.

Gloria Anzaldúa's meditation on *la frontera* and its production of a hybrid tongue subtends this conversation. Against the demands to conform to respectable and appropriate whiteness, Anzaldúa positions her wild tongue:

> I remember being sent to the corner of the classroom for "talking back" to the Anglo teacher when all I was trying to do was tell her how to pronounce my name. "If you want to be American, speak 'American.' If you don't like it, go back to Mexico where you belong." . . . Attacks on one's form of expression with the intent to censor are a violation of the First Amendment. *El Anglo con cara de inocente nos arrancó la lengua.* Wild tongues can't be tamed, they can only be cut out. . . .
>
> But Chicano Spanish is a border tongue which developed naturally. Change, *evolución, enriquecimiento de palabras nuevas por invención o adopción* have created variants of Chicano Spanish, *un nuevo lenguaje. Un*

lenguaje que corresponde a un modo de vivir. Chicano Spanish is not incorrect, it is a living language.⁶¹

Anzaldúa argues for a mestiza consciousness to accommodate this space that is penetrated by histories of Mexican indigeneity, colonialism, and Anglo imperialism. For the purposes of this chapter, I see this admixture as gesturing toward a form of belonging that is explicitly non-Oedipal in that it revolves around multiplicity (against the demand for one white paternal figure) and the ambiguities afforded by sensuality. Anzaldúa writes, "Indigenous like corn, like corn, the *mestiza* is a product of crossbreeding, designed for preservation under a variety of conditions. Like an ear of corn—a female seed-bearing organ—the *mestiza* is tenacious, tightly wrapped in the husks of her culture. Like kernals she clings to the cob; with thick stalks and strong brace roots, she holds tight to the earth—she will survive the crossroads."⁶² Reading *Untitled Fucking* through Anzaldúa, we see continuities in the discourse of survival, which can also become legible as threat—corn, cucarachas—and an insistence that penetration either through food or strap-on reveals an already complex set of imbrications and forms of belonging—even if disavowed.

I also can't help but think about the Tapatío ejaculate on Hawk Swanson's back. Might we read this as a sign that white feminism cannot actually be rid of women of color feminism, that it spreads its insights on the flesh and through its eroticism? Tellingly, Ibarra describes Tapatía as "Spic Jouissance." Although it is modeled after the Tapatío label, Tapatía features a photograph of Ibarra in a smile/grimace and lists among its ingredients "armargura, commodified negation, deadicated invader subjectivity, toilet water, Las 3 lupes, and Alternity, Cucharacha logic as a preservative."⁶³ Foregrounding bitterness, the affective labor of brownness, as well as eroticism—the bottle also reads "Es Una Puta ... Bien Jota" (which translates roughly to "a very queer whore")—Ibarra foregrounds the stain of difference, abjection, and appetite. Most saliently this dollop of spice shows us that objectification is not just about a simple oscillation between activity and passivity, but that in the space between saying and doing, there are multiple histories, multiple possibilities for pleasure, and multiple axes for penetration.⁶⁴ Importantly, this multiplicity also points us toward thinking with the distortions of normative kinship that can produce brown jouissance: racialization refigures mommy and daddy and what it might mean to take pleasure in "belonging." What has been called incestuous by an Oedpial and phallic order might be mined for alternate forms of belonging and sensuous pleasures. Instead of exclusion, these performances insist on critique, as well as the intimate proximity of difference and the multivalent delights that that produces.

4

Performing Witness

Voice, Interiority, and Diaspora

A young black woman stands in profile; she is bare-chested and unsmiling. There is a continuous line between the shadows on her back and her closely cropped hair. The image is bathed in red. White text overlaid on the photograph reads, "You became a scientific profile." In an adjacent photograph, an older black man with silvery hair gazes impassively at the camera in an image that highlights his wiriness; the textual overlay on this photograph reads, "A Negroid Type." These images are drawn from the Louis Agassiz collection at Harvard's Peabody Museum.[1] While Agassiz commissioned the daguerreotypes as part of his efforts to produce a visual taxonomy of physical types and support his theories of the inferiority of black people, Carrie Mae Weems incorporates them into her 1995–1996 photographic series, *From Here I Saw What Happened and I Cried*, as an illustration of the links between the commodification of blackness and the visible wounds of race. Yet in Weems' series, which consists of thirty-four nineteenth- and twentieth-century photographic images culled from various archives, there is also something else, something that enables us to think about brown jouissance in relation to voice and the project of witnessing.

Thinking brown jouissance in relation to the voice reveals the tension between the materiality of the body and the ineffable qualities of interiority. Voice, after all, is that which exceeds mere speech. Its granulations are products of movement, bodies, and histories—what I describe in relation to Weems's series as a version of diaspora—especially as it indexes a beyond. In his description of what he calls "jouissance beyond the word," Néstor Braunstein writes that "it is impossible to objectify, impossible for the *parlêtre* to articulate. It is this jouissance which prompts Lacan to say, 'Naturally, you are all going to be convinced that I believe in God.'"[2] Voice, then, links physicality to spirituality. To think voice in relation to a series of photographs, however, is another thing altogether, but voice comes through in the way that this series highlights Weems's performance of witnessing. This witnessing inheres in her tinting of the photographs—red mostly, but also blue—and her application of a textual overlay. Through these acts she amplifies the possibility of locating voice within the photographs, not only showing us the jouissance that lies beyond the word, but transforming these photographic objects into portraits of interiority, as well. Weems brings forth the voices of diasporic ancestors so that the relationship between spirituality and interiority is made manifest even as these photographs illustrate a history of black bodies as commodities. It is in Weems's interpretive tug between visual objectification and the possibilities of voice that brown jouissance lies.

Objectification, Commodification, and an Archive of Black Woundedness

From Here I Saw What Happened and I Cried was commissioned by the Getty Estate in Los Angeles as a companion piece to their 1992 exhibition, *Hidden Witness*, which depicted images from Jackie Napolean Wilson's collection of photographs of African Americans immersed in daily life throughout the nineteenth century. In his description of the image that gives the show its name, Wilson writes, "When I first saw this daguerreotype, it was the warmth of the family setting and the beauty of the land that first caught my attention; later I saw this man forlorn with shovel in hand leaning against the tree. . . . This slave gardener made the scene himself. He was the 'hidden witness' who saw this picture being created and was a witness to life at that time, and remained a testimonial to this day."[3] *Hidden Witness* recognizes the underacknowledged labor that African Americans performed as slaves or servants, displacing the ideology of the naturalized white family unit and highlighting its dependence on racialized labor. Wilson's project is recuperative: it brings together unexpected archives to consolidate images of quotidian black life, thereby allowing the viewer to consider the humanity of the subjects, who are often caught off guard and appear lost in thought, while drawing our attention to the labors of race.

In response to Wilson's eclectic, dreamy archive and its hints of racial uplift, Weems plays the more negative side of the affective register. As Weems explores what it is to witness, her installation summons grief, guilt, empathy, and sympathy in ways that both mask and unmask her racialized subjects. Instead of captions bearing names or identities, Weems's reprints show us objectified bodies, largely from nineteenth-century sources. In Weems's focus on the visual economy of race and its relationship to objectification, she illuminates Nicole Fleetwood's argument that "the notion of rendering/rendered is crucial to the formulation of blackness and blacks as objects and subjects of visuality and performance."[4] Writing further, Fleetwood argues that "the visual manifestation of blackness through technological apparatus or through a material experience of locating blackness in public spaces equates with an ontological account of black subjects. Visuality, and vision to an extent, in relationship to race becomes a thing-in-itself."[5] The histories of medicine, anthropology, and surveillance reinforce this claim because these disciplines rely on producing difference as visible and therefore quantifiable. For example, Simone Browne's recent work on re-centering blackness to demarcate difference in surveillance studies begins with a comparison between slave ships and Bentham's famous panopticon.[6] In these sets of arguments, we see that technologies of visual representation, including photography, are deeply imbricated in histories of consolidating race as visually knowable, transforming photographic subjects into specimens—examples of types rather than individuals. By delving into the photographic archive, Weems is explicit in her summoning of this history of visual objectification.

From Here I Saw What Happened and I Cried presents this violence in a doubled fashion, however. Weems shows us that there is violence inherent to the medium of photography, while also presenting images that speak to the violence (past and present) of slavery.[7] Part of what is at stake in Weems's series is the illustration of the delicate contours of the relationship between blackness and enfleshment. Here, we follow Hortense Spillers and her articulation of the relation between blackness, flesh, and rupture. Spillers argues that flesh is what bodies become through the violence of the transatlantic slave trade, but this flesh, she cautions, is seldom intact; it is "seared, divided, ripped-apartness, riveted to the ship's hole, fallen, or 'escaped' overboard."[8] These tears, and the discourse of woundedness, become scripted as precultural, rendering blackness vestibular and spectacular in its difference.

Because Weems's series plays with the wound, it activates cycles of spectatorical pleasure and empathetic shame, thereby allowing us to uncover the affective dimensions of enfleshment, the space where relations between racialization and gendering become written on the body through emotion. The spectacle of the black body in pain mobilizes empathy and sympathy, but also passivity.[9] This is to say that black pain induces sentiment, rather than action. In this understanding of race through visual dominance, we see a crystalization of a mode of interraciality in which blackness is related to woundedness and whiteness is linked with passivity and innocence—one cannot even begin to imagine acting. In her analysis of white innocence, Robin Bernstein argues that these images of woundedness also lead to a perception that black bodies can tolerate more pain and *should* be subjected to this violence. As evidence of this, Bernstein describes dolls as scriptive things that elicit racialized performances of violence. Bernstein writes, "Children of all races committed violence against dolls of all colors, but white girls specifically targeted soft black dolls for ritualistic and exceptionally violent abuse, which the dolls, of course, submissively endured."[10] In this violent play, blackness permits objectification and harm. In part, this is because violence is *not* imagined as producing pain—hence the production of white innocence as a lack of ability to conceive of black pain as well as insulation from white guilt. Black pain also hovers around projects of liberation, however. In her analysis of black feminist discussions of sexuality, Jennifer Nash argues that despite their aims to produce narratives of sexual liberation and possibility, many black feminists are still caught up in responding to these legacies of pain, especially in relation to representation: "A vibrant and varied archive that contains different theories of representation still manages to collectively perform the black female body as an injured site, producing an archive that is structured by a 'grammar' of woundedness."[11]

It is the explicit depiction of woundedness alongside the photographic and affective violence of spectatorship that make Weems's piece so complex. Her series summons the multiple forms of violence that have visited black Americans while also displaying the passivity of white Americans. Further, the title announces shame and sorrow at these spectacles of racist violence in relation to the act of crying: "From here I saw what happened and I cried." We have many options for understanding these tears:

as grief? Humiliation? Shame? Guilt? We might even use the title to understand the series in relation to racialized sentimentality as a genre.[12] In her analysis of the series, Jennifer Doyle notes that this mobilization of sentiment invites collective—perhaps even national—mourning at the history of slavery and of racism. She writes, "*From Here I Saw* might thus be read as indexing anger, frustration, and exhaustion, a depression by dint of routine: theft, exploitation, appropriation, resistance, grief, mourning, and recovery—followed by the requirement that the artist produce that cycle within her work."[13] The tears that Weems's series invokes invite us to critique the regimes of visuality that have objectified and harmed black people and to mourn the ways that we have been implicated within this system either as objectified bodies or as passive spectators; the textual "you" that circulates above most of the images allows for this shifting identification. In this way, the installation manipulates our affective response through either one or both of these circuits of bad feelings. Those who suffer are stuck in a cycle of violence and harm, while those who watch are rendered passive. Against the narrative of uplift hinted at in *Hidden Witness*, Weems's work suggests the impossibility of moving beyond that frame, prompting some, including Doyle, to ask whether Weems herself is participating in the same problematic dynamic that she unveils: "At what point does witnessing switch from being a point of resistance to being a point of collusion? How does one know the difference—is it a matter of how we look at something, how we feel about what we are looking at? What is the relationship between one and the other?"[14] *From Here I Saw What Happened and I Cried* appears to name the collective feeling that the series generates without giving us a way to think outside of that framework. As spectators, we remain stuck in the temporality of grief and its guilt, shame, and sadness.

But when we turn to Weems's comments on the series, we gain a different perspective. Weems argues that while she is "trying to heighten a kind of critical awareness around the way in which these photographs were intended," she is also working to "give the subject another level of humanity and another level of dignity that was originally missing in the photograph."[15] It is in this project of giving voice to her photographic subjects that I see Weems illuminating the possibilities of brown jouissance. She does this first by performing witness—rather than spectatorship—through her juxtaposition of text and image to produce interiority and, second, by drawing attention to the way that photography functions as a technology of reproduction and kinship, thereby altering our understanding of mothering.

Voice, Tears, and Interiority

One of Weems's strategies for returning humanity to the subjects in the photographs is to announce the opacity of their interiorities while simultaneously addressing them by the use of "you." This "you" is capacious, inviting both spectators—especially those who might identify with the photographs—and the long dead photographic subjects into dialogue with Weems. One particularly jarring example overlaid on a man's scarred back reads:

> Black and Tanned
> Your Whipped Wind
> of change howled low
> blowing itself-ha-smack
> into the middle of Ellington's Orchestra
> billie heard it too &
> Cried Strange Fruit Tears.

Here, we see that "you" can mean a lot of different things. In speaking to museum spectators, we can imagine that "your whipped wind of change" invokes the incomplete nature of civil rights movements in its suggested conflation between the wound depicted in the image and the contemporary viewer's experiences of racism. This allows the viewer to imagine that it is his or her body in the frame. Through apostrophe, Weems also summons interiorities that have historically been ignored—those of the people in the photograph. In speaking to them, however, Weems is not asking that we substitute their interiority for our own, but that we listen for their voices. It is significant that she does this by positioning them alongside Duke Ellington and Billie Holiday, which shifts the register of black pain away from the visual toward the opacity of sound. This allows us to consider voice in relation to interiority. The richness of this interiority is demonstrated, in turn, by how Ellington and Holiday signify. Here, I turn to Fred Moten's description of Holiday's voice:

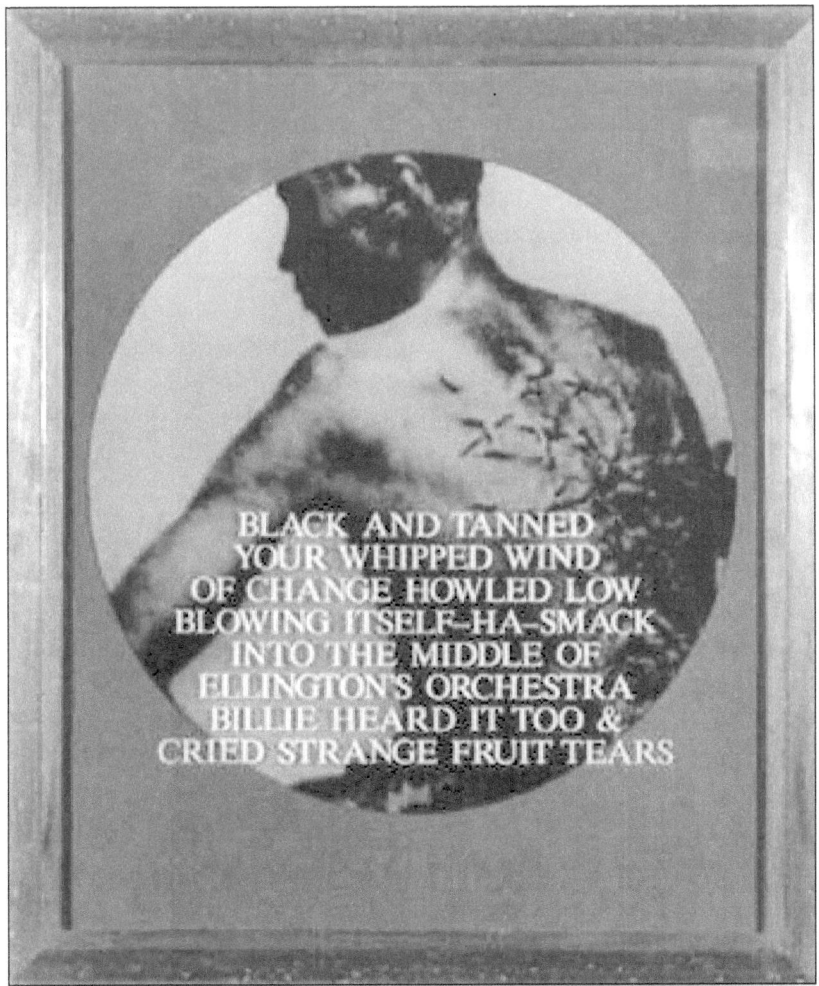

Figure 4.1. Black and Tanned Your Whipped Wind of Change Howled low blowing itself-ha-smack in the middle of Ellington's Orchestra billie heard it too & Cried Strange Fruit Tears. ©1995 Carrie Mae Weems.

The grained voice engrains, the sign of the mouth, which is the birth, the sign of a kiss, reading you like an analyst reads the signs; here that reversal, where the listener oscillates between the analytic positions, is now such that the listener is without knowledge and waiting on Lady to lecture, to free-associate.... She's on another thing, another register of desire. And that grained voice elsewhere resists the interpretation of the audience where the analytic positions are exchanged.[16]

In Moten's evocation of Holiday's interiority, we come toward opacity. Moten argues that Holiday's singing positions her interiority as unknowable, while prompting self-reflexivity in the listener. In other words, her singing announces an interiority, while leaving it to others to imagine themselves in relation to it. Further, by describing Holiday's voice as grained, Moten brings Roland Barthes into the conversation—specifically Barthes's argument that the grain of the voice, "the materiality of the body speaking its mother tongue" brings "not just the soul but *jouissance*."[17] For Moten, the materiality of Holiday's body does not just index pain (though that is present), but speaks to spirituality and pleasure, too: "She cuts literature like St. Theresa, with muteness and grain."[18] Brown jouissance, voice, and opacity come together in these lines. What Weems tells us with her juxtaposition of image and text and summoning of the sonic is that black interiority is found in the cracks around the visual and that within the register of the sonic, this interiority should be imagined through a prism of relationality and opacity rather than through a mandate of transparency. We are in the space of the something else that Weems creates from Agassiz's photographs.

Weems further distances herself from transparency by displacing her own interiority from the series. The titular "I" is not Weems, but Wilson. The title, *From Here I Saw What Happened and I Cried*, is actually a quotation from one of Wilson's captions in *Hidden Witness*. While we can understand this phrase through the spectacularization of the wound and the temporal stagnation of the black photographic subjects whose images she has enlarged and tinted—all of which are more conventional readings of Weems—what does it mean for Weems to use this phrase as her title? I read Weems's citation of Wilson as a strategic mode of creating distance in order to reveal the opacity of interiority. It also, however, signals that she is doing something different with the concept of witnessing. Instead of portraying witnesses, Weems *performs* witness through her emphasis on the relationship between her and the images and in the way that she acts as a mediator between the images and the installation spectators. This performance of witness is about fleshiness and relationality.

Witnessing announces Weems as a self who exists profoundly in relation to others. She produces her own opacity by juxtaposing text and image so that the relation between her, these photographic ancestors, and museum spectators becomes complicated. We are presented with voices, but we do not know whose. Are we listening to Weems, the people in the photographs, or an unannounced voice from elsewhere? Thinking with voice and witnessing is important because it highlights the elements of fleshiness that come through Weems's performance of witness. By witnessing, Weems is actively listening to the photographs—challenging the idea that photography is only about the visual and illuminating Moten's argument that photographs "in general bear a phonic substance."[19] Further, this "I"—which we imagine to be Weems's flesh—allows us to think of Weems's interiority as infusing the installation through her manipulation of the prints, which are not only enlarged but tinted blue or red, perhaps suggesting rage, sadness, or any number of emotions. It is significant that the two blue-tinted images, "From Here I Saw What Happened" and "And I Cried"—which depict an African woman whose gaze is directed toward the rest of the series in "From Here" and back over it in "And I Cried"—bookend the show. In addition to gesturing toward the diasporic, as the only images that are overlaid with an "I" they further illustrate the distance between the images that Weems has resignified—"A Scientific Type"—and her own interiority.

Weems's circumspect invocation of tears is also an important part of this simultaneous display of fleshiness and opaque interiority. If Weems is crying, might we find a kinship between these salty emissions and photography's liquidity? Perhaps crying in the darkroom offers its own politics? I come to this fusion of photography and crying by way of imagining the alchemy behind these scenes of fleshy capture. Photography's techniques of making the visible permanent through the chemical capture of light seems an apt counterpoint to the tear's imbrication within racialized discourses of woundedness. Both traffic in fixity and fiction. Here, the ambiguity of tears is an asset. Even as they illuminate

Figure 4.2. Carrie Mae Weems, "And I Cried," Baltimore Museum of Art. ©1995 Carrie Mae Weems.

the violent ruptures caused by colonial histories, they offer a way to see beyond woundedness. Further, in perceiving "the tears" as evidence of Weems's witnessing, we move into the alchemical—the space of transformation where flesh might shift from wound into something else. Specifically, I argue that these tears transform photographs of objectification into portraits—illustrating the mobility that underlies liquidity.

Liquidity, here, reveals something about the relationship between affect, flesh, and the possibility of expression. More specifically, it leads us to think with the face—the origin point of tears. While we do not actually see anyone in tears, it is through a consideration of the tear that we can restore interiority to the subjects of these photographs. By transforming these photographs into portraits, these images become people who might cry or laugh or reveal their interiority in countless possible ways. For Brian Wallis this transformation occurs because Weems's subject position allows her to relate to those in the photographs as individuals rather than types. He writes, "She saw these men and women not as representatives of some typology but as living, breathing ancestors. She made them portraits."[20] In thinking with this difference through the images that Weems uses from the Agassiz archives, for example, the suggestion that these are portraits rather than depictions of specimens draws our attention to hints of personality in the crevices of the face, emotions in the eyes, affect in the posture. Instead of registering these prints as examples of African Americans during slavery or in terms of measurement or form, viewing them as portraiture suggests affect. In this we see that Weems's transformative (and tinted) tears have shifted our attention away from the affect that is projected onto the images and toward the possibility of understanding these images as expressive.[21]

Expressivity also allows us to think through the tears that we do not see. The invocation of a crying face—whether it is Weems's or someone else's—*and* Weems's denial of the spectatorial pleasure of a crying face, which might lead to catharsis or an imagined absolution of guilt, force us to dwell on the interiority hidden beneath these violently produced images. This ambiguity allows us to see the importance of thinking with opacity. In this Weems also issues a subtle rejoinder to the concept of blackness as a "hidden witness"; in her series, not only are these portraits of black people *not* hidden within the cloak of white normativity, but they and their expressivity are essential to the performance of witnessing. They are front and center—an emphasis amplified by Weems's use of black matting around the images to focus our attention on the center of the frame. This focus on the photographic forces us to think *with* the images of black people in pain to find something new, something not overly signified. In Barthes's parlance we might ask what is the punctum? What affectively pricks us?[22]

Instead of tears, what we see is the complex relationship between surface and depth *and* subject and object. How we perceive what is going on in the images depends entirely on perspective, but the possibility of ambiguity, which is where I locate interiority, is crucial to allowing flesh to signify differently. This is a space where many things are possible. It is the space where Tina Campt and Kevin Quashie locate the quiet. Campt writes that "quiet is a modality that surrounds and infuses sound with impact and affect, which creates the possibility for it to register as meaningful."[23] For Campt, the quiet is part of an "everyday practice of refusal."[24] Likewise, Quashie argues that quiet enables us to imagine a wider range of possibilities for blackness and to begin to theorize black subjects. He writes, "Quiet . . . is a metaphor for the full range of one's inner life—one's desires, ambitions, hungers, vulnerabilities, fears. The inner life is not apolitical or without social value, but neither is it determined entirely by publicness. In fact, the interior—dynamic and ravishing—is a stay against the dominance of the social world; it has its own sovereignty."[25] Quashie's insistence that interiority allows for a space separate from domination allows us to think about both the value of ambiguity and the form of political work that Weems's installation does. Interiority is the space that Spillers demands black intellectuals take up when she urges a reconsideration of psychoanalysis. She argues that interiority can act as a balm against the sociological construction of subjectivity, which Fanon argued vociferously against and which activates pernicious circuits of sentimentality. Spillers describes interiority as "persistently motivated in inwardness, in-flux, it is the 'mine' of social production that arises, in part, from interacting with others, yet it bears the imprint of a particularity."[26] Traditionally, interiority is expressed through speech, but as Spillers points out, "To speak is to occupy a place in social economy, and, in the case of the racialized subject, his history has dictated that this linguistic *right to use* is never easily granted with his human and social legacy but must be earned, over and over again, on the level of a personal and collective struggle that requires in some way a confrontation with the principle of language *as a prohibition*."[27] The denial of interiority and speech is, after all, part of the process of enfleshment. Voice, that sonic space of expressivity that exceeds language, signals interiority while remaining opaque. This is what makes Weems's use of apostrophe radical: it hails a quiet, but not silent interiority.

Refracted through the ambiguity of the quiet and its "level of intensity that requires focused attention," these photographic voices are amplified through Weems's performance of witness.[28] This illumination of voice also draws attention to all of the ways that flesh evades technological capture. Importantly, Michelle Stephens argues that the gap produced by fleshiness is one that centers relation. Rather than focus on the question of authenticity or liveness, the voice activates circuits of openness toward the other. She writes, "Lacan privileged voice, sound, and the ear as important aspects of, as he termed it, an invocatory drive. This was precisely because of the ways in which, unlike the image and the gaze, the circuit of desire to hear the self, to hear the other, and to be heard as the other hears us, can never be completely closed."[29] In using Weems to think with the relational dimension of voice, however, we gain access to long-dead ancestors in a way that exceeds the portrait.[30] It is not just that these images have their interiority restored; their identity as a bounded series also allows us to think about the self as collective and diasporic. This Weems achieves by drawing attention to photography as a technology of reproduction and mothering.

Making Kin: Diaspora, Affect, and Mechanical Reproduction

In arguing that Weems presents selfhood as collective and diasporic, I also argue that Weems allows us to see the ways in which performing witness is a form of gendered labor. This restoration of gender operates against the ungendering that traditionally accompanies enfleshment, what Saidiya Hartman describes as the fungibility of blackness, which is part of the enslaved's transition into the commodity.[31] This re-gendering is part of what emerges when we consider the work of photography in terms of reproduction, which, in turn, allows us to see that Weems's performance of witness is also one of mothering in that it produces new forms of kinship.

The ungendering that accompanies the processes of enfleshment is achieved, according to Spillers, through slavery's violation of the norms of the psychoanalytic family. The emergent family structures collapsed the law of the Father with normative whiteness and made maternity synonymous with reproduction and labor, thereby making mother and father impossible positions for the enslaved to inhabit and leaving the Oedipal family structure unachievable. These psychoanalytic consequences left blackness outside of the symbolics of gender. Spillers writes, "In other words, in the historic outline of dominance, the respective subject-positions of 'female' and 'male' adhere to no symbolic integrity."[32] Under these conditions of powerlessness, "we lose at least gender difference *in the outcome*, and the female body and the male body become a territory of cultural and political maneuver, not at all gender-related, gender specific."[33] This unmaking of gender has deep and important consequences. Most immediately, it threatens the possibility of subjectivity. This difficulty emerges most potently when we read Spillers in conjunction with Judith Butler. In *Gender Trouble*, Butler argues that even as gender is not an inherent attribute of the subject, it is integral to its formation because it enables legibility. Gender, Butler argues, is the product of repeated, stylized acts that are part of historically produced binaries and the heterosexual matrix.[34] Since these performances of gender lie at the core of the subject's identity, Butler articulates a subject who is perpetually in the state of becoming male or female. To exist in a state of un-gendering, then, denies the possibility of subjectivity. This difficulty around subjectivity is part of why I argue that *From Here I Saw What Happened and I Cried* restores interiority not subjectivity.

Indeed, we see this instability in Weems's reprints of Agassiz's photographs of bare-chested slaves, which do not adhere to the conventional gendered divisions of portraiture and present both male and female slaves in the same way. Weems's use of "you" throughout the series also serves to preserve the instability of gender even as the images themselves—a female nude presented as a "playmate for the patriarch" while the subsequent image of an older woman holding a white child reads "and their daughter"—expose the gendered division of labor. Further, if we consider Weems's use of photography as a technology of reproduction—in its multiple meanings—we can see a space for re-thinking mothering. Here, I argue that we think Weems's photographic enterprise and its relation to liquidity as not only about the provocation of chemical reactions and interiority but also as a form of reproduction and kinship. This is to say that Weems's performance of witnessing creates important connections between Weems and the photographs that she reproduces. This connection is not just about the infusion of interiority, but about the constitution of kinship wherein linkages are wrought through voice, darkroom chemicals, and flesh. Returning briefly to the analogy that Moten draws between the voice, mouth, and birth in his analysis of Holiday—"The grained voice engrains, the sign of the mouth, which is the birth, the sign of a kiss"—I argue that Weems's witnessing enables us to consider the fleshiness of the voice through the lens of mothering.[35]

Specifically, I argue that Weems's reprinting of these archival images is a form of taking up what Elissa Marder terms the *maternal function*. Differentiating the mother from the maternal function, Marder links the latter with technologies of reproduction and "the capacity for self-replication."[36] While this form of reproduction may feel obvious in the case of photography, the maternal function is also about grappling with the lost maternal body—a form of mourning that is deeply important to thinking with blackness, gender, and sexuality. Marder makes this connection through an analysis of Barthes's *Camera Lucida* and grief. While photography represents the mechanized possibilities of reproduction, it also offers a way to both mourn and connect with the lost maternal body. She writes, "The photographic medium is often represented as a prosthetic maternal body that is simultaneously defined by and contrasted to the body of the biological mother.... To the extent that these [photographic and cinematic] technologies aim to usurp the maternal function, they are often deployed as a means of regulating or warding off anxieties that are provoked by the inevitable experience of loss that real separation from the mother invariably demands."[37] Marder's emphasis on marking the link between photography, reproduction, and loss gives us an alternate perspective on Weems's work as a photographer.

When we consider her enlargements a labor of reproduction and mourning, we can imagine Weems as not only disrupting circuits of sentimentality, but also producing paths of kinship born from chemical bonds. Blood is replaced with saline, which recalls the oceans that often separate diasporic communities. Calling the links between Weems and her photographic subjects kinship is important, not just because it brings attention to other emotional currents that swirl within the violent histories of displacement, but because it allows us to think gender and race in concert with agency, specifically, the agency of mothering. This agency is about creating connection, upending expectations, and scripting alternate futurities. While Weems probes difficult history, she also restores the possibility of less negative affects to her subjects by restoring their interiorities and emphasizing her connectedness—kinship—to them through a form of gendered labor.

And labor, it is. For this series, Weems selected images that spoke to her. She photographed them—because many of the images were daguerreotypes and so could not be reproduced without first being photographed. She enlarged the images and tinted them by replacing the metallic silver in the emulsion with dye, so that the photographs appear blue or red. Then, she placed a circular black mat around the images and covered them with glass inscribed with words. This is a multistep and multilayered process that required Weems to perform a great deal of care both in her thought process and in her handling of the photographs. It is this layer of care that is important in our consideration of Weems's process. While I am not arguing that Weems makes herself into a mother *or* a child through her act of mechanical reproduction—especially since Moten might argue that photography itself is emblematic of the collapse between becoming-material and becoming-maternal that ungendering entails—she does enlarge her network of kinship, producing a sort of affective diaspora. She links herself to people in the photographs and invites us to think about the modes of connecting—salinity and tactility—between then and now.

One of these modes of connection is the diasporic, which Weems summons through her use of an African woman to bookend the series. By having this blue African woman flank red African American portraits, Weems connects Africa to the United States while also underscoring the multiplicity of affects at work in this diaspora. Does this blue indicate these women's sadness at the fate of their diasporic kin? In of the bringing together of Africa and the United States we cannot help but think of slavery and separation, but we also see the activation of a particular fantasy of home, or more particularly the idea of a temporally static motherland. Though I have been calling this relationship

Figure 4.3. Carrie Mae Weems, *From Here I Saw What Happened and I Cried*, installation view, Center of Contemporary Art, Seville, Spain, 2010. ©2010 Carrie Mae Weems.

"diasporic," it differs from traditional notions of diaspora in that it is not about the relationship to a particular nation, but about the affective pull of the imaginary of a place. This connection is one of loss, but it is also one that speaks to optimism and the possibility of a restoration of kinship alongside violent rupture.

In this duality, we might profitably also think about the ways in which Weems's diaspora is enlarged through the process of selling her photographs. On the one hand, the question of copyright, brought to the fore in one way through Harvard's threatened suit against Weems, illustrates the complex imbrications of commodification (especially in relation to photographs from the Agassiz archive) and circulation. Specifically, this tangle enables us to ask, as Yxta Murray does, whose images these are:

> But whose daguerreotypes are they? Should Agassiz have ever been able to claim a right to these pictures? And, by extension, should Harvard? Agassiz pirated these images through capture and exploitation. No legitimate law should recognize this violent taking of property rights. Allowing the Agassiz daguerreotypes to remain in Harvard's custody sustains a

brutal offense, and erases instead of bears witness to the violent past. In the interests of peace, the law should transfer the property to new hands: this would involve transforming the daguerreotypes' title from that of the University to those who bear the closest lineal relationship to the subjects of the daguerreotypes, being Drana, Renty, Jack, and Delia.[38]

But, thinking with this same question of property in relation to Weems's own circulation and sale of the photographs still marks these images, or at least those manipulated in the manner that Weems does, as the property of entities who are not the enslaved. They become Weems's intellectual property and the art collector's or museum's private property. On the other hand, however, following the arguments that I have laid out here, these images' circulation, especially when understood as part of Weems's artistic and activist oeuvre, suggests that this movement might also register as an enlargement of diaspora and kinship.

In this promiscuous fusion of kinship and diaspora, I connect Weems's work to that of Audre Lorde, who describes an expansive version of kinship that centralizes race, geography, and maternity. Lorde theorizes kinship in her discussion of what it is to be a daughter and think affectively about history, ancestors, and migration. In an open letter to Mary Daly critiquing the white and European focus of *Gyn/Ecology*'s female lineages, Lorde writes, "To dismiss our black foremothers may well be to dismiss *where* European women learned to love."[39] This emphasis on maternity and place is deeply important for Lorde's theorization of kinship and affective connection. We see this throughout her biomythography, *Zami: A New Spelling of My Name*, and in Lorde's travels.[40] She traveled through West Africa—Senegal, Togo, Ghana, and Benin—for the first time in 1974 and moved to Saint Croix toward the end of her life. Her biographer, Alexis De Veaux, describes these trips as spiritual voyages: "Leaving Dahomey, and Africa, saddened her, and she wasn't ready to go. But Lorde took from Africa what she needed: a spiritual location; the knowledge of original ancestors; a corporeal reality that was unique, timeless, and complex, and a lust to operate upon the world's stage. When her time in Africa was over, Africa in Lorde had just begun."[41] This fusion of mother and place is inscribed not only on *Zami*'s pages, but on the poetry that emerged afterward in *The Black Unicorn*, published in 1978, which marked the beginning of Lorde's writings on Africa, the maternal, and the sensual. In the poem "Dahomey," for example, Lorde is explicit about the fact that her relationship with the mother is spatial:

> It was in Abomey that I felt
> the full blood of my fathers' wars
> and where I found my mother
> Seboulisa.[42]

Lorde uses the occasion of visiting Abomey, the former capital city of Dahomey (now called Benin), to reference ancestral paternity and maternity, but it is notable that the paternal is marked by violence while the maternal signals a spiritual kinship. Indeed, Seboulisa, whom Lorde imagines as the Mother of us all, is a goddess to whom Lorde refers throughout her writing from this time forward. Likewise, in *The Cancer Journals* she compares herself to the Dahomey one-breasted women warriors and places herself in a maternal lineage of African women. These examples show us that Lorde's invocation of Africa is not necessarily located in a search for ancestral bloodlines; rather, it is about seeking affective maternal connections. In her analysis of Lorde's writings, Michelle Wright argues that this move to incorporate African and American heritages underscores Lorde's deployment of "diaspora as the new collective model for Black subjectivity."[43]

While this production of kinship and diaspora is premised on loss and might profitably be imagined as part of a repertoire of extended mourning, I would like to heed David Eng's caution against linking diaspora to the "normative impulse to recuperate lost origins, to recapture the mother or motherland, and to valorize the dominant notions of social belonging and racial exclusion."[44] Instead, I would like to think of these diasporas as queer in the sense of generating new possibilities for kinship. Neither Weems nor Lorde is invested in the nation, but they *are* interested in feelings and the queer possibilities of these feelings. In her work on decentering nation from diaspora, Gayatri Gopinath argues that queer diaspora not only disrupts hierarchies of origin but also produces sites of novel difference: "A queer diasporic framework productively exploits the analogous relation between nation and diaspora on the one hand, and between heterosexuality and queerness on the other: in other words, queerness is to heterosexuality as the diaspora is to the nation."[45] These spaces of difference may be colored by loss, but speak to emergent eroticisms and affects underlying the formation of kinship. In *Territories of the Soul*, Nadia Ellis draws on José Esteban Muñoz's discussion of utopia to conceive of diaspora as a queer horizon produced by desire, always present and always slightly out of reach. She writes, "In retaining striking traces of the gap between *here* and *there*— between the possibilities spied on the horizon and territory currently occupied—these modes produce urgent feelings of loss, desire, and zeal that mark them, like Muñoz's utopian horizon, as queer."[46] If the creation of diaspora is born of loss, it also enables us to imagine reworking this type of excess through an alternate language of eroticism and care, which Weems and Lorde perform through their work.

Importantly, in imagining these new diasporas, we must remember that Lorde's use of diaspora is not ungendered; it is explicitly premised on a version of matrilinearity. Like Lorde, Weems resurrects the matrilineal, though she does so in more subtle ways. Her mode of connecting with ancestors via her laborious photographic process imbues reproduction with affect and touch. Despite reinforcing Weems' position within a network of kinship, rather than necessarily producing her as mother, I term this work "mothering." It is not merely that the photographs are reproduced, but that Weems does so with obvious care: each photograph requires being listened to and handled. In this way, we see that this performance of photographic witnessing veers away from Moten's critique of photography as a silencing of the mother in favor of "an imperial descent into self."[47] Instead, *From Here I Saw What Happened and I Cried* amplifies voice, thereby resurrecting the opacity of the photographic form, an opacity that Moten refers to as "the invocation of a silenced difference, a silent black *materiality*, in order to justify a suppression of difference in the name of (a false) universality."[48] This materiality gives the photographs life and embeds them within circuits of the erotic. This form of making possible is part of the work of mothering. As Alexis P. Gumbs argues, it is explicitly political and pedagogical: "The pedagogical work of mothering is exactly the site where a narrative will either be reproduced or interrupted. The work of Black mothering, the teaching of a set of social values that challenge a social logic which believes that we, the children of Black mothers, the queer, the deviant should not exist, is queer work."⁴⁹ For Gumbs, this politicization of mothering is queer because it speaks to a practice that has historically been denied to black women and to futures that have not yet come into being. Campt argues that this version of futurity is a type of black feminist praxis, writing that "the challenge of black feminist futurity is the constant and perpetual need to remain committed to the political necessity of *what will have **had to** happen*, because it is tethered to a different kind of 'must.' It is not a 'must' of historical certainty or Marxist teleology. It is a responsibility to create one's own future as a practice of survival."⁵⁰ As such, this performance of witness also gives us a mode of reconsidering the work that goes on in the darkroom. The future is not yet fixed, but we can see possibility in this version of the vestibular.

This is where I return to brown jouissance and its ability to make the ambiguity of grief or joy into something else. In *From Here I Saw What Happened and I Cried*, voice and its fleshiness not only facilitate the creation of interiority, but also enable the creation of a sort of affective diaspora. Here, I ask us to think not only about the fact that Weems brings together these archival images to stand together under her name, but that she marks their connection by tinting them red or blue. Through their coloration, they have been baptized by Weems's fleshiness to point toward a way to reckon with diaspora and the production of kinship. By reading Lorde into Weems, we see that making kin is a project necessitated by processes of racialization. Making kin stands as a rebuke against slavery's dismantling of nuclear families and removal of agency. This is not a project to recover the individual; it is one that insists, instead, on highlighting the production of a collectivity. By making kin through her performance of witness, Weems displaces the individual with the diasporic collective and opens our imaginations toward rethinking the work of mothering: we see connection, care, mourning, and possibility.

Spirituality, Kinship, and Witnessing

Through Weems's performance of witness we see the importance of dwelling on the fleshiness of the voice as it pertains to interiority, mothering, and diaspora, but the solicitation of voice also brings us toward the spiritual. Here, I return to Braunstein's description of jouissance beyond the word in order to think with the particular forms of excess that are part of the voice's ephemeral qualities. On the one hand, voice is imagined to enjoy a particular relationship to authenticity: Katherine Brewer Ball writes that "although the voice seems to flow from nowhere in particular, vaguely originating somewhere in the throat of the mouth, it is imagined to be indelibly attached to the core of the body and mind, and even to bridge the two. The voice reflects the subject at the center of the body, the inner being; it is 'the hidden bodily treasure beyond the visible envelope.'"[51] On the other hand, absent the sonic dimensions of voice, how do we describe exactly what Weems's performance is amplifying? The spiritual, I argue, signals a particular form of fleshy excess. In thinking with spirituality, we see that it is born from materiality and yet exceeds it. I see this excess in relation to the brown jouissance mobilized by voice and witnessing in that it shows us the contours of interiority without necessarily manifesting the tangibility of a body. In Weems's amplification of voice, she makes her interiority diffuse. We see traces of *her* corporeality in her care and production of kinship, yet this performance exceeds Weems. This alternate métier of excess—the space of the collective and indescribable—is what I term "the spiritual."

In both Barthes's and Moten's discussion of the grain of the voice, spirituality is an important undercurrent. For Barthes, spirituality is located in the breath—that which brings together emotion and body—and its mysterious relationship to voice. He writes, "The breath is the *pneuma*, the soul swelling or breaking, and any exclusive art of breathing is likely to be a secretly mystical art (a mysticism leveled down to the measure of the long-playing record)."[52] While he juxtaposes the breath with the corporeality of jouissance—"It is in the throat, the place where the phonic metal hardens and is segmented, in the mask that *signifiance* explodes, bringing not the soul but *jouissance*"—when we turn to Moten, we can see how the sonic is actually the place where spirit and matter meet.[53] In describing the power of the commodity that speaks, he writes, "If the commodity could speak it would have intrinsic value, it would be infused with a certain spirit, a certain value given not from the outside, and would, therefore contradict the thesis on value—that it is not intrinsic."[54] Moten's insistence on the resistance of the object by way of sound—not necessarily speech—allows us to read voice as spirituality, especially in relation to blackness and its history of commodification. This rereading is especially important for imagining that voice can provide resistance to the objectification that photography produces. From this perspective Weems's project of restoring interiority reminds us of interiority's nonphysical aspects.

This excess is part of the challenge to epistemology that brown jouissance offers. Luce Irigaray, for example, describes spiritual excess in relation to unreason and dynamics that physics or other sciences, for example, cannot account for. She writes, "What is left uninterpreted in the economy of fluids—the resistances brought to bear upon solids, for example—is in the end given over to God. Overlooking the properties of *real* fluids—internal frictions, pressures, movements, and so on, that is, *their specific dynamics*—leads to giving the real back to God, as only the idealizable characteristics of fluids are included in their mathematicization."[55] This is to say that there is always an excess of interactivity that rationality cannot account for. That she makes this argument in relation to fluidity, a space where she locates subversive dimensions of femininity, is significant in that it leads us to imagine ways in which brown jouissance's mobilization of liquidity helps us to enact or conceive of a new politics—a new version of materiality between subject and object, a version of agency that is relational, and a way to think affect alongside the flesh. Historically, we can locate genealogies of unreason, spirituality, femininity, and alternate imaginaries of agency in the realm of the religious. Ashon Crawley, in particular, argues through a reading of the Black Pentecostal Church that performances of embodying voice—spirits who work through corporeal vessels—disrupt notions of subjectivity, agency, and reason.[56] Thinking brown jouissance in relation to spirituality is not about not recognizing or fleeing violence, but about understanding its ripples as multiply layered and present in a fleshiness that is not necessarily physically tangible.

However, I also want to veer away from arguing that spirituality is the catch-all category for theorizing racialized excess.[57] Instead, I am interested in how we might fuse the diasporic and the spiritual in order to deepen our conception of brown jouissance, specifically how thinking with the spiritual invites us to think about Weems's diaspora as a form of connection that rejects certain mandates of objectivity and rationality.[58]

It is in the name of this diffuse form of collectivity that we also gain a way to rethink the relationship between spirituality and photography—namely, the late nineteenth-century practice of spirit photography. Nicholas Pethes situates this genre within a history of scientific experiments designed to make visible what could not be seen by the naked eye. He writes, "Accordingly, the new medium became an important part of the spiritualistic movement at the turn of the twentieth century. In its attempt to establish occult practices as empirical facts, this movement—most notably represented by the Society for Psychical Research (SPR), founded in London in 1882—applied experimental methods and technological devices to document psychic phenomena such as telepathy, telekinesis and communication with the dead."[59] While spirit photography is no longer considered part of a legacy of rational scientific practice, this impulse to make connections and kinship between the present and the past shows us a way to read Weems's project as a subversion of photography's attachment to projects of objectification and domination. Like spirit photography, *From Here I Saw What Happened and I Cried* brings together disparate temporalities in order to forge kinship. That it does so through voice and the performance of witnessing, technologies of the body that we might relate to "telepathy, telekinesis and communication with the dead," is not incidental. The series speaks to a mode of thinking the fleshiness through an alternate genealogy of reason and outside of the demands of the tangibly physical.

Spirituality further gives us occasion to reexamine Weems's tears. Tears offer a way to think about the connection between individual and communal outside of the demand for mourning. The spiritual becomes its own form of diaspora, albeit a deliberately promiscuous one. It is this queer diaspora that produces connection through an alternate understanding of how space and time become collapsed through fleshiness. For how can Weems witness what she was not alive to behold? It is not the question of relatedness, but an investment in thinking the self collectively, soliciting connection not through literal lineages of kinship, but through performances of witnessing and opacity. In performing witness, Weems listens, tethering her body to these photographic subjects in affective, amorphous, and spiritual ways.

5

Weeping Machines

Automaticity, Looping, and the Possibilities of Perversion

Neapolitan (2003) invites spectators to sit on a bench covered in a crocheted cozy to watch a television that plays a fourteen-minute loop of Nao Bustamante watching a projected loop of the end of the Cuban film *Fresa y Chocolate* (1993). Bustamante cries during the final scene, pausing only to wipe her eyes with a hanky before she rewinds to re-watch the end and cry again. Patty Chang's *In Love* (2001) pairs a monitor that shows Chang and her mother locked in a passionate kiss with another monitor showing a video of her doing the same to her father while tears stream down everyone's faces. As the film progresses, the action unspools backward; we see that what appeared to be a kiss was both of them sharing an onion. With *Neapolitan* and *In Love*, Bustamante and Chang perform women on the verge. While Bustamante and Chang cry and cry and cry, catharsis is just out of reach. Just as spectators begin to imagine resolution, the videos begin again.

Bustamante's and Chang's inhabitations of hysteria and perversion reveal the divergent ways that racialization positions these performances of responsiveness as excessive. This version of brown jouissance is akin to what José Esteban Muñoz calls "brown feeling," which "chronicles a certain ethics of the self that is utilized and deployed by people of color and other minoritarian subjects who don't feel quite right within the protocols of normative affect and comportment."[1] These brown feelings are Muñoz's mode of describing "the ways in which minoritarian affect is always, no matter what its register, partially illegible in relation to the normative affect performed by normative citizen subjects."[2] I come to this articulation of brown jouissance by combining Muñoz's investment in thinking with feeling as a mode of non-normativity with Dana Luciano's argument that affective comportment be linked to sexuality. While Luciano centers her discussion on grief, she invites us to think more broadly about emotionality in relation to sexuality. Luciano writes that grief "constitutes a crucial dimension of the *dispositif* of sexuality itself: the modern intensification of the body, its energies, and its meanings."[3] Hence, I argue that we can understand Bustamante's and Chang's performances of emotion as part of a constellation of sexuality because they are legible through norms of labor, intimacy, and brown femininity.

Bustamante's crying can be indexed to stereotypes of the overly sensitive, hysterical Latina, while Chang's crying can be attached to the specter of the insensate assimilated Asian American. Through their occupation of opposite sides of the spectrum of "appropriate" emotionality, Bustamante's and Chang's performances of crying illuminate the complexity of brown feminine performances of emotion. These performances oscillate between grief, happiness, relief, and pain and resist any fixed reading. That is what makes them arresting works of art to think with, but in their divergence each also highlights the contours of what constitutes normative comportment and the underlying assumption that black and brown people do not *feel*, they merely react. This is a legacy of the linkage of interiority to whiteness that Denise Ferreira da Silva describes in *Toward a Global Idea of Race* when she differentiates between the subject and Other. As I wrote in the introduction, the subject occupies "the stage of interiority, where universal reason plays its sovereign role as *universal poesis*," while the Other is assigned to the realm of the external as an "affectable I."[4] This notion of affectability, reactivity, and responsiveness is what I connect with automaticity.

Automaticity, which occupies the register of the un-thought and robotic, issues a challenge to the norms of affective comportment because it suggests sensation without—or at least out of joint with—feeling. I argue that this notion of automatic responsiveness can be found in several post-Enlightenment discourses. We can trace this genealogy through a history of automata, which in the late eighteenth century became invested in replicating internal processes—witness the popular defecating duck whose appearance Jessica Riskin attributes to designers wanting "not only to mimic the outward manifestations of life, but also to follow as closely as possible the mechanisms that produced these manifestations."[5] We can also locate automaticity in theorizations of the body as mechanical, which led to a cleavage between authenticity and acting. Joseph Roach, in an explanation of Denis Diderot's philosophy of acting, describes it as approximation, because the body is "a virtually soulless machine possessing vital drives but no will."[6] Roach further describes Diderot's perception of the eighteenth-century actor as "imitating the exterior signs of emotion so perfectly that you can't tell the difference; his cries of anguish are marked in his memory, his gestures of despair have been prepared in advance; he knows the precise cue to start his tears flowing."[7] Automaticity, then, renders corporeality and emotionality suspect, positioning them in relation to theatricality and insincerity and against ideologies of authenticity.

Bustamante and Chang, I argue, play with this idea of automaticity, highlighting the ways that it undergirds how minoritarian performances register, but also using it to subvert these norms through their performances of excessive theatricality. These performances challenge the norms of intimacy between performer and spectator and activate multiple frameworks of opacity in their confounding of transparency, domesticity, and temporality.

Emotional Excess, Vibrators, and Melodrama

While we do not see what makes Bustamante cry, we bear witness to her rapt attention. Light from the television flickers across her face as the music swells and tears stream down her face. Her shoulders heave, her mouth emits a few low sobs, and her nose runs. The scene ends, and Bustamante reaches for the remote control to rewind the clip. We hear the same music and see Bustamante cry again. She takes a sip of water; she uses the remote to rewind. In this performance of automatized sensation and emotional looping, Bustamante plays with what it is to perform the excessively emotional Latina. By suturing this mode of theatricality to the loop, however, Bustamante resists the overdetermination of this stereotype in favor of illuminating the orgasmic and masturbatory pleasures of the brown hysterical body and its domestic excesses.

Bustamante's inhabitation of the emotional Latina has had particular resonance with critics. Lindsey Westbrook, reviewing the piece in *Artweek*, frames *Neapolitan* as a performance of Chicana mourning. She writes:

Figure 5.1. Nao Bustamante, still from *Neapolitan*. ©2003 Nao Bustamante.

Nao Bustamante's *Neopolitan* is also brand new and deals with several themes that recur in her work; emotionality, vulnerability and stereotypes of gender and Mexican-American culture; we watch her watching a scene from the Cuban film *Strawberries and Chocolate*. She is making herself cry, periodically rewinding the tape and wiping her eyes on a Mexican flag hanky. The work is profoundly self-conscious, of course, and, for that reason, cynical. But it is also genuinely sad, expressing sorrow and mourning, perhaps, for the current world situation.[8]

Proposing that the hanky is merely a colored dish towel, Muñoz argues that Westbrook's review highlights the "various ways in which brown paranoia is not something that can be wished away, no matter how much we would like to fully escape the regime of paranoia," while also calling attention to the subversive possibilities of Bustamante's performance—namely, that by reading her Mexican American identity alongside her crying, depression and the depressive position become strategies of minoritarian critique and signal the possibility inherent in opacity.[9] What is important about the difference between Westbrook's and Muñoz's interpretations of Bustamante's performance is the status accorded to her crying. For Westbrook, Bustamante's crying is decipherable as part of Bustamante's sorrow at being a minoritarian subject; hers are the tears of overdetermination, intertwined with the wound of representation and its relationship to violent geopolitical histories. Westbrook reads Bustamante as participating in a ritual of mourning. Muñoz, however, understands Bustamante's tears as a strategic form of self-determination in which she navigates these colonial histories, but also plays with them and with the expectations that they produce. Muñoz reads her performance within his theorization of "feeling brown" and positions her tears as a representational strategy that acknowledges minoritarian subjects' estrangement from affective norms, but rewrites this non-normativity as a mode of performing optimism that simultaneously recognizes historical trauma.

Bracketing the question of whether or not *Neapolitan* fits within the genre of mourning, I focus on the piece as a performance that plays with racialized concepts of automaticity. By this I mean that Bustamante's excessive crying signals a history of perceiving brown female responsiveness, particularly Latina emotionality, as automatic—less thoughtful and more reactive—and that Bustamante's own framing of her performance plays with the repetitive pleasures of this automaticity.

Indeed, Bustamante's performance of excessive emotion can be positioned within a history that links black and brown people and white women to sensation rather than sensibility. In elaborating on this dichotomy further, Kyla Schuller argues that women were characterized as impressible, which is to say that their bodies and minds were overly responsive to their external environments. For Schuller,

> Impressibility of *character* describes emotional excitability above and beyond its stimulating impression. Anglo-Saxons, at the top of the evolutionary ladder, possessed the most highly differentiated physical, mental, and psychological profiles, such that woman's "form" is more unlike that of men. The bodies and minds of civilized women, on account of their being more childlike than men's, retained more plasticity; correspondingly, their hyper-impressibility triggered responses exceeding the stimulating impression.[10]

These taxonomies not only positioned "excessive" emotional response outside the realm of the civilized, but by the same logic also registered the emotional responses of women, and brown and black people as excessive and non-normative.

Muñoz himself has written much on the non-normativity of Latinx affect. While he frames the stereotype of the "hot 'n' spicy spic" against the idea of whiteness as lack, excess is still a key term in his discussion: "The 'failure' of Latino affect, in relation to the hegemonic protocols of North American affective comportment, revolves around an understanding of the Latina or the Latino as affective excess. . . . Thus the 'hot 'n' spicy spic' is a subject who cannot be contained within the sparse affective landscape of Anglo North America. This then accounts for the ways in which Latina/o citizen-subjects find their way through subgroups that perform the self in affectively extravagant fashions."[11] Similarly, writing in a psychoanalytic vein, Antonio Viego describes the untranslatability of traditional Latino maladies such as "los nervios" and "attaques."[12]

Further, within this space of the emotionally excessive, sensation becomes linked to a temporality of the present, which further demarcates it as uncouth. In contrast to sentiment, which is what civilized men possess as an internalized psychic structure that requires a narrative temporality of past, present, and future, sensation is a corporeal response that exists only in the now. Luciano writes, "'Sensation' signals a mode of intensified embodiment in which all times but the present fall away—a condition simultaneously desired, in its recollection of the infantile state, and feared, in its negation of social agency."[13] Those who experience only sensation exist in the present; they do not exhibit agency since the narrative structure of time is foreclosed to them.[14] This fetishization of the moment and the imagined corporeal excess of these sensational bodies mark them as out of sync with normative society. Through her use of the loop, Bustamante plays with what it is to inhabit the present. She is always crying, automatically performing responsiveness, and always out of joint.

Interestingly, in her artist statement, Bustamante embeds her understanding of this performance within the realm of mechanized sexuality, which nuances our understanding of the way she frames excessiveness and automaticity. She refers to the final scene of *Fresa y Chocolate* as "an emotional vibrator of sorts."[15] The film, directed by Tomás Gutiérrez Alea and Juan Carlos Tabío tells the story of what becomes a friendship between a university student, David, and a gay artist, Diego, in Cuba in 1979. It is a story about the seductive nature of ideas, the power of art, and exile. At the end of the film, Diego leaves Cuba to avoid persecution, and the men embrace. Bustamante describes the appeal of this scene thus: "In this scene the two main characters hug, that's it, they hug, a plump moment of relief and connection for the emotional body. The music swells and so do my eyes. I cry every time, inducing a momentary emotional response by technical manipulation of my psyche."[16] If the film functions as a technology to elicit response, then what viewers watch is Bustamante's excessive responsiveness. The barrage of tears enters the realm of the sexual not only because the installation produces a type of voyeurism (we watch Bustamante watch), but also because Bustamante understands her response within the frame of sexuality.

In Bustamante's invocation of the vibrator, two different ideas about mechanical sex become simultaneously operationalized. On the one hand, we are allowed to think about our current era as one in which all sex is mediated in the way that Luciana Parisi suggests: "In the age of cybernetics, sex is no longer a private act practiced between the walls of the bedroom. In particular, human sex no longer seems to involve the set of social and cultural codes that used to characterize sexual identity and reproductive coupling."[17] Her comments speak to the way in which interactions with machines have restructured sexuality, sexual relations, and identity. Parisi focuses on this invasion of technology through the notion of "mediated sex." In this view machines (nonhuman ones especially) are tools that enable humans to have sex with each other in numerous different ways. We certainly see this at work in Bustamante's suggestion that the end of the film is a technology that facilitates her emotional climax. On the other hand, the vibrator also raises the specter of sexual response as itself mechanical. This idea is behind the attention to anatomy and physiology that William Masters and Virginia Johnson ushered into modern sexual thought by using Ulysses, their technologically enhanced dildo, to help map out female sexual response for their ground-breaking 1966 book, *Human Sexual Response*. Masters and Johnson's carefully measured results were based on the interventions of film and photography. Couples were filmed during intercourse, women were filmed masturbating, both manually and with Ulysses, which took intravaginal photographs at rapid intervals during orgasm. The use of these technologies speaks both to the interconnectedness of cinema and science and to the desire for precision that automation was perceived to provide. Unlike the women used in the study, Ulysses was not subject to subjective interpretations of truth. Although the women's comments were used to ascertain whether orgasm had taken place, they became part of a knowledge loop that ricocheted between their statements and the physiological data gleamed in the laboratory. In this instance it is Ulysses' *approximation* of humanity that is valued; partial physical similitude was coupled with the mechanical absence of feeling. Ulysses' ability to record but not interpret and to penetrate but not feel were prized above all else, in a way that is emblematic of what Peter Galison calls a *machine ideal*—"the machine as a neutral and transparent operator that would serve both as an instrument of registration without intervention *and* as an ideal for the moral discipline of the scientists themselves."[18] Although Masters and Johnson acknowledged the potential for different responses with Ulysses and with a partner, they used data from their research to argue for their *sameness*, a rhetorical strategy that reopens the question of Ulysses' subjectivity. In defending the use of Ulysses as an appropriate sex object, they wrote: "In view of the artificial nature of the equipment, legitimate issue may be raised with the integrity of observed reaction patterns. Suffice it to say that intravaginal physiologic response corresponds in every way with previously established reaction patterns observed and recorded during hundreds of cycles in response to automanipulation."[19] In this statement Ulysses is assumed to produce the same physiological effects as masturbation, which, in turn, is already assumed to produce the same effects as intercourse. Through this argument for the data's simultaneous difference and sameness, we see the dilemma of simulation. In this case, using the machine to simulate sex opens the category of sex. If copulation with a machine provides the same result as human intercourse, what is the difference between the two? Transposing these insights to the installation unearths the ways that Bustamante exploits her body's learned response to a particular stimulus, displaying her body's automaticity.

The automaticity of the vibrator also suggests an alternate dimension to thinking about the loop—a mechanical temporality that produces the same results over and over again. Lauren Berlant argues that the loop (which Bustamante watches and which we watch), allows us to see the forms of agency and ambiguity that Bustamante is playing with. Berlant writes, "She is reveling in the kind of self-imitation that constitutes pleasure, whether or not it feels good."[20] Berlant situates this ambiguous affective performance within Muñoz's description of the oscillation between subject and object, which minoritarian subjects perform. For Berlant the loop not only signals the porosity of subject and object, but also highlights the minoritarian subject's particular interaction with forms of historicity—by being both "caught" in modes of projection and able to manipulate that form of stasis. Berlant writes that the loop "enacts a desire to be in a temporality that is impossible to destroy as long as the technology can hold the world up—here, a world of longing and displacement from so many objects, enduring as long as there is memory, electricity, broadcast satellites, and batteries in the remote. It matters that the thing that brings Bustamante's video object to her is called a remote, even though she holds it: that is the remote's magic, to deny its own name. It's a limited magic."[21] Technology, then, is vital in creating Bustamante's agency (and our voyeuristic pleasure). It highlights both Bustamante's relationship to automaticity and the pleasure of this mode of embodiment. Additionally, by insisting on a repetition of the present, Bustamante moves toward a jouissance of existing in the now. Brown jouissance is part of this insistence on feeling with the moment against the demand to present feeling in accordance with the norms of chronology.

Further, in Bustamante's description of the film's final scene as a "vibrator of sorts," we see that she is equating the film's moments of catharsis with sexual release. In this way, she harkens back to the vibrator's late nineteenth- and early twentieth-century function as providing relief for hysterical women through orgasm.[22] Within the context of hysteria, orgasm, as induced by the vibrator, was posited as the solution to the larger structural problems of femininity. Generally imagined as a pathology related to "overcivilization," hysteria became a technology of race-making that furthered racial divisions between women, positioning white women within the category of the frigid and black and brown women in that of the hyperfecund and hypersexual.[23] Laura Briggs writes, "It is in this arena that the racial discourse of nervousness emerged in a very familiar form, one that had already been (and would continue to be) reiterated often in Euro-American culture: 'overcivilized' women avoided sex and were unwilling or incapable of bearing many (or any) children, 'savage' women gave birth easily and often and were hypersexual."[24] Briggs argues that these dual discourses underline the ways that white women's "struggle for social and political autonomy from white men" was framed not only as a threat to masculinity, but as a racial threat.[25] In this way we can see Bustamante's inhabitation of the hysterical woman not only as about indexing the overly emotional Latina, but as about posing a direct threat to whiteness through hypersexuality as signaled by the vibrator *and* Bustamante's linkage of automaticity to pleasure.

Additionally, Bustamante nuances this hypersexuality by attaching it to the domestic. Whereas scholars have argued that hysteria emerged as a form of embodied protest against the confines of domesticity in the late nineteenth century, Bustamante invites us to explore her sensational excess within the domestic space of the coz(s)y, which provides the setting for these repeated scenes of crying.[26] Doyle writes, "The installation is full of pleasure and care; we see this in the artist's obvious affection for the film and the loving hand applied to the installation itself, in which the television becomes a homey shrine."[27] She describes Bustamante's installation in detail:

> The monitor is shrouded in domestic ornaments and grandmotherly doilies—not genteel white lace but a riot of garish orange and yellow. The monitor is cloaked in crocheted yarn; little tassels adorn every corner and dot the blanket that wraps around the monitor's base. The headphone's earpieces and wires have cute coverings, turning them into adorable caps. The bench is covered in its own tailored outfit. A black crow perches atop this mountain, wearing a crocheted hat. The installation is customized for each appearance. Electric cords, outlets, and power strips all wear yarn cozies that take the artist several days of continuous labor to fashion.[28]

While the coziness of the installation brings Bustamante's pleasure within the framework of melodrama and the feminine pleasure of sentimentality, it also hints at a deeper menace: that of the mundane comingling of pleasure and the violence of racialization.

The cosies and their excessiveness—both in color and number—recall what Muñoz has called *Latino camp* and names as a minoritarian strategy of survival.[29] That Bustamante has so obviously labored to create

Figure 5.2. Nao Bustamante, *Neapolitan,* installation view, at the Broad, Los Angeles, CA, 2017. Courtesy of the artist.

them is a statement about her relationship to this aesthetic, the feminine space of the home, and the forms of labor that go into crafting. Jeanne Vaccaro argues that craft "evokes the remunerative, utilitarian, ornamental, and manual labor and laborers—the feminine, ethnic and 'primitive.' A philosophy that subordinates labor, the manual, and the sense of touch to abstraction, rationality, and the sense of sight operates in a political economy of devaluing bodies."[30] Further, Lacey Jane Roberts suggests that crafting itself is queer because of its relationship to the anachronistic and the slipperiness of its designation as something professional or amateurish: "Institutions, practitioners, curators, and critics have often claimed the word *craft* cannot be defined, and this ambiguity is largely viewed as a negative quality. While craft represents a large scope of labor practices, methods, skills, mediums, and makers, it typically is embedded with a tinge of nonnormativity and otherness."[31] For Julia Wilson Bryan it is these very qualities that allow craft to highlight alternate forms of relating to materiality and knowledge production: "Craft draws its very strength from its anachronistic quality and its ties to traditions, both its adherence to conventional artisanal labor and also its more messy reinventions. Handmaking maintains its integrity in response to and in opposition to industrialization. . . . Craft embodies its histories in its materials."[32] What Wilson Bryan draws our attention to is the very particular micro-historical relations embedded in Bustamante's installation—Who taught her to craft and how? Why these colors?—which produce meaning, though much of it is opaque to the viewer. Through the materiality of craft, however, we also see that the handmade, which Vaccaro describes in relation to "the politics of the hand, that which is worked on, and the sensory feelings and textures of crafting," is central to thinking about the form of agency that Bustamante is putting on display.[33]

Through crafting, we see an appeal to an excessiveness that is not codified by the relentless racializing gaze. Instead, we see an alternate aesthetics of tactility and softness, the labor of the marginalized, and a domesticity that stitches together pleasure and difficulty through technology—or manipulations of the hand. Through the cosy, *Neapolitan*'s teary spectacle gives way to the possibility of pleasure, subversion, and a shifted sensoria. The space of racialized excessiveness may not be pleasurable, but Bustamante offers ways to think around that by inviting you into her space and overwhelming you with tactility.

It is through her hailing of the domestic that Bustamante generates a scene of intimacy. Yet this intimacy is not about transparency, but about genre and the opacity that it offers. I come to this argument by thinking through Bustamante's mobilization of melodrama, a term that both Muñoz and Doyle use to describe Bustamante's mode of watching *Fresa y Chocolate*. In Bustamante's performance of automatic crying, she draws attention to the ambiguous nature of crying in that her tears fall without necessarily being coded as mourning or sadness, but instead of attaching particular meaning to Bustamante's response, I take Muñoz's and Doyle's disparate analyses of the last scene of the film as further evidence of Bustamante's performance of opacity.

For Muñoz, the film is about "the way in which queerness can finally not be held by the nation-state.... Queerness is the site of emotional breakdown and the activation of the melodrama in the installation.... I would thus position Bustamante's art object as a corrective in relation to the homophobic developmental plot. Queerness, the installation shows, never fully disappears; instead it haunts the present."[34] This analysis sutures the domestic with the nation-state and reads Bustamante's crying as part of the film's queer excess. In the film, queer excess and exile from the nation-state is literalized in Diego, whose departure from Cuba precipitates the hug from David, who has spent much of the film learning to respect Diego, Diego's homosexuality, and his critiques of the government. José Quiroga reads the film as working to soften the perception of the government as anti-homosexual while expelling the concept of a gay identity from national consciousness in order to prioritize Cuban nationalism.[35] Bustamante's crying, however, prevents queerness from actually being removed from the nation-state. For Muñoz, Bustamante's melodramatic response is part of a larger statement about the ways affect can revive queer possibilities in its oscillation between the scale of the nation and the domestic. We might also profitably think with Elizabeth Anker's discussion of melodrama as a form of national rhetoric in *Orgies of Feeling*. While Anker discusses melodrama within the context of the United States in order to produce national heroes and villains, we might think about what it means for Bustamante, who is Mexican American, to watch a Cuban film in which Cuba stages its own drama in which those who stay are heroic and accepting of difference while queers are exiled.[36] Does the drama of exile mirror her own familial histories of migration across borders? Is there something about the relationship between Mexico and Cuba, which was uniquely friendly until 1998, that facilitates this connection? Do these shared national residues form part of the film's ability to function as an emotional vibrator?

In her reading of Bustamante's relationship to *Fresa y Chocolate*, however, Doyle, is more invested in situating Bustamante's viewing within a history of feminine viewing habits. She emphasizes the pleasures of the domestic. She writes, "At the heart of *Neapolitan* is a scene of indulgence, the treat of a weepie"[37]—a genre that "offers a fantasy escape for the identifying women in the audience," according to Laura Mulvey: "The illusion is so strongly marked by recognizable, real and familiar traps that escape is closer to a day dream than to a fairy story."[38] Thus, Doyle's hailing of Bustamante's viewing pleasure as akin to that of watching "a weepie" places us solidly in the realm of feminized domesticity and fantasy. This is the space that for Doyle is marked by indulgence and that we can read as masturbatory owing to its relationship with both the vibrator and fantasy. Ien Ang connects melodrama with a resistance to the banality of everyday life. Instead of revealing its artifice, melodrama infuses the daily with excessive emotion. Ang writes: "The melodramatic imagination is therefore the expression of a refusal, or inability, to accept insignificant everyday life as banal and meaningless, and is born of a vague, inarticulate dissatisfaction with existence here and now."[39] While melodrama offers the balm of emotionality, it also threatens to evacuate specificity in favor of responsiveness and repetition. Here, Tania Modleski points out the importance of melodrama's temporality of non-progress, which enables this feeling of indulgence and escape. She writes, "Unlike most Hollywood narratives, which give the impression of a progressive movement toward an end that is significantly different from the beginning, much melodrama gives the impression of a ceaseless returning to a prior state."[40] The language of melodrama, then, vacates the content of interiority by focusing on swirls of feeling rather than their particular province. Melodrama introduces the idea of inhabiting an affective reality in which progress is not the goal, but a masturbatory excess of tears is.

Endurance, Assimilation, and Perversion

At the onset, Patty Chang's installation provokes spectators' discomfort because it appears as though we are watching something deeply perverse—an adult child passionately kissing her parents, in front of a camera no less. In this performance of excessive parental affection, we see a different register of automaticity—one that brings endurance, perversity, and the specter of being insensate to the fore. The flagrant nature of this perversity announces itself as a failure of assimilation and brings our attention to the residue of racialization. As a discourse, assimilation is, of course, deeply fraught. Bracketing the question of who is allowed to participate and what it means to posit whiteness as normal, I read this installation as a critique of assimilation. Although assimilation is just one road toward what Jeffrey Alexander describes as the incorporation of difference, the theory behind assimilation relies on the idea that difference can be erased for certain groups while also imagining that some residue remains. Alexander writes, "Assimilation is possible to the degree that socialization channels exist that can provide 'civilizing' or 'purifying' processes—through interaction, education, or mass mediated representation—that allow persons

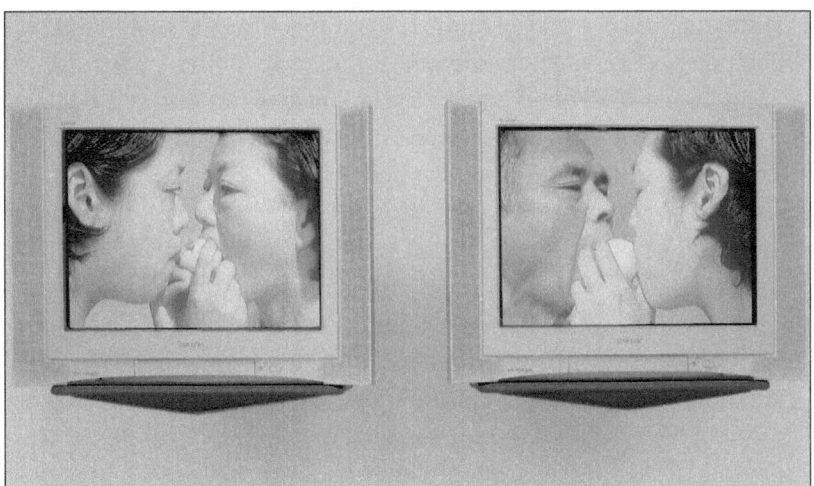

Figure 5.3. Patty Chang, *In Love*, 2001. Two-channel video installation, 3 min., 28 sec.; dimensions variable. Solomon R. Guggenheim Museum, New York. Purchased with funds provided by Janet Karatz Dreisen, 2002.

to be separated from their primordial qualities. *It is not the qualities themselves that are purified or accepted but the persons who formerly, and often still privately, bear them.*[41] In Alexander's mention of the importance of pedagogy for thinking assimilation, we move toward theorizing the loss that accompanies it, which David Eng and Anne Anlin Cheng have written about as a form of racialized melancholy as well as an unstated understanding of the assimilative body as passive slate for inscription—which, in turn, speaks further toward Muñoz's assessment of whiteness as lack.[42]

In lieu of melancholy, however, Chang foregrounds the possibility of perversion. This sensual potentiality gives voice to the assumption that assimilation cannot tame what Celine Parreñas Shimizu describes as "perverse interiority," though the actual nuances of this perversity remain unknowable.[43] Further, by revealing what one might imagine to be tears of shame to be onion-induced, Chang suggests that she (and her parents) might be shameless, thereby refusing normative affective codes of behavior that one might thrust upon the situation and activating the idea of automaticity (solicited by the onion instead of emotion). We might consider this invocation of shamelessness part of Chang's engagement with the trope of Asian and Asian American female hypersexuality, whose legacy Parreñas Shimizu describes as "a vibrant combination of fantasy and reality charging the fashioning of the self that moralism, or the power of puritanical discourse, and scopophilia, or the love of looking, cannot accommodate."[44] The embrace of this excess is political in that it acts as a "productive perversity" which challenges "the power of normalcy, especially in limiting definitions of sexuality," while also enabling a way "to make sense of one's punishment and disciplining as Asian American women hypersexualized in representation."[45]

This perverse excess, however, is also part of an economy that understands Asian and Asian American femininity through the lens of passivity. Parreñas Shimizu works through this dichotomy in her analysis of Annabel Chong, the Singaporean porn star who became famous for starring in *The World's Biggest Gangbang* in which she had penetrative sex with 251 men in one session. Parreñas Shimizu reads Chong's performance of bottoming and her persona as a model minority, which she establishes by discussing her life as a student and subsequent career in IT, as two elements that play into the ideology of Asian passivity. The form of passivity embodied in the idea of the model minority is what offers the possibility of assimilation and is part of the mobilization of the mundane, which Ju Yon Kim uses to describe particular Asian and Asian American performances of racialization. Kim writes, "The mundane, as something enacted by the body that is not necessarily of the body, inserts a productive uncertainty whereby the prerogative to manage racial others can be channeled into efforts to change their behaviors. Yet the presumed incompleteness of these endeavors, exemplified by Homi Bhabha's 'almost the same, but not quite' colonial subject, affirms the very boundaries that such efforts are meant to erase."[46] Kim traces this tension between viewing Asian and Asian Americans as possessing difference that is easily (almost) erased through habit in her discussion of Chinese laborers, Japanese war brides, Korean shopkeepers in the wake of the LA riots of the 1990s, and the myth of the model minority. She writes, "Associated variously with an American work ethic, Confucian values, or an inhuman mechanical efficacy, the same model minority traits lauded for exemplifying American self-sufficiency can just as easily signify an un-American lack of playfulness, and even forebode the ascendance of Asia."[47] Here, we see the double valence of passivity in the model minority as passivity comes to signify the tendency toward uncritical labor *and* the threat of automaticity as part of the baggage of racialization. This is a different idea of automaticity than that which Bustamante plays with; it is an idea of automaticity that is connected to histories of capitalism and globalization. It is an automaticity that is not about an excessive emotional response to a stimulus, but automaticity as symptomatic of an inability (or lack of desire) to maintain a self in the face of prevailing structures. Its underside is endurance.

Eric Hayot connects this idea of automaticity with mechanization and the impulses of capitalism to extract as much labor from subjects as possible. In his analysis of the coolie stereotype, he writes:

> The coolie's ability to endure small levels of pain or consume only the most meager food and lodging represented an almost inhuman adaptation to contemporary forms of modern labor. . . . An "absence of nerves," remarkable "staying qualities," and a "capacity to wait without complaint and to bear with calm endurance" were all features of Chinese people in general described by Arthur Smith in his 1894 *Chinese Characteristics,*

the most widely read American work on China in the late nineteenth and early twentieth centuries ... The coolie's biologically impossible body was displaced ground for an awareness of the transformation of the laboring body into machine.[48]

Rachel Lee argues that Hayot's analysis "underscores the 'impossible biology' of the coolie's body—and its alignments with both 'past and future, animal and superhuman' capacities—as well as the 'possible end to suffering via indifference' palpable in the late nineteenth and early twentieth centuries."[49] For Lee, this relationship between mechanization and endurance works to produce Asian American bodies as fragmented—both in the sense that capitalism demands fragmentation for efficiency and in the sense of being seen as superhuman (requiring less nutrition, for example, than others), on the one hand, and animalistic (lacking in nerves), on the other.

By using the onion to solicit tears, Chang alludes to her body's position within this racialized economy of automaticity, but she challenges the charge of passivity both through her active engagement with her parents and through her mobilization of the perversity of endurance. While Hayot and Lee both point to the suggestion that Asian American bodies are seen as able to endure, performances of endurance are usually considered the province of white masculinity in that they indicate an ability to use suffering to bolster one's sense of self. Kent Brintnall argues that tableaux of masculine suffering (such as presented by Mel Gibson, Francis Bacon, and Robert Mapplethorpe) highlight the reification of privilege that can occur in the face of pain. Brintnall writes, "Although suffering can signify vulnerability, weakness and limitation, enduring pain and injury requires resilience. Similarly, while display of the male body can both render it an object of erotic contemplation and reveal the fabrication of the masculine ideal, it can also mark the body *as* ideal, worthy of attention and admiration. This allure can, at the same time, make the masochistic trial itself appealing."[50] Brintnall evokes masochism as a way for us to understand how performances of masculinity rely on a narrative of triumph over woundedness. His suturing of eroticism and racialization is instructive for my analysis of Chang's performance, however, because it points to the ways that her performance of endurance adheres to altogether different conventions. Not only is the scene of suffering quieter than those that position the male body as imperiled—we see Chang and her parents only from the shoulders up, which suggests that it is not her body, but her mind that is imperiled—but the specter of masochism does not resolve itself into a privileged position. Instead, it furthers the spectacle of Chang's racial difference. By this I mean that it invokes the specter of Asian female masochism that haunts Annabel Chong's performance in *The World's Biggest Gangbang*. If we read Chang and her parents' performance as part of an economy of masochism rather than endurance, we see that both automaticity and this sexual excess are part of the coding of brown femininity as flesh.

Chang's mobilization of tears, however, undercuts this relationship between racial excess and automaticity when we focus on the role of the onion. Chang describes *In Love* as a direct citation of Marina Abramovic's 1995 piece *The Onion*, in which Abramovic eats an onion in its entirety while her voice records a list of banal annoyances. This is a performance of endurance that calls attention to the trials of femininity. Doyle describes it thus:

> The act of eating the onion begins as a perversely masochistic variant of using an onion to shed artificial tears—an external provocation to cry over a life not interesting enough to cry about. As the loop of complaints repeats itself, we watch her struggle over her own instinct as she takes one large bite from the onion after another. We hear her moan and whimper as she chokes it back, skin and all. (This aspect of the performance is almost erotic.) Over time she disintegrates before our eyes: her composed face collapses in abjection and grief.[51]

Doyle sees this piece as resonating with viewers' disgust because they find themselves empathetically tasting the onion's bitterness as they watch Abramovic eat. The viewer, then, moves from questioning whether Abramovic's tears are authentic toward pondering their deeper meaning. Doyle narrates, "In the end, it is not the authenticity of her tears that you question but their artificiality, in part because as you watch this video it is hard not to have a physical reaction in sympathy with the manifest difficulty of eating a raw onion while suppressing the impulse to gag. . . . Here what starts as a theatrical production of artificial tears appears to morph into real tears over the artificiality of the performance of her daily life."[52] Feeling zings through the circuits of sympathy, viewers cannot help but project onto Abramovic and her alimentary-induced suffering. By contrast, we might read Chang's use of the onion as a theatrical trick, since it elicits tears *without* feeling and thereby highlights the difference between the "realness" of Abramovic's performance and the lack of authenticity in Chang's. Further, the reverse temporality of Chang's piece blocks spectatorial projections of empathy because viewers do not understand that an onion is being eaten until the end. Instead viewers meet the (artificial, real?) threat of incest and its relationship to the specter of racialized perversity head-on. This temporal confusion solicits corporeal identification and empathy in very different ways. In an interview with Eve Oishi, Chang says that she was drawn to Abramovic's piece, but felt sad in response to watching the video: "I felt it was sad to be having this experience alone. Sharing an awful experience with another person binds you together. . . . As I thought about this awful yet exquisitely touching act, I imagined . . . the least likely people I would want to do it with . . . my parents. And this is why I attempted to make *In Love*."[53] In this way, the focus is less on the act of eating than thinking the onion as an object that connects Chang to her parents. Through the onion, all three of them veer close to incest, enduring its proximity as well as its noxious fumes. By using an onion to triangulate her relationship to her parents, Chang suggests that kinship is a matter of food, endurance, eroticism, and love.

In Love becomes a piece about her relationship with her parents, returning us to the specter of incest and allowing us to position Chang's piece alongside the plethora of incest memoirs that emerged in the United States and Canada in the late 1990s and early 2000s. Gillian Harkins reads incest memoirs as a genre unto themselves—"a dominant trope for a national culture in crisis, without its moorings in cold war security rubrics or the rationalities of welfare statism."[54] Incest narratives, Harkins argues, garnered much of their force from the refashioning of the family under neoliberalism, making it "into the synecdoche for all broader social relations," and asserting that "family values were cultural, not economic or political per se."[55] These memoirs elaborated the production of modern neoliberal subjects by focusing on self-reliance, confession, and self-narration. While earlier fictionalized narratives of incest from the 1970s, such as *I Know Why the Caged Bird Sings*, *The*

Color Purple, *Corregidora*, and *The Bluest Eye*, all authored by African American women, explored incest as a way to "interrogate the use of race and racial hierarchies to devalue black female children in ways that subject them to increased sexual vulnerability," the spectacularization of incest reread these critiques as examples of African American familial pathology.[56] The difference between these two visions of the incest narrative is powerful. On the one hand, we get a critique of national structures of care, and on the other, we see an articulation of autonomy and privatization. It is telling, I think, that this shift also occurs through a generic transformation—we move from narrative (and occasionally autobiographical fiction) to memoir.

In Love falls between these two modes of narrativizing incest. On the one hand, it plays with the idea of confession, thereby summoning the agency and resistance of that discourse—though it fails to coopt confession's production of interiority, preferring, instead, to display the opacity of perversion. On the other hand, it also activates the specter of incest as a way to highlight the assumptions that surround Asian Americans even as it works to undermine those ideas by revealing the assumption of incest to be a cinematic trick. However, I also want to suggest that by showing the videos in reverse temporality, Chang plays with the past/future temporal orientation of automaticity. Most saliently, however, *In Love* differs from these models of incest narratives in that Chang cannot be isolated as the sole protagonist. She is always pictured in relation to her mother or father. In this way, I argue, Chang highlights the willingness of parents to endure—perhaps this is a different form of love than the primarily sexualized love of incest. This is about the parental bond and its fleshiness, which comes to the fore through Chang's manipulation of tears to illuminate facets of racialized excess. Importantly, the piece is also about eating. As its description on the Guggenheim Museum's website suggests, "Chang examines the territory of the primal, parental connection in her work *In Love* (2001). . . . [Parents and child] bite into it slowly, pausing as they take turns offering it to each other, as if it suggests the proverbial, forbidden fruit. Parents and child swallow before they take additional bites, blinking hard to hold back tears from the onion's sharpness and pungency."[57] Not only are these family members tolerating the onion, they chew it, swallow it, and exchange its morsels so as to nourish the other. Here, we might think about the relationship between eating as part of the realm of the mundane and the imagined controls enacted to police Chinese American people through diet. This is part of the legacy that Chang, born in the Bay Area, recollects through this performative eating. Kim writes:

> Dietary preferences were not simply a matter of taste, but intrinsic to the American worker's "character," and essential to fulfilling the responsibilities of a republican government. Offering its own theory of consubstantiation, the state senate located the body politic in the very meat and bread consumed by the nation's citizens. The presumed irreconcilability of "meat" and "rice" as metonyms for American and Chinese ways of living set distinct racial limits on the struggle for workers' rights by suggesting that the very "stuff" of Chinese and American labor differed.[58]

By reading Chang through this history, I want to suggest that *In Love* also shows the generational pain of assimilation: after all, the white onion they share is sharper and harsher than scallions or green onions more traditionally associated with Chinese food. In this reading, the reverse temporality of the piece is also significant in that it prevents us from reading this as a static triumphant narrative of assimilation, the onion is reconstituted in the end. The mastication that we watch unfold in slow sensual time does not dissipate difficulty even as it might call upon the bonds of kinship—diasporic and otherwise.

The veneer of foreignness, which haunts Chang's installation in its manipulation of perversity and through its critique of discourses of assimilation, is part of what Karen Shimikawa labels "abjection." Through her analysis of Asian American performance, Shimikawa argues that Asian Americans are perpetually positioned as external to Americanness through the suturing of nation, race, ethnicity, and bodily identity. Shimikawa writes, "Read as abject, Asian Americanness thus occupies a role both necessary to and mutually constitutive of national subject formation— *but it does not result in the formation of an Asian American subject or even an Asian American object.*"[59] By drawing on Shimikawa's discussion of Asian American identity as occupying the space outside of subject and object, we can situate Chang's performance within the parameters of brown jouissance. Like Bustamante, Chang manipulates our sense of time—here, playing with the idea of Asian Americans as simultaneously occupying the past and future. In Chang's piece, we begin with the future and end with the past, leaving the present opaque and unknowable. It is in the opaque present, however, that we find perversion. Chang's tears call attention not only to the persistent foreignness of the Asian American body and the impossibility of assimilation, but also to the possibility of pleasure in that space in between, a space that Shimikawa describes as "a movement between visibility and invisibility, foreignness and domestication/assimilation."[60] It is precisely this wavering between abjection, pleasure, and pleasure in abjection that exceeds the matrix of overdetermination and produces brown jouissance.

Temporalities of the Present and Brown Jouissance

While Bustamante and Chang perform different aspects of automaticity, what unites their versions of brown jouissance is that these performances occur in relation to the loop, which invites us to think about the relationship between sensation and temporality. By showing their performances in a loop, Bustamante and Chang keep them in the register of the present. Time does not advance beyond this moment of crying, which is repeated endlessly for visitors to the installation. In the case of *Neapolitan* this repetition amplifies the affective resonance of Bustmanete's performance of crying. Instead of containing her tears to a few iterations of re-viewing *Fresa y Chocolate*, the loops bleed into each other to produce more hysteria and more melodrama. No matter when one begins watching, the cycle of tears feels endless. For Chang's *In Love* the effect of this looping is more complicated. Since the two monitors show different loops, which may or may not be synced to each other, the viewer has varying understandings about the relationship between the onion and tears. This means that it is possible to watch the entire cycle so that the performances are juxtaposed, which means that one is always aware that the kisses are not kisses, but chewing. However, one could also enter at a moment when the onion is revealed, rendering the kiss a shocking outcome as the video starts again, or one could watch "from the beginning" and see the kiss turn into an onion. Although these scenarios embed the spectator within different narratives of what is at stake, each one relates

Chang's performance to perversion and crying. What shifts is whether the onion or the kiss is a cheap trick. Is Chang using the onion to produce the veneer of perversion or is the kiss an excessive cover-up for the onion? Either way, Chang's excess falls within the realm of the perverse (even as that space may be the perversely unfunny).

That these larger loops speak to the tensions that emerge from the installations themselves is not surprising, but the doubled nature of these manipulations of temporality should give us pause. After all, Bustamante is also playing with looping within the video, while the force of Chang's critique lies with her use of reverse temporality. Since I have been arguing that the forms of automaticity that Bustamante and Chang perform have to do with race and sexuality, I want to suggest that their disparate modes of staying in the present—through technological temporal manipulation—also have to do with race and sexuality and the temporal dimensions that they call forth. Generally, brown bodies are imagined as atavistic, which we see in Schuller's discussion of nineteenth-century beliefs about sensation and evolutionary time. This is not an altogether unfamiliar argument. In *Sensational Flesh*, I made a similar set of claims. I argued, through a reading of Frantz Fanon, that black masculinity was seen as hewing to the temporality of the biological, which is to say that which is outside the temporality of civilization, while also arguing that black female sexuality could not be imagined as occurring outside the moment of chattel slavery. In these formulations, temporal stagnation was pernicious since it did not allow for agency or subjectivity. Bustamante's and Chang's suspension of progress, however, is doing something different.

Their loops foreclose narratives of progress and focus on the pleasures in dwelling on the unfinished. They also reorient the relationship between sensation and temporality. Rather than imagining that hysteria or perversion stop time, these bodily performances generate their own temporality, which is distinct from the conventionally narrativized time of progress in which there is a past-present-future. This is a temporality produced through the oscillation between subject and object. Bustamante and Chang mobilize the stagnation that the hysterical Latina and perverse Asian American woman inhabit and imbue it with their own affective energies. Through their theatrical amplifications of their modes of being objectified, Bustamante and Chang illuminate the subversive possibilities of the temporal stagnation that accompanies objectification. In Bustamante's and Chang's installations, the distinctions between past, present, and future blur into each other through the loop to suggest that brown jouissance carries with it its own sense of time related not to the external, but to the internal dimensions of sensation. In this way, we might imagine that Bustamante and Chang have created their own versions of reality in which reliving the impact—some might term it "trauma," but I want to stay with the ambiguity of Bustamante's and Chang's assessments—of inhabiting the excess of a brown female body provides comfort, if not resolution or catharsis. This is the comfort of existing in the loop, of existing in repetition, of existing in an affective and emotional reality of one's own choosing.

This temporality of brown jouissance is akin to one that Berlant describes as elliptical. In an interview in *ArtForum*, she describes elliptical thinking as thought that "both tracks concepts and allows for unfinishedness, inducing itself to become misshapen in the hope that by the time you return to the point of departure, so many things will have come into contact that the contours of the concept and the forms associated with its movement will have changed. How can our encounter with something become a scene of unlearning and engendering from within the very intensity of that encounter?"[61] In Berlant's description the unfinishedness of the ellipses enables her to unlearn what she thought she knew about something. Even as she returns to the beginning time and again, the narrative switches. Living in the present, even and perhaps especially when that present is self-created, is also about change even if it is not the same type of progressive shift that we have been trained to anticipate via repetition with a difference. Within any imagined stasis, there is always a dense thicket of possibility. This is where it becomes important that Bustamante and Chang refuse catharsis. In Bustamante's endless crying, we see pleasure, grief, and masturbatory excess. In Chang's narrative of kiss to onion, the questions of incest and masochism go unanswered, leaving us with a perverse opacity. These are particular pleasures that might disappear with more time or narrative. Instead, they remain contained in the loop—giving us space within the present to think with these repetitions and their pleasures, to think with sensation and to be in the time of brown jouissance and its multiple iterations of the present.

6

Femme Aggression and the Value of Labor

The film starts with a close up of plastic doll furniture. A yellow dresser, blue chairs, and a pink couch are arranged as a living room set on a small white rug. After the camera lingers on these objects, it pulls back to reveal a pair of legs in yellow, strappy, patent-leather espadrilles walking toward the set. We hear the heels click toward the furniture and suddenly—a cut. One foot crushes the couch, the other the green television. More steps and destruction follow. The camera zooms in on moments of impact to show rubber soles enacting plastic destruction. The legs lift and come down again—breaking things and kicking away the detritus. The legs are relentless. They seek out objects with pointed toes, only to crush them anew, even using the rug—a knitted square—for leverage. The legs walk away only after each object has been thoroughly crushed and kicked, so that all that remains is some debris and the knit square.

This is not the only film of its ilk. Maureen Catbagan's series *Crush* (2010-2012) consists of multiple such videos. Each features Molly Caldwell in different patent leather heels crushing plastic toys in different rooms. In one she wears a pair of burgundy high-heeled Mary Janes to stomp on a yellow plastic saxophone. It breaks apart across a white tiled bathroom floor. In another, her legs are clad in black lace tights while her silver strappy stilettos act as the instruments of destruction. In yet another, Caldwell wears large-holed fishnets and black peep-toe pumps. The small brass buttons on the shoes offset the toy's exposed electronic control panel.

These films traffic in feminine aggression. One of the ways we see this is through the emphasis on the size difference between legs and furniture. Though Caldwell's legs would appear large in comparison to the small toy furniture, Catbagan's decision to position the camera at eye level with the furniture at a medium distance amplifies the sense of Caldwell as a looming, destructive—yet also feminine—presence. In some ways this is a confounding piece to use to think about brown

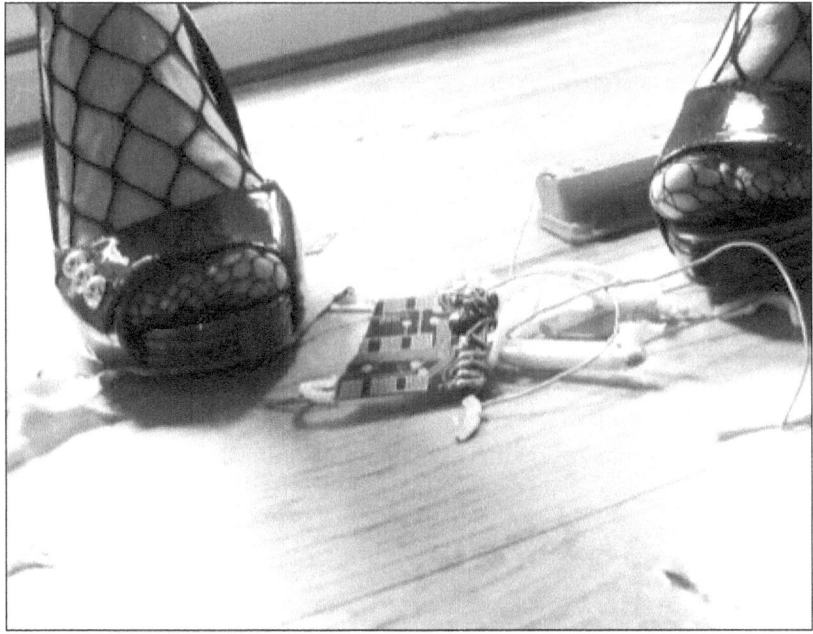

Figure 6.1. Maureen Catbagan, still from *Crush*. © 2010 Maureen Catbagan.

jouissance—its central object is white femininity; yet, I suggest we think about Catbagan, who is Filipino, as illuminating the excesses of affective labor, which transforms our perceptions of femininity, the fetish, and mimesis. *Crush* ultimately shows us the possibilities of invisibility and lingering with materiality.

Artifice and Misery: Narratives of White Femininity

Through the imaginary of Caldwell as giantess, *Crush* recalls the 1958 film *Attack of the Fifty-Foot Woman*. Famous as a B-movie and sci-fi classic, the film attracts admirers for its artifice and emphasis on feminine excess. It stars Allison Hayes as an heiress (Nancy Archer) in an unhappy marriage with Harry, who is cheating on her with Honey. Honey and Harry plot to get rid of Nancy and keep her money. Honey suggests various ways to make Nancy believe that she is mentally unstable, so that she is readmitted to the asylum where she spent some time after a previous separation from Harry. Chance intervenes in the form of satellites that fall into the California desert before Nancy's eyes. No one believes her story of a giant man in search of her diamond, so she asks Harry to accompany her into the desert in order to track him down. They find the giant, and Harry, scared, runs away and abandons her. The next morning, Harry is with Honey, and Nancy has been found on the roof of the pool house, where she remains unconscious. Harry, feeling fortunate, celebrates with Honey. This, however, is short-lived as Nancy begins to grow and become a giant. In this state, she is desperate and seeks out Harry—destroying much of the town in the process. Eventually she finds him and ends up crushing him, after which she is killed by an exploding power plant.

The film's popularity is due to its ridiculousness. The plot, the low-budget special effects—papier-mâché hands and projections of giants roaming the California desert, which recall early cinema's spectacles of distraction—and portrayal of white domestic femininity as pathological, which we see through the frequent discussion of the protagonist as unbalanced and irrational, combine to make audiences feel as if they are in on the joke.[1] Whereas Kara Walker's giant Sugar Baby indexes feelings of vulnerability for many spectators, Nancy mobilizes aggression; *she* is the threat. Further, in this movement away from realism, the film plays as a quasi-feminist rejoinder to patriarchy.

This tarrying with affective distortion positions the B-movie alongside pulp and camp as a minoritarian genre. Pulp's popular narratives bring together lust, danger, and a whiff of the tawdry, providing a glimpse of unconventional and (potentially liberated) femininity by emphasizing domesticity's discomforts. Camp offers critique through artifice and exaggeration. Susan Sontag writes, "Camp is a certain mode of aestheticism. It is one way of seeing the world as an aesthetic phenomenon. That way, the way of Camp, is not in terms of beauty, but in terms of the degree of artifice, of stylization."[2] *Attack of the Fifty-Foot Woman*'s emphasis on threatening femininity brings together domestic unhappiness and artifice to highlight the ways that the constellation of white femininity is affectively undergirded by misery and ontological insecurity.

The fundamental instability of white femininity, which Joan Riviere appears to admit in the middle of her 1929 essay "Womanliness as Masquerade," has been very attractive to feminist interpreters. Riviere writes,

"The reader may now ask how I define womanliness or where I draw the line between genuine womanliness and the 'masquerade.' My suggestion is not, however, that there is any such difference; whether radical or superficial, they are the same thing."[3] Stephen Heath argues that this statement reveals femininity's fundamental relationship to artifice through its emphasis on mimicry, thus positioning the essay to provide a political intervention into femininity, performance, and social norms.[4] This conflation of white femininity and artifice is often emphasized when scholars turn to drag. In *Gender Trouble*, Judith Butler draws on Esther Newton's description of drag's play on the difference between inner and outer selves to argue that "drag fully subverts the distinction between inner and outer psychic space and effectively mocks both the expressive model of gender and the notion of a true gender identity."[5] What Butler draws from Newton and what is integral to this theorization is that camp's reliance on the distance between "real" and "artificial" femininity reveals the very artifice of femininity and gender more broadly.[6] As Butler writes, "*in imitating gender, drag implicitly reveals the imitative structure of gender itself—as well as its contingency.*"[7] From this perspective the reveal of artifice functions as a critique of discourses that would seek to argue that domestic femininity and patriarchy—its structuring force—are "natural" and should be replicated without question because of this naturalness. This denaturalization of gender, described here specifically in relation to white femininity, though potentially liberatory, also produces an ontological insecurity that manifests itself through misery.

When we return to Riviere, we see that the affective underside of masquerade is unhappiness, an unhappiness produced by femininity's constraints—especially those of the domestic variety—despite the promises suggested by its instability. As Butler argues, this means that "the process of gender incorporation [is located] within the wider orbit of melancholy."[8] Indeed, Riviere's essay is as much about misery as it is about masquerade. While melancholy and misery are certainly not reducible to each other—melancholy refers to the unhappy affect produced by the inability to separate from the lost object, while misery refers more generally to a state of discomfort—this aura of unhappiness is the dominant current in understanding the relational aspect of the masquerade. Indeed, the lack of "pure enjoyment" is what detaches womanliness from its masquerade. In her analysis of psychoanalytic patients suffering from this form of unhappiness, Riviere takes pains to note the flawlessness of these women's performances, writing that they "maintain social life and assist culture; they have no lack of feminine interests, e.g. in their personal appearances, and when called upon they can still find time to play the part of devotees and disinterested mother-substitutes among a wide circle of relatives and friends. At the same time they fulfill the duties of their profession at least as well as the average man."[9] Against this portrait of success, however, Riviere argues that womanliness is attached to these women's unhappiness because it "did not represent [their] main development, and was used far more as a device for avoiding anxiety than as a primary mode of sexual enjoyment."[10] Interestingly, this lack of sexual enjoyment does not foreclose orgasm, which Riviere notes, happens frequently, but this orgasm is deficient in that "the gratification it brought was of the nature of a reassurance and restitution of something lost, and not ultimately pure enjoyment."[11] Although Riviere does not specify what exactly does constitute pure enjoyment, its absence leaves the feminine subject's unhappiness diagnosable vis-à-vis her sexual self. This important schism links sexuality with subjectivity explicitly and articulates womanliness/femininity with passivity and happy objectification. Butler interprets this objectification as part of the difficulty of the heterosexual matrix, which refuses to grant women the status of active sexual subjects. Butler writes that the woman's appropriation of masculine sexual desire (signaled by her nonenjoyment of womanliness) is "the predicament produced by a matrix that accounts for all desire for women by subjects of whatever sex or gender as originating in a masculine, heterosexual position. The libido-as-masculine is the source from which all possible sexuality is presumed to come."[12] Mary Ann Doane positions this conflict about activity and passivity in the realm of spectatorship: "When she masquerades, Joan Riviere's famous patient renounces her status as the subject of speech (as a lecturer, as an intellectual woman with a certain amount of power), and becomes the very image of femininity in order to compensate for her 'lapse' into subjectivity (i.e., the masculinity in Riviere's analysis) and to attract the male gaze. Masquerade would hence appear to be the very antithesis of spectatorship. Subjectivity."[13] These interpretations of Riviere reveal that the instability of the feminine position is about the relationship between being and doing—and woman's capacity to do has always been mediated through other subjects.

This agency through mediation is a form of ontological insecurity, and it works to produce femininity as synonymous with objectification, which also helps us to understand the racial contours of Riviere's analysis more clearly. In the space between pure enjoyment and misery, the social is injected into the frame of analysis. When Riviere's central analysand chafes at her social position and the limits of the external world, the outside world becomes marked as hostile, threatening, and immiserating. In this situation womanhood becomes linked with Sara Ahmed's trope of feminist killjoys, who "disturb the very fantasy that happiness can be found in certain places: it is not just that feminists might not be happily affected by the objects that are supposed to cause happiness but that their failure to be happy is read as sabotaging the happiness of others."[14]

Riviere's essay produces an analysis of white womanhood that pivots on the inability to achieve "full enjoyment." We can connect this space of unhappiness with *Attack of the Fifty-Foot Woman*'s Nancy Archer, a character whose unhappiness is prevalent enough to have been medicalized and is remarked upon by all of the characters. Even when she is transformed into a giant, Nancy is waiting—waiting for Harry to come home after his trysts with Honey, waiting for their marriage to get better, and waiting to become happy. She is in the midst of a performance of unhappy passivity. While Riviere restricts her subject's unhappiness to the guilt that she feels for wielding the phallus, the social aspects of misery creep in when one delves more deeply into the racial context that Riviere narrates, but does not parse. Amidst Riviere's description of the masquerade, two imagined scenarios appear in rapid succession, both of which complicate our understanding of how guilt and misery are functioning in this situation. The first is a recurring childhood fantasy in which the woman is attacked by a black man and defends herself by succumbing to his advances. The second, an elaborate dream, positions the patient alone in a house, washing clothing when a black man enters the home, and she endeavors to seduce him. As Ann Pellegrini and Jean Walton note, this appetite for destruction recalls Fanon's analysis of white women's fantasies of being raped by a black man—"a Negro is raping me"—in *Black Skin, White Masks*, fantasies that derive their power from female masochism.[15] This interpretation allows us to read Riviere's patient's fantasies as a mode of securing her desired punishment. This appeal to masochism further sutures white femininity to misery since this masochism would be a mark of "pure enjoyment."

As Elizabeth Wilson argues in *Gut Feminism*, most narratives of feminine aggression suggest that it turns inward to become depression or masochism.[16] In Riviere's essay we see this as melancholy and misery, but reading with the minoritarian gives us another perspective. While Sontag's theorization of camp has often been imagined to be synonymous with upper middle-class gay male life (here we might consider David Halperin's *How to Be Gay* as an updated articulation of these constellations of white middle-class gayness), José Esteban Muñoz argues that camp can be employed as a strategy of disidentification for minoritarian survival.[17] Muñoz argues that camp should be read, not merely as a style, but as a strategy for dealing with the dominant culture: "It is a measured response to the forced evacuation from dominant culture that the minority subject experiences. Camp is a practice of suturing different lives, of reanimating, through repetition with a difference, a lost country or moment that is relished and loved. Although not innately politically valenced, it is a strategy that can do positive identity- and-community-affirming work."[18] For Muñoz the distance that camp provides is not between artifice and sincerity, but between the dominant culture's dictates of representation and a self-presentation that is otherwise. Camp offers an alternative to the status quo's assignation of unhappiness to particular subjects. Camp provides a way of feeling embraced by remaking objects in ways that better suit survival.

It is through the lens of camp and other minoritarian genres, then, that I suggest we view Catbagan's *Crush* as trafficking in overt aggression rather than misery. As a director, Catbagan accomplishes this transformation in optics by undoing the heterosexualization of white femininity and introducing the specter of the femme. While Riviere's analysis of white femininity relies on the repression of homosexuality, which haunts all public women, Catbagan and Caldwell embrace this queerness. Caldwell's femme-ness is manifest not only in her patent-leather shoes, but in Catbagan's framing of her.

While sexual orientation is best understood relationally, normative assumptions link gender performance to orientation. This produces confusion when it comes to the femme, whose performance of femininity is assumed to connect her to heterosexuality. Generally, femmes are made visible as queer women when they are seen as part of a couple. Historically, femmes have been most recognizable when paired with butches, whose overt masculinity marks the relationship as legibly sexual, in part because the butch-femme dynamic is assumed to recall heterosexual norms of attraction. By making explicit the sexual economy that she is a part of, the butch makes the femme recognizable as something other than heterosexual. From this perspective, we see that having Catbagan at the helm is part of what produces Caldwell as femme. Though we do not see them, we can understand Catbagan as inhabiting a queer position, both because of their Filipino-ness and because of their (non-white male) inhabitation of the director's role—that is, of the one who controls the camera's gaze.

When we read Caldwell's performance as femme, instead of attaching to potential narratives of misery, her stomping registers as a form of feminine agency. Some of this agency is related to the reveal of gender's masquerade and its subversion through desire. In *Gender Trouble*, Judith Butler describes the terms of this subversion as queering heterosexual identity: "Lesbian femmes may recall the heterosexual scene, as it were, but also displace it at the same time. In both butch and femme identities, the very notion of an original or natural identity is put into question; indeed, it is precisely that question as it is embodied in these identities that becomes one source of their erotic significance."[19] Here, we see that femme identity is examined as a performance that subverts gender norms by illuminating the performative nature and nonoriginality of all gender. Madeline Davis also makes explicit this connection between femmes and subversion, writing that femmes are queer because they are "women who look and act like girls and who desire girls. We're just the queerest of the queers. It makes me laugh, but it also makes me feel so different. For butches, their masculinity makes them seem more 'normal.' We're kind of like those women in the 'lesbian' porn movies— long hair, lipstick—except we're real. We desire everything about our butches—even their womanness. I think that's pretty queer."[20] These readings of the femme emphasize the ways femme-ness can be a space of performance, play, and subversion. Through its invisibility, femme identity acts as a critique of heteronormativity and normativity in general. Lisa Duggan and Kathleen McHugh argue that this invisibility offers a twist on how one can understand the normal: "although seemingly 'normal,' [the femme] responds to 'normal' expectations with a sucker punch—she occupies normality abnormally."[21] Indeed, Caldwell's performance of stomping on toys offers a rejection of domesticity in literal ways. Her heels suggest that social immiseration is not going to be handled passively, but instead dealt with as an immediate radical rejection of domestic norms.

Caldwell's performance of femme-ness is not sui generis. It arises from citations of normative gender identity, which themselves are embedded within a particular historical moment. The citational nature of femme-ness has two important simultaneous effects: it creates a present that differs from the past, and it reifies a certain version of the past. As Elizabeth Freeman notes in *Time Binds*, this iterative process "consolidate[s] the authority of a fantasized original, even if citationality itself unsettles the idea of an origin."[22] We see this in *Crush*'s subtle recall of 1950s femininity as manifest in *Attack of the Fifty-Foot Woman*, which itself (most notably through its iconic poster) recalls pulp, and lesbian pulp, in particular. Ostensibly produced for a male audience, the genre, according to Yvonne Keller, facilitated the production of American lesbian identity by presenting a world of possibility for its readers. Pulp widened access to representations of lesbianism and presented same-sex relationships as erotic rather than pathological.[23] Access, positive representation, and information made pulp especially appealing in the homophobic environment of the 1950s. Keller argues that this is especially illustrated through cover art, which signals the genre's coherence more than the actual content.[24] Such covers, Keller writes, were "sensationalist and overtly lesbianism, or at least 'deviant' or overly sexualized." These fierce women offered portraits of unconventional and potentially liberated femininity—femininity that occupied a strikingly different world compared to the femininity that circulated outside of the books. Jennifer Worley writes, "Embedding a desire for escape from normative mid-century gender roles in sensational stories of queer passion and urban adventure, these narratives produced the position of the lesbian as not simply one of sexual preference, but as one of profound dissatisfaction with the culturally proscribed apparatus of heterosexuality: Marriage, motherhood, domesticity, and family."[25] In other words, the protagonists of the pulps illuminated possibilities for feminine non-normativity and feminism in addition to making visible female queerness. Reading Caldwell as femme not only makes explicit the implicit critiques of patriarchy and heteronormativity present in these 1950s texts, but also offers us a way to read femme-ness as a strategic resignification of femininity to express aggression.

The transformation of misery into aggression that we see in *Crush* has to do with harnessing the affective distortions of the minoritarian genres of B-movies, camp, and pulp, so that the ontological instability of white femininity is oriented toward femme aggression. The possibility that is unleashed through white femininity's instability allows us to see the transformative power of affective labor *and* think more critically about the relationship between labor and value. Lingering in the space of aggression also presents us with a particular formation of feminine pleasure. Caldwell's performance of aggression is about an extension of herself outward; her affect travels, and the boundaries between self and other break.

Fetish, Labor, and Destroying the Domestic

While Caldwell's performance is integral to *Crush*'s presentation of femme aggression, Catbagan's presence also impacts our understanding of the stakes of the films. We must be mindful that it is Catbagan's vision as director—their edits, their zooms, their soundscapes—that frames the way we can understand Caldwell's performance. The decision to frame the films in relation to the idea of the fetish allows us to think about the relationship between objects and labor while reading through their Filipino identity complicates the scenes of domesticity that Caldwell smashes.

Playing with the idea of the fetish is an explicit part of Catbagan's aim as a director. In describing *Crush* on their website, they write that the videos illustrate the fetishization of feminine destruction: "Visceral feminine destruction is fetishized as toys are demolished by specifically chosen heels."[26] Indeed, the title of the series refers to a fetish in which people respond sexually to women in heels crushing objects—be it toys, insects, or even small animals. In the versions of these fetish videos that circulate via YouTube, women in high heels are shown in static long shots stomping on objects such as routers, cigarettes, or food items. The allure of the videos is their unedited nature, which draws out suspense about whether the object will bend or break and whether the heels or the floor will be ruined. Catbagan's highly edited films with fast cuts and close-ups of destruction are a different beast altogether. They forego suspense in favor of focusing on aggression. But it is through these contrasting images of destruction that we see an alternate vision of embodied sensuality.

In psychoanalysis, the fetish acts as a metonym. In an early articulation of fetishism, Sigmund Freud argues that these cherished objects, generally shoes, velvet, or underwear, are stand-ins for a phallus.[27] He later refined this definition to argue that fetishism is the result of a boy's horror at realizing that his mother does not possess a penis. Unable to deal with his mother's "castration," the boy imagines an object to be his mother's missing phallus. According to Freud, the fetishized object is a "substitute for the woman's (the mother's) penis that the little boy once believed in and—for reasons familiar to us—does not want to give up."[28] These fetish objects, then, represent the mother's phallic power while simultaneously acknowledging her lack of power. In the transfer of affection from mother to object, the phallus retains its power, and femininity's relationship to objectification is further reified. In making humans into objects, however, Freud's discourse of fetishism also reveals the complex falseness of the dichotomy between humans and objects.

To think the fetish in relation to the object is to make it disappear under the weight of human desire, displacement, and fantasy. David Marriot writes: "Fetishism (or at least its structure) always has to do with repudiation and loss. That it commemorates a loss, but a loss that is simultaneously recognized and denied (perhaps it is recognition that it denied?), but substituting a sign, a sign that preserves the loss it effaces like ice preserves the muddy footprints of passersby."[29] Marriot emphasizes the desire for this object's disappearance despite the actual impossibility of this act. Thinking with Freud, Emily Apter suggests that his fetishist operates within "the realm of the simulacrum, generating a copy or surrogate phallus for an original that never was there in the first place."[30] These shifts between avowal and disavowal reveal fetishism to be "an ambiguous state that demystifies and falsifies at the same time, or that reveals its own techniques of masquerade while putting into doubt any fixed referent."[31] This version of fetishism is about masquerade and the ability to become-object or embody passivity. Already, we see echoes between this version of the fetish and the imaginary that surrounds white femininity. Both pivot around the idea of ontological insecurity.

Crush highlights the ways that white femininity, as an opaque object, is fetishized, thereby illuminating the overlap between discourses of fetishization and racialized desire.[32] In his discussion of the fetishization of black men, Frantz Fanon argues that racial fetishism is at the root of stereotype and phobia, both of which are discourses that traffic in distance from reality.[33] On the one hand, this provides the possibility of opacity, which Marriot describes as a form of freedom: "Politically, fetishism leaves us unfree within our representations but frees us from the presuppositions and outcomes of mutual exposure to ourselves and others."[34] On the other hand, the possibility generated by this opacity is also deeply feared. Anne Anlin Cheng describes this anxiety as invisible, pervasive, and deeply threatening to a modernist order that wants to categorize: "As a psychical structure that signals, rather than averts, the contagion between the known and the unknown, the material and the imagined, the visible and the invisible—fetishism may signal more than a symptom of colonial desire, it may index a set of tenacious problems underlying what it means to value someone or something."[35] Fetishism, then, is about the deep comingling of these anxieties with pleasure. It is about the pleasures of difficulty—difficulty in understanding what constitutes an appropriate relationship with objects, fantasy, and difference. It provides us with a narrative of constraint (in its flattening), possibility (through opacity), and value.

Yet Catbagan transforms this story. By presenting femme aggression rather than lingering lovingly on the objects, *Crush* highlights the evacuation of female agency within the conventional fetish videos and shows us something else. In addition to addressing fantasies of white femininity, *Crush* brings us toward thinking about the circuits of labor that the fetish invokes. When we watch the high heels destroy the toys, are we witnessing an impulse to decouple capitalism and desire, a rejection of the commodity, or a privileging of the flesh? Does the hardwood floor domesticate the uncontainability of the flesh, the visceral, in all of its destructive glory? In showing us the potential fury that underlies femininity, Catbagan unveils our desire to see femininity as an active agent in addition to illuminating the labor that femininity performs. This process of showing labor is part of what shifts concepts of value away from the object toward affect.

In this choreography of destruction, the toys are stripped of the magic of the commodity, and we see, instead, feminine labor and aggression. Perhaps *Crush* is Catbagan's version of a critique of commodity fetishism? Commodity fetishism is Marx's mode of making sense of the difference between an object's objective value and its value as a commodity, which is to say its value becomes inflated beyond its use-value and separate from labor. The process of commodification transforms the object into "a thing which transcends sensuousness" in that the object is severed from its connection to actual laboring hands.[36] Capitalism's ability to transform labor into an abstract value—money—obscures the social interactions underlying these transactions, making value inhere in the objects rather than the labor that produced them. This creates a relationship with objects instead of people and renders human relationships alienated: "Men are henceforth related to each other in their social process of production in a purely atomistic way; they become alienated because their own relations of production assume a material shape which is independent of their control and their conscious individual action."[37] Marx's elaboration of the fetish does not contain anything of the language of substitution that we see in Freud; instead, it hews toward thinking with magic and animism to understand how objects become infused with human properties and social relations to become desirable. For Marx, the commodity calls up a form of false idolatry because it obscures the relationship between labor and objects. It is problematic because it makes men into atoms, which is to say isolated entities separate from each other and from the fruits of their labor.

Crush's performance of feminized labor is especially arresting because the objects that Caldwell destroys—plastic domestic scenes—are imbricated within the realm of the commodity in several ways. First, the objects themselves are part of the global economy of plastic trinkets, which are manufactured in the global South and circulate as toys before becoming waste. In this way, they usher both race and class onto the scene through the reminder of the commodity's movement and the racialized component of labor that has gone into the production of these objects. This shift toward the global invokes race in a way that is not about skin color and the potentiality of opacity, but about the specific affective and material work of laboring bodies in multiple geographies. Additionally, the objects are also representative of the instruments of domestication that transform women into commodities. This double valence brings race and gender onto the scene in ways that show their complex relationship to labor, specifically the domestic labor that women have performed or are expected to perform. This labor is different from the labor of decoration or masquerade that Riviere invokes. The feminine labor that Catbagan rejects is that of keeping house and reproducing the family—labor that some 1970s feminists demanded be classified as work. Kathi Weeks writes, "Feminists insisted that the largely unwaged 'reproductive' work that made waged 'productive' work possible on a daily and generational basis was socially necessary labor, and that its relations were thus part and parcel of the capitalist mode of production. What had been coded as leisure was in fact work, and those supposedly spontaneous expressions of women's nature were indeed skillful practices."[38] While Catbagan's intervention into these debates is through the matrix of destruction, it is important to keep this feminine labor and domestic work in mind as we focus on the heels rebelling against that world order.

Catbagan's critique gains extra charge because of Filipina migrants' role within the field of domestic service. Rhacel Salazar Parreñas describes Filipino women as "the quintessential service workers of globalization" because of the disproportionate number of women who leave the Philippines to perform domestic service in other countries.[39] This migration has been spurred by processes of globalization that have created turmoil within the Philippine economy and created demand for service workers elsewhere. Because of its colonial history in the Philippines, the United States is a particularly popular destination. Importantly, the work that many of these migrants perform (though proportionally fewer in the United States than elsewhere) is feminine labor, what Parreñas describes as "the labor needed to sustain the productive labor force. Such work includes household chores; the care of elders, adults, and youth; the socialization of children; and the maintenance of social ties in the family."[40] Through this lens we see that Catbagan's critique of domestic labor also carries with it a colonial history and a complex understanding of gendered labor and work, since the presence of the Filipina domestic worker enables other women to enter the workforce through a different economy in what Parreñas argues "could be read as a process of rejecting gender constraints for different groups of women in a transnational economy."[41] In this portrait of feminine labor, it is not just that feminine labor is tied to the domestic, but that it is profoundly tied to dislocation.[42]

This geopolitical spatialization of labor also serves as a reminder that brown jouissance itself is the product of black and brown labor. Because this labor is born from the flesh, however, its fleshiness disrupts the assumption that labor is ever a straightforward form of value added. Denise Ferreira da Silva argues that this excess fleshiness disrupts the characterization of the feminine body as an economic and symbolic given within the confines of productivity. Da Silva writes, "For her body only enters accounts of racial violence as always already in the juridical, economic, and ethical register of coloniality-patriarchy-slavery, that is, in accounts of domination, in bondage, marriage, and rape. My intuition here is that the sexuality of the female body refers to a power other than the sovereign's . . . one that is beyond and before the re/productive capabilities of the fe/male native/slave body."[43] Black and brown flesh enters the scene as a Thing, which, da Silva argues, "hosts the possibility of violence, of that which threatens to undo any resolution; because it is a mediator, it necessarily unsettles the limits of justice itself."[44] Da Silva urges us to stay with this violence because it offers the possibility of unsettling categories, disrupting assumptions about value, and transforming labor into something else—namely, desire. This appropriation of desire—the concept deeply tethered to interiority and the sovereign subject—by fleshiness unleashes a new world of possibilities for da Silva. She writes:

> I am interested in a frame of intervention that appreciates the body as a referent of The Thing, without (outside) modern signification, that is, one that exposes precisely that referent Hegel's version of sovereign reason has protected in interiority, namely, desire. To be sure, by evoking the body in the register of excess (value [form and force] + violence), I do no more than to track its disavowal, to indicate how, when desire threatens to become a descriptor of the Other as Subject, the racial subaltern subject (the affectable I), it is immediately returned to the proper place, to the white side of value, from where authorized violence is done in the name of a regulated desire.[45]

This territory of Thingness is that which is inhabited by blackness and brownness. It is the space where the power of materiality and violence are illuminated and transformative. These transformations are how brown jouissance offers a way to rethink labor and value. If the commodity is produced when the labor that produces objects is absented, remembering that brown jouissance is labor allows us to revalue labor as an entity unto itself instead of dwelling on the commodity. This focus on labor and its fleshiness—its affective excess—is distinct from the fetish's emphasis on objects and the logic of substitution. It does not rely on ontological insecurity, but rather insists on valuing the unruly (possibly aggressive) fleshiness of materiality.

The Question of Value

A radical praxis would then stay with The Thing, exposing the constitutive violence; it releases free radicals and virtual particles, which by unsettling—through affection, intention, and attention—expose the relationship that is knowledge itself and its effects.
—Denise Ferreira da Silva, "To Be Announced: Radical Praxis or Knowing at the Limits of Justice"

While Catbagan's body does not appear anywhere in the frame, it is their flesh, their materiality that frames the films. In this way, I suggest that we view Caldwell as a proxy for Catbagan because she enacts aggression on their behalf without the distraction or spectacle that angry black and brown bodies produce. In her discussion of the unhappiness that angry black women cause, Ahmed writes, "It is not just that feelings are 'in tension' but that the tension is located somewhere: in being felt by some bodies, it is attributed as caused by another body, who thus comes to be felt as apart from the group, as getting in the way of its organic enjoyment and solidarity."[46] This to say that this form of racialized anger elicits irritation because it interrupts the fabric of social belonging. The aggression that Catbagan shows through Caldwell's performance is that which rejects the status quo, but it is not the anger of an outsider. Rather, it is the aggression that comes with familiarity. This familiarity is twofold. It is produced through Caldwell's white femininity and through

Catbagan's status as Filipino, which connects them to a country that has a particularly complex relation to the United States because of its status as former colony. Sarita See writes, "A racial formation that emerges out of the colonial construction 'foreign in a domestic sense,' Filipino America is a simultaneously inassimilable *and* assimilable entity in the 'house' of the American empire."[47] Yet, within both identitarian—white and Filipino—constructions of "belonging," the films highlight affective excesses that disrupt. Here, I read the performance of Caldwell's femme aggression alongside (and perhaps as a proxy) manifestation of Catbagan's rebellion against model minority status, which Christine Bacareza Balance describes as "the punk aesthetic of 'gleeful opposition to decorum and propriety' by expressing itself in ways that 'fl[y] directly in the face of the "polite Asian"' stereotype."[48] These forms of rage, Balance argues, help to specify the incoherence of the term "Asian American" while also announcing possibilities for resistance under its umbrella: "As a mode of identification, ['Asian American'] holds the possibility of being a 'deliberative and motivated thing: experiential rather than biological, grounded in the present as much or more than in the past.'"[49] Balance translates this form of protest into an "attitude," which "performs the affective labor of transforming alienating episodes into common understanding."[50] From this perspective, Caldwell's femmeness becomes important for Catbagan because she enables Catbagan to locate aggression in and through the familiar.

In particular, Catbagan's rejection of the fetishization of white feminine misery and their mobilization of Caldwell as femme introduce ambiguity about the value of whiteness, which we might register as an aspect of "the familiar." In her analysis of neoliberalism and the Philippines, Neferti X. M. Tadiar uses Marx to argue that the alignment of blackness and brownness with corporeality and labor has led to a valuation of whiteness as that which is unmarked. This, in turn, produces value through an alienation from this corporeality. She writes, "Value reflects the racialized relations of its production, in particular the alienation of and from racialized labor as a suprasensible 'quality' of unmarked, immaterial, even spectral power. The white subject is, simply put, the realization of the subjectivity of the vanishing mediator."[51] For Tadiar this separation of whiteness from materiality signals a particularly American form of imperialism. It results in enterprise, which Tadiar describes, citing Richard Dyer, as a process in which "the white spirit organizes white flesh and in turn non-white flesh and other material matters: it has enterprise. Imperialism is the key historical form in which that process has been realized. Imperialism displays both the character of enterprise in the white person, and its exhilaratingly expansive relationship to the environment."[52] For Tadiar this separation between the material and the unmarked has particular resonance for the Philippines because it signals the ways in which whiteness continues to have value despite (or because of) its reliance on black and brown materiality.

In displaying white femme labor and rendering their own body invisible, Catbagan challenges the status of whiteness as unmarked and immaterial. In part this is because Caldwell's labors do not circulate within the realm of productivity—except insofar as they produce waste. But, the question of value emerges from Catbagan's removal of self from the frame—thereby denying the contemporary liberal desire to see black and brown subjects at work, creating the surplus labor familiar to many of us as the labor of diversity. Grace Hong narrates this transition, writing that "racial capital transitioned from managing its crises entirely through white supremacy to also managing its crises through white liberalism, that is, through the incorporation and affirmation of minoritized forms of difference."[53] Catbagan's refusal of the spectacle of racial difference and the labor of diversity work makes the question of value central. Drawing on Lindon Barrett, Lisa Marie Cacho argues that, "the 'object' of value needs an 'other' of value because 'for value "negativity is a *resource*," an essential resource. The negative, the expended, the excessive invariably form the ground of possibilities for value.'"[54] This to say that the production of value is reliant on relegating something (some people) to the periphery and making it (them) invisible, while also hiding the violence of this disavowal, as Barrett argues in relation to his discussion of the relationship between race and value: "Violence is posited as the subsequently occluded origin of value. This model understands value as a principle of order that concertedly overlooks its forceful, initial intervention into what it constructs as 'disorder,' a principle that subsequently sublimates its ineluctable violence through the fetishization of boundaries."[55] Catbagan's critique of the discourse of fetishism and mobilization of Caldwell as proxy acknowledges this violence, yet it also rejects the boundaries that it might produce.

To this, we might ask what type of value Catbagan is asking us to reflect on? What lies between the valued and the valueless? One immediate register is the shifting value of disposability, which brings to mind the toys that Caldwell crushes and those who made them. Hong describes these workers of the global South as "nonlaboring subjects, that is, the populations that are surplus not to production but to speculation and circulation" and are "useful for their intrinsic lack of value."[56] This lack of value facilitates capital's flexibility and hovers adjacent to abjection. However, Catbagan doesn't actually ask us to stay with these objects and imagine their place in the universe; instead, *Crush* allows us to ask what the production of valueless (disposable) objects suggests about the value of labor itself. The invisible, material surplus of these acts of destruction, I argue, offers insight into the affective reorientations of the value of brownness.

By employing Caldwell as proxy, Catbagan uses Caldwell's femmeness to destabilize the value of whiteness while also reorienting our relationship to the labor that Caldwell performs. As a vehicle for enacting Catbagan's rage, Caldwell shows the utility of white femme labor in terms of Tadiar's discussion of whiteness as the vanishing mediator. As concept, however, proxy does more than suggest a certain type of white fungibility, and instead allows us to think with the concept of mimesis— that popular postcolonial term for the pedagogical process of approximation, for which the Philippines is often singled out as exemplar. This, in large part, is due to its history of multiple colonizations, but it is also because of the Phillipines's history of exporting certain types of labor. Lucy Mae San Pablo Burns argues that mimesis is a particularly Filipino strategy of performance. She writes, "The recognition of Filipinos on the global stage rests on and wrestles with their remarkable ability to 'perform back' what they have imbibed through their colonial education."[57] Against the idea of mimesis as a form of automation—here we see the difference between the films of *Crush* and those of Patty Chang and Nao Bustamante—I am interested in mimesis's affective excesses in relation to similarity. In this, I follow San Pablo Burns, who writes, "My interest in mimesis, used here interchangeably with imitation, consequently lies specifically in the material and affective labor it takes to imitate."[58] San Pablo Burns's instruction to stay with the material and affective labor of imitation—its fleshiness—brings us back to aggression. Catbagan's work shows us how aggression transforms acts of citationality—that of the fetish videos and white femininity—into something else. Catbagan's use of aggression as the primary affect in the *Crush* series illustrates mimesis's cutting edge and the ways that mimesis can be transformative. Aggression, here, shores up the self as agential, creative, and material. This aggression is both a recognition of indebtedness to these citational sources and a critique of them. In her description of Filipino art strategies, See argues that "these artists unexpectedly reverse dominant American narratives of immigrant assimilation. According to the 'immigration mythography' of assimilation, racialized subjects undergo a transformative process of adjustment and accommodation proper to successful absorption into the body politic, a process that reinforces the nation-empire. In contrast, the Filipino Americanist integrationist desire for America paradoxically leads to the disintegration of the empire."[59] This is to say that the mobilization of assimilation, which is where we might position acts of mimesis, is actually what reveals the cracks of imperialism. In contrast to Chang's critique of assimilation through her embrace of foreignness, what we see in Catbagan's work is an inhabitation of assimilation that produces excessive affect—aggression—as critique.

These endless possibilities of proliferation and excesses of affect, in turn, bring us to the viral. It is notable, I think, that Catbagan offers not just one film of Caldwell's acts of destruction. This multiplicity intensifies *Crush*'s play with the transformational powers of mimesis and speaks to the ways that virality functions to undercut the question of value. In her analysis of YouTube virality in relation to Asian American identity, Balance argues that the videos must contain an emotional hook, which often hinges on a certain produced vulnerability. Balance writes, "In other words, to catch an already distracted viewer's attention, viral videos must exude an air of amateur production—versus the slick, professional, and therefore controlled aesthetics of mainstream Hollywood or television sources—and mobilize key signifiers that resonate with a particular community or subculture."[60] Balance's foregrounding of the amateur qualities of the videos returns us to a consideration of the role that B-films, camp, and pulp play as intertexts for Catbagan's films. Although their films are edited and polished so that they are not amateur, this summoning of minoritarian genres and their relation to subculture (here we should also include the YouTube fetish videos as well) positions them within its affective orbit. These viral Youtube "performances of affect and participation," Balance argues, "point to this virtual diaspora's simulated and representational elements and, in turn, to the performative and affective dimensions of the 'symbolic ethnicity' of Asian Americans."[61] This is to say that virality, as a performative dimension, brings into question the notion of value by emphasizing the symbolic nature of cohesion—in Balance's argument through the sign of the "Asian American"—the relation between virality and replication, and the intangibility of vulnerability. Virality cannot be just about labor; it is about the materiality of the body and the ways that that materiality penetrates the viewer—we might recall briefly the spectacle of Ibarra's gloved hands. The viral is, after all, often characterized as "corruptive, mobile, and infectious."[62] In virality, excessive affect is smuggled in under the guise of the familiar.

In the absence of consumable racial difference and productive labor, Catbagan offers mimesis, but this is mimesis with a difference, albeit of a very different sort than Carrie Mae Weems' labors of affective reproduction. What we see is not that mimesis—which Catbagan's films contain multiple strains of in their mobilization of camp, pulp, the femme, and the YouTube video format, including the film's existence as a series—produces subversion, but that mimesis reorients value. Tadiar argues that mimesis can "carry out new imperatives and possibilities of consumption in an age of 'mechanical' or technological reproducibility though in a labor-intensive, rather than capital-intensive form."[63] What we witness in *Crush* is the wasteful labor of aggression, a labor without product, which offers instead value in its affective charge and in its ability to make brownness signify differently, or rather to defer the question of its signification by insisting on the material in conjunction with the affective. This is an unusual position; traditionally the question of material value is considered in relation to labor power, and it circulates separately from that of the value that stems from desire. Meg Wesling builds on Gayatri Chakravorty Spivak to develop the concept of "queer value" to "suture together two domains too often understood to operate autonomously: the psychic realm of desire and the material realm of accumulation and exchange."[64] Queer value is useful, Wesling argues, because it enables us to think with multiple economies simultaneously.[65] For Wesling this means an interrogation of the question of complicity between intellectuals and the global circuits of labor that enable their work. *Crush* illustrates these forms of complicity while also illuminating the power of the flesh.

Invisibility and Brown Jouissance

Thinking with the proxy and mimesis brings us toward invisibility, which, it is important to note, is not the same as absence. I have traced the ways in which Catbagan's materiality can be located in directorial choices and the excessive affect that emerges from *Crush*. The films' use of the sonic offers another mode for us to think with invisibility. In the films, we hear the crush of the toys as they are ground into the floor, the sound of heels hitting the ground, and hiss of objects falling apart all set against a backdrop of Catbagan breathing. The sonic excess, I argue, leads us to rethinking the commodity, the fetish, and becoming-atomic. In the crush of destruction, we hear what Fred Moten describes as the commodity's scream. Moten reads Marx's ventriloquization of the commodity as a mode of arguing that value emerges from exchange: "The commodity discovers herself, comes to know herself, only as a function of having been exchanged, having been embedded in a mode of sociality that is shaped by exchange."[66] Against this, however, Moten argues that the commodity's value preexists exchange and that the resistance of the object can be located in the scream—notably that of Frederick Douglass's Aunt Hester, whose scream upon being whipped "embodies the critique of value, of private property, of the sign."[67] The commodity's scream is the space of brown jouissance; it illustrates the oscillation between subject and object and the fleshy excess of the sonic. In relation to questions of value, the crunch of the toys may register as the excess of the object's materiality, but it is also symptomatic of its excision from exchange—its embeddedness within a circuit of un-useful labor. As such, this "scream" emerges as a symptom of both Caldwell's wasteful labors *and* Catbagan's affective framings. We hear these sounds because Catbagan wants us to; they remind us that we are in their world, where visibility does not occupy a privileged space.

When we think with the noise generated by these crushed toys, we can register the commodity's scream as critique *and* creation. The act of destruction at the heart of these videos—stomping—is also one of creation—the creation of more, the creation of waste, excess, the unwanted, but possessed. In its activation of an alternate economy of value, this production of excess is a mode of working through the collapse between the material and the maternal that Moten argues blackness occupies. This iteration of brown jouissance accepts the maternal (the literal creative force here) as the material, even as it exists in a space of excess and lack, which is to say that there is both an excess of objects and a lack of desire. Catbagan has created a universe populated by objects that beget other objects outside of the circuits of desire. In fact, we have an "excess of lack," which circulates to the sound of crushed objects. This destruction does, indeed, illuminate "the fetish of desire." Value cannot circulate in the object, but is located in the invisibility of Catbagan's and Caldwell's affective labor.

This value of invisibility is further underscored by the persistence of Catbagan's breath, which we hear throughout. Their breath signals bodily presence without a body—a trace of personhood, a trace of flesh. Their breath also reminds us simultaneously of the vulnerability of personhood and the triangulation of voyeurism. Both of these elements bring us back to the spatial. *Crush* invites us to think with global economic circuits in addition to the atomic and the cosmic. Catbagan mobilizes these related, but slightly oppositional registers in two ways: through the scream of the commodity and through their own breath, which marks not only their presence but also the potential of invisibility. This is a different becoming-atomic than Marx describes in his complaint about the absence of connection to the worker. The destruction of toys gestures toward becoming-atomic by emphasizing the smaller and smaller fragments that are created through destruction—the material maternal means that we are all atomic—while Catbagan's breath brings us toward the register of the vibrational. That we can hear/feel the breath but not see Catbagan suggests that the invisible is what holds the universe together and what provides the conditions of possibility for being. This rescripts the excess of lack as its own form of maternity—one that combines the material and the spatial by invoking the universe.

Coda

Elsewhere, Is the Mother a Place?

Throughout this book, I have examined works of art and asked us to feel for the epistemological, to feel for brown jouissance's relational selfhoods, sensuality, and politics, but, here, at the book's very end, I address the idea that hovers below the surface—the feminine. Femininity, I argue, has become a disappearing horizon—unable to be imagined without collapsing under the weight of materiality. However, by foregrounding relationality in content and form, this book offers an alternative narration of femininity, one that opens us toward a suturing of queerness and femininity while keeping us attentive to the flesh. I come to this queer femininity, because thinking processes of racialization in relation to femininity, as this book has done, stretches its boundaries in particular ways. This occurs because femininity produced within the sphere of pornotropic capture must already be thought outside of the bounds of traditional femininity. Remembering Hortense Spillers's discussion of the pornotrope, we see that black and brown women become estranged from femininity on multiple levels: "In this play of paradox, only the female stands *in the flesh*, both mother and mother-dispossessed. This problematizing of gender places her, in my view, out of the traditional symbolics of female gender, and it is our task to make a place for this different social subject."[1] This queer femininity, then, exists outside of the symbolic—tied not to the father and recognition, but to the mother.

To invoke the mother is to set off waves of existential panic. Motherhood, in particular, has been understood as a limitation for women. Shulamith Firestone famously wrote that "the heart of woman's oppression is her child-bearing and child-rearing role."[2] Likewise Lynne Huffer writes, "The mother . . . is, in fact, the most extreme expression of the construction of the feminine as negativity: absence, invisibility, meaninglessness, silence, loss."[3] In becoming a mother, then, a woman is transformed from subject (or proto-subject) into a void, a being that exists to sacrifice. In order to give to her offspring, she denies herself. To combat this existential and cultural space of negation, Firestone offers a dream of artificial reproduction, which would distribute the maternal function (to use Elissa Marder's phrase) among the population and effectively destroy the mother as a cultural object.[4] In these analyses the mother is read as an absence, a lack, an obstacle to both female transcendence and feminist progress. Motherhood is femininity gone wrong—too far. What is grafted onto the idea of motherhood is the idea of self-denial and lack of agency. A mother is someone for whom others come first, or at least she is someone for whom others *should* come first. As Barbara Johnson points out, this association with self-denial is a way to discipline women whose ambitions are seen as too heady: "She may be a CEO, but she's *childless*."[5] In Johnson's example, this woman is too selfish, too self-realized, and motherhood would be a way to temper that.

But, thinking with Spillers and brown jouissance, I argue that queer femininity is not necessarily attached to motherhood or self-denial, but it emerges through an insistence on keeping the mother at the center of projects of selfhood and intimacy. This model displaces the Oedipal in its prioritization of the oscillations between Other, object, and Thing. The mother is the first provider of care (regardless of gender), who introduces the child into sociality. For Melanie Klein, these encounters with otherness occur first at the maternal breast. The infant, she argues, divides the world into what she terms the "good (gratifying) and bad (frustrating) breast": the infant introjects the good breast, which offers sustenance, and expels the bad breast.[6] This divides the world into interior and exterior, establishing the parameters for selfhood and marking the world spatially and affectively. Meira Likierman describes this process of projection as the child's "displacement of instinctual forces from the interior arena of his psyche outwards, [which] invest[s] the world with a qualitative variety of affect" and argues that it happens in tandem with introjection, a process in which "aspects of the external world are taken into the self and incorporated by the mind."[7] Introjection and projection create an imagined division between the self and the rest of the world over which one does not have agency. The task of the infant is to work through this division in order to understand the m/Other as separate, but whole (good and bad) and to achieve a depressive position, which involves "an awareness of vulnerability, dependence, and guilt."[8] The mother, but more precisely those who provide care, then, is the first object for one to test the boundaries of self. She is the object on whom one is dependent and from whom separation initiates selfhood.

Klein's model of object relations is deeply sensual in that the infant uses a variety of strategies to assess the boundaries of the self. After all, what are projection and introjection other than alternate ways of crafting externality through feeling? In bringing the external inward (via introjection) and linking the internal to the outside (via projection), exteriority gains textures and folds. It is this maneuvering that leads Gayatri Chakravorty Spivak to describe the work of the infant as that of translation. She writes, "The human infant grabs on to some one thing and then things. This grabbing (*begreifen*) of an outside indistinguishable from an inside constitutes an inside, going back and forth and coding everything into a sign-system by the thing(s) grasped. One can call this crude coding a 'translation.' In this never-ending weaving, violence translates into conscience and vice versa."[9] For Spivak this shuttling between the interior and the exterior leaves the mother's body as the unknowable site of difference—what I have described throughout the book as opacity. The infant's selfhood is formed through this action of producing interiority, but there is no illusion that objects are not part of this affective and corporeal pull nor is there any desire to see the process as anything other than violence. Through this we can see that grappling with the mother produces a rich world where the presumed goals of subjectivity—individuality and omnipotence—are undermined. Not only is individuality revealed to be the product of violence, but it is also shown to be impossible: one is always in a state of coexistence and immersed in violence. Vulnerability is the underside of fantasies of omnipotence, and love and hate must be woven together in order to provide a path toward existing ethically as a self in the world. Opacity and sensuality come together in this work of producing a self in relation to the mother.

These opaque and sensual relationships with the mother are evident in thinking about the dynamics at work in the pieces of art that I examine—some of which explicitly summon the mother or perform various modes of reproduction—but when we dwell on race in relation to the mother, these relationships become even more complicated. To be a pornotrope is to already exist in a process of violent enfleshment that shapes the possibilities of being. Further, pornotroping has historically also been accompanied by a violent erasure of mothers and mothering. In the brutal separation of kin that accompanied the transformation of people into flesh through slavery, Spillers argues, the paternal became synonymous with whiteness while the maternal was often experienced as an absence—"mother-dispossessed."[10] Building on this, Fred Moten argues that this inability to be a mother and to be mothered produces an impossible distinction between maternity and reproduction. He describes this convergence as "a *being maternal* that is indistinguishable from a *being material*."[11] This is to say that the black mother cannot be thought outside the parameters of commodification—an equivalence that allows us to see the ways that the specter of the lost mother haunts blackness. The brown mother, too, has been disappeared. Thought in tandem, these black and brown maternal absences occur in relation to global capitalism, specifically in relation to the movement of bodies and the effect that this has on kinship. We know that the unequal flow of global capital requires some forms of migration that break families apart, which we can imagine as an extension of slavery's violent wrenching of mothers from their offspring. This is to say that that the specter of the lost mother haunts black and brown fleshiness in ways that Saidiya Hartman describes as the "gendered afterlife of slavery and global capitalism."[12] In these contexts, capitalism relies on black and brown flesh to be material (and maternal), while denying access to maternal labor to black and brown children. Joshua Chambers-Letson describes this paradox succinctly: "As a result of the commodification of black women's reproductive labor, their singularity and subjectivity is often occluded behind the (misnomer) of 'the mother.' That is, they disappear behind the name 'mother,' 'maid,' or, worse, 'mammy.'"[13]

While the absence of the black and brown mother might produce generative forms of queer kinship, which E. Patrick Johnson describes as "reconfiguring of the very notion of 'family,'" thinking with the psychoanalytic, I am interested in the ways that this complication of kinship introduces melancholy into the maternal dynamic.[14] Importantly, this is a very different form of melancholy than that produced by the foreclosure of the mother, which the Oedipal complex enacts. In Judith Butler's description of the mother as the original site of the subject's desire, we see the work of taboo and melancholy. She writes: "If the mother is the original desire, and that may well be true for a range of late-capitalist household dwellers, then that is a desire both produced and prohibited within the terms of that cultural context."[15] This forbidden desire, in turn, constitutes the subject through its quest for what can never be fulfilled. However, desire, in these terms—threaded through with the (im)possibility of omnipotence and subjectivity—is not the form of attachment to the mother that is at work in brown jouissance.

Grappling with this missing black and brown maternal as a "person of color" offers a unique set of challenges because one must also contend with whiteness, which produces its own psychic distortions. Anne Anlin Cheng argues that having to assimilate to a white culture produces melancholy at the unattainability of whiteness for black and brown subjects, while the simultaneous repression of the necessity of racial otherness (to sustain white dominance) manifests itself as melancholy as well. Cheng writes:

> The terms thus denote a complex process of racial rejection and desire on the parts of whites and nonwhites that expresses itself in abject and manic forms. On the one side, white American identity and its authority is secured through the melancholic introjections of racial others that it can neither fully relinquish nor accommodate and whose ghostly presence nonetheless guarantees its centrality. On the other side, the racial other . . . also suffers from racial melancholia whereby his or her racial identity is imaginatively reinforced through the introjections of a lost, never-possible perfection, an inarticulable loss that comes to inform the individual's sense of his or her own subjectivity.[16]

In these formations of melancholy, whiteness (unsurprisingly) takes the place of the father, and the mother (again) becomes coded as the racial other. Through this we can read the black and brown mother as doubly repressed.

This form of motherlessness does not revolve around taboo but on reconciling with one's fleshiness and the mutability of selfhood. The resistance of the object, as Moten describes it, is also the space of attachment to absent brown and black mothers and the arena of brown jouissance. Here, we remember Moten's discussion of the maternal trace on the commodity. Moten writes, "This presence of the commodity within the individual is an effect of reproduction, a trace of maternity. Of equal importance is the containment of a certain personhood within the commodity that can be seen as the commodity's animation by the material trace of the maternal—a palpable hit or touch, a bodily and visible phonographic inscription."[17] What Moten's suggestion about the relationship between animation and materiality tells us is that these maternal traces, embodied in various formations of selfhood and expressed through aesthetic excesses, can be apprehended by paying attention to the sensual. Here, we can find black and brown maternal absence and the traces of attachment that emerge from this lacuna in the multiple permutations of relational selfhood that we find in brown jouissance. Thinking the black and brown m/Other requires that we attend to sensuality, aesthetics, and embodiment. Brown jouissance, then, could also be read as a project of recovery and survival. In finding permutations of selfhood that exceed the "I," we come close to the missing matter of these black and brown mothers.

This space of difference and coexistence, I argue, resides in thinking about the black and brown mother as a place, an *elsewhere* that is always adjacent to black and brownness and accessible through the sensual.[18] This elsewhere registers the black and brown mother as a figure akin to Kara Keeling's black femme and Nguyen Tan Hoang's Asian male bottom, who Hoang writes, "cannot be accommodated or made to make sense within commonsense regimes of sexuality [and] sociality.... This failure of intelligibility is due to her status... that exceeds conventional organizations of subjecthood based on the requirements of compulsory heterosexuality."[19] To think the mother as a place, not a void, works toward a framework of generativity, fleshiness, and sensuality. Black and brown mothers have haunted the pages of this book, sometimes appearing and sometimes absent, but always hovering. Here, in lieu of trying to discern *who* a mother might be, I focus on *what* it might mean to locate her as an elsewhere, a formulation that enables us to think of her as simultaneously present (at least psychically) and not. This move away from Oedipus is also a move away from an ethos of recognition and a temporality of development. Instead, I move toward thinking space and time together to produce geographies of intimacy. This is not about producing the maternal as homeland, but about reaching toward the black and brown maternal as horizon. We might think of this maternal elsewhere in relation to José Esteban Muñoz's description of queerness: "Queerness is a longing that propels us onward, beyond romances of the negative and toiling in the present. Queerness is that thing that lets us feel that this world is not enough, that indeed something is missing."[20]

I see an articulation of this maternal horizon, this elsewhere, in Audre Lorde's *Zami: A New Spelling of My Name*, which registers mother not as lack, but as place. The book's prologue begins with an explicit move away from the Oedipal toward the matrilineal: "I have felt the age-old triangle of mother father child, with the 'I' at its eternal core, elongate and flatten out into the elegantly strong triad of grandmother mother daughter, with the 'I' moving back and forth flowing in either or both directions as needed."[21] Lorde is also quick to connect this mutable "I" to place, writing, "Woman forever. My body, a living representation of other life older longer wiser. The mountains and valleys, trees, rocks. Sand and flowers and water and stone. Made in earth."[22] While *Zami* tells the story of a black lesbian in New York in the 1950s, these moments of reflection are peppered with musings on the mother and her place in the schema of love, hate, and selfhood. The narrative itself begins with Audre (Lorde's eponymous heroine) traveling to her mother's homeland: "When I visited Grenada I saw the root of my mother's powers walking through the streets. I thought, this is the country of my foremothers, my forebearing mothers, those Black island women who defined themselves by what they did."[23] This displacement does not last long, but it sets the stage for the recollection of Audre's early years as she comes to terms with the world that her mother has created for her. In the biomythography, Audre's mother's omnipotence melds together with an eroticism that becomes Audre's lesbianism, creating a sensuous brew of tactile mother love, lesbian desire, and diasporic yearning. Some of Audre's memories of her mother take the form of erotic fantasy: "Years afterward when I was grown, whenever I thought about the way I smelled that day, I would have a fantasy of my mother, her hand wiped dry from the washing, and her apron untied and laid neatly away, looking down upon me lying on the couch, and then, slowly, thoroughly, our touching and caressing each other's most secret places."²⁴ The epilogue, in particular, is explicit about the fusion of the maternal, the erotic, and the spatial:

> Once *home* was a long way off, a place I had never been to but knew out of my mother's mouth. I only discovered its latitudes when Carriacou was no longer my home.
> There it is said that the desire to lie with other women is a drive from the mother's blood.²⁵

Throughout, Lorde speaks not of recognition, but of relating, and not of progress, but of ancestors and children. The mother, here, is more than psychic space of loss, however; she is flesh and possibility; more precisely, she is a condition of possibility—here we might recall Tina Campt's invocation of the conditional tense to speak of black feminist futurity.²⁶ Restoring the spatiality of the mother gives flesh, material, to this possibility.

Lorde's approach to the mother, who is both actual and fantasy, both there and not, is explicitly sensual. She marks this love as erotic in ways that illuminate the impotence of any possible Oedipal narrative. This is to say this mother love illustrates the impossibility of thinking Oedipality—and its resultant structuring of subjectivity and desire—in relation to blackness and brownness while showing us familial dynamics and sensuality (explicitly not sexuality) outside of that frame.²⁷ One could stop at this suggestion of incest, but that would be to insist on a regime of sexuality, a regime that cannot find orientation outside of possession or desire. Lorde, herself, offers clues toward this different place by mobilizing the figure of the woman loving woman. Toward the end of *Zami*, she writes, "But that is why to this day I believe that there have always been Black dykes around—in the sense of powerful and woman-oriented women—who would rather have died than use that name for themselves. And that includes my momma."²⁸ Angelique Nixon describes Lorde's choice to "explore her identity and her home through her maternal line and the stories of women in Carriacou . . . as the foundation of her identity as a black lesbian warrior poet."²⁹ And, the term *Zami*, as Lorde and Nixon remind us, "is a Carriacou word for women who worked together as friends and lovers," which is to say as participants in an economy that did not revolve around men.³⁰

Into the vacuum of theorization on black female sexuality that Evelynn Hammonds and Hortense Spillers decry, Lorde describes a sensual, political black lesbianism.[31] Interspersed between poems about the agony of slow black death in *The Black Unicorn*, Lorde dwells on different forms of touch between women. In "Woman" Lorde writes,

> I dream of a place between your breasts
> to build my house like a haven
> where I plant crops
> in your body[32]

In "Woman," the "I" desires touch, to sow it desires to make "you" productive. In another poem, "Meet," Lorde writes, "Tasting your ruff down to sweetness" and "Or the taste of each other's skin as it hung / From our childhood mouths."[33] Here, the "you" is devoured through the mouth. In these moments when Lorde calls up hands and tongues and textures and tastes, she is calling forth an embodied and active sensuality.

Sarah Chinn argues that Lorde's explicit descriptions of lesbian sex are a direct manifestation of what Lorde describes in "Uses of the Erotic" in that they are "about a sensory connection with others, 'the sharing of joy, whether physical, emotional, psychic, or intellectual,' that embraces the entire body, that 'flows through and colors . . . life with a kind of energy that heightens and sensitizes and strengthens all . . . experience.' The erotic infuses and intensifies the experience of the body, linking the sensory with the spiritual."[34] These spaces suggest alternative ways to consider how to approach the mother and the lesbian. In "Meet," for example, Lorde interrupts descriptions of sex to reference children—

> as our hands touch and learn
> from each others hurt.
> Taste my milk in the ditches of Chile and Ouagadougou . . . now you
>   are my child and my mother

—and thereby brings together the mother and the black lesbian in an unexpected way.[35] Lorde's insistence on having sensuality, desire, woman loving, and politics meet in the same space is deliberate. The radicality of insisting on a language of sex for queer black female bodies rescripts the ways that coalition might be enacted; it renders the sensual political in large part, because this queer feminine—here, it is the mother, the lesbian, and the woman-loving woman—offers a challenge to epistemologies of sexuality.

In their estrangement from a phallocentric economy, the mother, the lesbian, and the woman-loving woman sit alongside each other, each providing versions of what I read, using Denise Ferreira da Silva, as Luce Irigaray's female lover. Da Silva describes this site as one of radical potential: "Irigaray's 'female lover' is a productive critical tool because she is also in her flesh . . . her uncomprehensible desire, that sexual which is the female's unresolvable (undeterminable, unpredictable, unmeasurable) power. What can she allow us to say that has not been said before?"[36] Da Silva draws on Irigaray because her critique of phallocentrism insists on positioning the body as the site of excess and theory. Instead of a linguistic rejoinder to masculinity, she offers the power of the body and its materiality through a reordered sensorium and sensuality. In *Zami*, this emphasis on a femininity with appetites occurs through economies that are outside of a white and phallocentric order—through the diasporic mother and the lesbian: remember the way that Lorde explicitly brings mother into a lineage of queer femininity. This set of crossings is important because it illustrates the force of the critiques that blackness, brownness, and queerness offer while also gesturing toward epistemologies that center these feminine figurations. This disruption is a mode of insurgence. As Joshua Chambers-Letson reminds us: "To stand in the flesh, in this capacity, is to transform (and perform) the ungendering of black (female) flesh into a condition of possibility, thus opening up new ways of doing gender, being a being, being black, being in the body, and being together."[37]

The queer feminine is an expansive idea. On the one hand, I use it to describe black and brown femininities that are estranged from normative modes of white femininity. On the other hand, I am also arguing that the queer feminine is what is activated when we look to the mother as horizon, as elsewhere. The queerness of the queer feminine is in some ways akin to E. Patrick Johnson's description of "quare" in relation to "queer":

On the one hand, my grandmother uses "quare" to denote something or someone who is odd, irregular, or slightly off kilter—definitions in keeping with traditional understandings and uses of "queer." On the other hand, she also deploys "quare" to connote something excessive— something that might philosophically translate into an excess of discursive and epistemological meanings grounded in African American cultural rituals and lived experience.[38]

Johnson's attention to both the non-normative and the excessive as well as his attention to quare as a "theory in the flesh" speak directly to the queer feminine as born from sensual excess.

Kyla Wazana Tompkins reads quare as a call for a methodological shift toward materiality. Tompkins writes, "Such a methodology, I argue, necessarily shifts us away from a focus on representation, linked as it is to visuality and textuality, and toward what [Johnson] terms materiality, understood here as the tense and ongoing work of living within the thickened experiences and sensory orders of daily life."[39] In thinking with method, we see that tarrying with the queer feminine is part of the work of prioritizing the sensual because queer femininity signals a shift away from an economy of recognition toward multiple embodied modes of being-with. This is a "thickening" of the relation to the mother—an enfleshment of sorts. Middle English offers a term for this regrowth of flesh—*regendre*—and, indeed, a regendering is what is at stake here.[40]

Returning to Lorde, we feel this regendering and sensual knowledge production in her description of her mother combing her hair in *Zami*:

> I remember the warm mother smell caught between her legs, and the intimacy of our physical touching nestled inside of the anxiety/pain like a nutmeg nestled inside its covering of mace.
>
> The radio, the scratching comb, the smell of petroleum jelly, the grip of her knees and my stinging scalp all fall into—*the rhythms of a litany, the rituals of Black women combing their daughters' hair.*[41]

This embodied move toward her mother—as a recollection of care, ritual, and pedagogy—is the space of the queer feminine. Lorde fills this memory with a whirl of smells, sounds, and touches. She marks herself and her mother as part of a multigenerational, diasporic selfhood and illuminates the contours of an intimacy that insists on the material. The queer feminine inheres in this fleshy mode of knowledge-making and self-production, and this transmission of knowledge is endless—perpetually inviting people to feel with this experience and insert themselves into this lineage.

I ask us to dwell on queer femininity in order to highlight what comes from thinking with sensuality, fleshiness. This order of knowledge, I argue, is spatial because it resists the mandate of depth even as it traffics in self-creation. This is a spatiality of possibility, of the always-already, of not-quite-return or homeland, of embrace, plurality, spirituality, and sensuality. This transformation enables contemplation of femininity in relation to possibility *and* violence. It is an *elsewhere* to sexuality, to phallocentrism, to white supremacy. It is what emerges from and yet exceeds the pornotrope.

What this reimaged dynamic especially shows us is that race disrupts attempts to think sexuality as the primary frame of difference.[42] This modification is not just about inclusion, but a question of epistemology. The epistemological whiteness of sexuality is what separates discourses of incest from those of natality, according to Gillian Harkins. Race becomes appended to the discourse of the population, which keeps sexuality implicitly coded as white and relegates black and brownness to its excesses.[43] Foucault's *History of Sexuality*, then, becomes, as Rey Chow points out, a history of the ascendancy of whiteness.[44] These histories, in turn, offer insight into why the black and brown mother and queer femininity disrupt sexuality with sensuality and shift us away from a discourse of desire and individuality toward plural, porous selves and multiple modes of being-with. A queer femininity underlies brown jouissance's movement toward epistemologies of fleshiness. They are epistemologies that operate within the arena of the spatial, mobilizing opacity in lieu of transparency, sensuality instead of recognition, and regendre-ing instead of incest. This movement, I argue, following Britt Rusert's reading of Deleuze, we might read as a form of minor science. She writes:

> As a method that depends on sense perception, continual observations, and a mobile, searching orientation toward the world, there is indeed something fugitive about empiricism itself. Fugitive science makes good

on the active experimentalism of experience that lies at the heart of empiricism: it reanimates the Latin sense of experiment, *experior*: to test or to try. Instead of hardening observations and trials into theorems and facts, it tarries in the multitude of experience, continually poses problems (for the state and the state of slavery), and transforms the passivity of knowledge production into the activity of invention.[45]

An invitation to think with the flesh, with the sensual, then, is an invitation to make new knowledges and new politics.

ACKNOWLEDGMENTS

To write a book feels like a wondrous thing. This book, in particular, emerges from the generosity of those around me. I am deeply grateful for those who have shared their work, their thoughts, and their lives with me.

First, I would like to thank Lyle Ashton Harris, Kara Walker, Judy Chicago, Mickalene Thomas, Xandra Ibarra, Amber Hawk Swanson, Cheryl Dunye, Carrie Mae Weems, Nao Bustamante, Patty Chang, and Maureen Catbagan. Some of these artists I know and others I do not, but all have created works of art to inspire radical forms of thought.

I have also had the benefit of being enmeshed in several supportive academic and intellectual communities. The early stages of this book were developed in conversations with the Sexual Politics and Sexual Poetics Collective, so I thank them for listening and nudging the project forward: Kadji Amin, Katie Brewer Ball, Ramzi Fawaz, Zakiyyah Iman Jackson, Uri McMillan, Roy Pérez, Jennifer Row, Shante Smalls, Jordan Stein, and Damon Young. At Washington University in St. Louis, I thank my colleagues in the Women, Gender, and Sexuality Studies Department: Rebecca Wanzo, Trevor Sangrey, Linda Nicholson, Bahia Munem, Julie Moreau, Jeffrey McCune, Donna Kepley, Andrea Friedman, Mary Ann Dzuback, Amy Cislo, Rachel Brown, Barbara Baumgartner, Cynthia Barounis, and Jaime Ake. The Voice and Sexuality working group has been a particular source of delight and thought over the past several years, thanks to: Anna Bialek, Cynthia Barounis, Pat Burke, Denise Gill, Dana Logan, Jasmine Mahmoud, Paige McGinley, Rhaisa Williams. Thanks to Rebecca Wanzo and Jean Allman at the Center for Humanities for providing generous support for the project. I am also grateful for support from Pannill Camp, Adrienne Davis, Diane Lewis, Anne-Marie McManus, Mel Micir, Anca Parvelescu, Anika Walke and the wonderful students I have been fortunate enough to share classroom space with. This project was being completed as I began my position at George Washington University, but I am already grateful to colleagues there for thinking with me as it neared completion. Within the broader reaches of academia, I have also benefited enormously from friendship, guidance, and conversations with John Andrews, Anjali Arondekar, Anna Bialek, Tyler Bradway, Jayna Brown, Josh Chambers-Letson, Rebecca Colesworthy, Niamh Duggan, David Eng, Danny Fox, Leon Hilton, Summer Kim, Isaac Nakhimovksy, Tavia Nyong'o, Ann Pellegrini, Roy Pérez Joe Pierce, Alex Pittman, Emily Owens, Elliot Powell, Chitra Ramalingam, Ivan Ramos, Jordy Rosenberg, Riley Snorton, Gus Stadler, Karen Tongson, Hentyle Yapp, Jeanne Vacarro, and Nasser Zakariya.

There are also several individuals who have spent hours reading, discussing, and thinking about brown jouissance. They have given me citations, nudges, and inspiration. Most importantly, however, they have also spoken to me about other things, enriched my life with their presence, and provided an abundance of celebration. For their friendship, I thank Kadji Amin, Emily Bolton, Larissa Chernock, Stephanie Clare, Ankur Ghosh, Michael Gillespie, Uri McMillan, Paige McGinley, Jennifer Nash, and Jasbir Puar. However, I share my deepest debt of gratitude to Maureen Catbagan, who has been integral to the shaping of this book and its larger political project. Through countless hours of conversation, many, many drafts, many dinners, and much art, Maureen has pushed me toward the forest, toward the parts of thought that I found scariest and hardest. I am grateful for their strength, their generosity, their brilliance, and their care. Where I hesitated, they insisted. This book would not have been possible without their and our collaboration.

This book and this life would not have been possible without the guidance and support of my family, who keep me grounded and also let me see the clouds. Thank you for your care, love, and willingness to share in joy with me, Camille, John, Thomas, and Ashley.

Throughout the writing and thinking process, I have been profoundly grateful to have had the opportunity to share parts of this book with many communities, including: the University of California, Los Angeles, the State University of New York, Stonybrook, Haverford College, Indiana University, Wesleyan University, the Queer Worldings workshop at McGill University, the Center for the Study of Gender and Sexuality at New York University, Northwestern University, the Sex Conference at University of Pennsylvania, the Hortense Spillers Symposium at Cornell University, George Washington University, Illinois State University-

Normal, Rutgers University, Georgetown University, Saint Lawrence University, University of North Carolina, University of Washington, York University and the Sexuality Studies Institute, the Feminist Theory workshop in Dubrovnik, Croatia, the State University of New York, Cortland, the American Studies Association, the National Women's Studies Association, and the Association for the Arts of the Present. I am enormously grateful for the conviviality, suggestions, and intellectual engagement that emerged in these spaces.

I am also extremely grateful to have received funding from a Ruth Landes Memorial Fellowship in 2015. This grant enabled me to take a year's leave, which gave me mental space to dream up and begin this project. A 2017 Arts Writer's Grant from the Creative Capital | Andy Warhol Foundation Arts Writers Grant Program gave me more time and money to complete the project. I am deeply grateful to these funding bodies for believing in the project and supporting it materially. I am also grateful to Washington University in St. Louis and The George Washington University for allowing me to take advantage of these grants and to the Center for Humanities for funding summer research on the project.

Finally, *Sensual Excess: Queer Femininity and Brown Jouissance* has benefited enormously from support from New York University Press. I thank Josh Chambers-Letson, Tavia Nyong'o, and Ann Pellegrini for their sustained conversations about the book and including it in the Sexual Cultures series. Eric Zinner, Lisha Nadkarni, and Dolma Ombadykow have guided the book through the publication process with grace and speed. I am grateful for comments for reviewers, anonymous and not, and indexer Josh Rutner. I thank Nao Bustamante, Xandra Ibarra, Amber Hawk Swanson, Maureen Catbagan, and the Guggenheim Museum for giving me permission to reproduce their works of art. Portions of the manuscript have been published in altered form elsewhere. A version of the introduction appears as "Surface-Becoming: Lyle Ashton Harris and Brown Jouissance," *Women and Performance* 28, no. 1 (2018): 34–45, a version of the first chapter appears as "Queering Sugar: Kara Walker's Sugar Sphinx and the Intractability of Black Female Sexuality," *Signs: Journal of Women and Culture* 42, no. 1 (2016): 1–22; and small portions of "On the Orgasm of the Species: Female Sexuality and Sexual Difference," *Feminist Review* 102 (2012): 1–20 appear in chapters two and four. I am grateful for permission to reprint portions of those essays here.

NOTES

INTRODUCTION
1. Moten, *In the Break*, 104.
2. Griffin, *If You Can't Be Free, Be a Mystery*.
3. Jones, "The 'Eternal Return,'" 950.
4. Ibid.
5. Jennifer Nash and José Esteban Muñoz both use the term "ecstasy" in reference to feeling beyond the self. For a genealogy of ecstasy see Nash, *The Black Body in Ecstasy*, and Muñoz, *Cruising Utopia*.
6. Deavere Smith, *Lyle Ashton Harris*, 1.
7. Ibid., 2.
8. Deleuze and Guattari, *A Thousand Plateaus*.
9. Alice Jardine criticizes Deleuze for his appropriation of the feminine position in his concept of becoming-woman. In "Woman in Limbo: Deleuze and His Br(others)," Jardine argues that the feminine is posited as a step toward freedom, but its materiality is never considered as a thing unto itself. Further, Gayatri Chakravorty Spivak addresses the Eurocentric nature of Deleuze's project in her essay "Can the Subaltern Speak?"
10. Deavere Smith, *Lyle Ashton Harris*, 7.
11. Ibid.
12. Weheliye, *Habeaus Viscus*, 113.
13. Berlant, *Cruel Optimism*, 100.
14. Spillers, "Mama's Baby, Papa's Maybe," 227. Here and elsewhere, emphasis in original unless otherwise noted.
15. Ibid., 206.
16. An initial inquiry into work in Afro-pessimism would include Sexton, "The Social Life of Social Death," and Wilderson, *Red, White, and Black*, which are widely hailed as some of the inaugural texts of the movement.
17. Weheliye, *Habeaus Viscus*, 91.
18. Ibid., 91.
19. Ferguson, *Aberrations in Black*, 13.
20. Ibid., 14.
21. Morgensen, *Spaces between Us*, 31.
22. Spillers, "Mama's Baby, Papa's Maybe," 206; King, "Interview with Dr. Tiffany Lethabo King."

23 Musser, *Sensational Flesh*.
24 Weheliye, *Habeaus Viscus*, 2.
25 Fleetwood, *Troubling Vision*, 29.
26 Ibid., 112.
27 Ibid.
28 Muñoz, "Feeling Brown, Feeling Down," 676.
29 Ibid., 679.
30 Ibid., 684.
31 León, "Forms of Opacity."
32 Britt Rusert's *Fugitive Science: Empiricism and Freedom in Early African American Culture* offers another recent example of how one might begin to approach this process.
33 Stallings, *Funk the Erotic*, 3.
34 Ibid., 6.
35 Ibid., 7.
36 Ibid., 7/8.
37 Braunstein, "Desire and Jouissance in the Teachings of Lacan," 104.
38 Jacques Lacan, quoted in ibid., 107, fn. 8.
39 Braunstein, "Desire and Jouissance," 107.
40 Da Silva, *Toward a Global Idea of Race*, 31.
41 Glissant, *Poetics of Relation*, 190.
42 Chen, *Animacies*; Tompkins, *Racial Indigestion*; McMillan, *Embodied Avatars*.
43 Holland, Ochoa, and Tompkins, "On the Visceral," 392.
44 Bradley, "Other Sensualities," 130.
45 Amin, Musser, and Pérez, "Queer Form," 234.
46 Doyle and Getsy, "Queer Formalisms."
47 Musser, *Sensational Flesh*, 21–2.
48 Silverman, *The Miracle of Analogy*.
49 Buse, "Photography Degree Zero," 42.
50 Among others in this constellation I am thinking here of Nash, *The Black Body in Ecstasy*; Horton-Stallings, *Funk the Erotic*; Rodríguez, *Sexual Futures, Queer Gestures, and Other Latina Longings*; and Cruz, *The Color of Kink*.
51 See, for example, Boyarin, "What Does the Jew Want?": Fuss, *Identification Papers*; Pellegrini, *Performance Anxieties*; and Walton, *Fair Sex, Savage Dreams*.
52 Fanon, *Black Skin, White Masks*; Memmi, *The Colonizer and the Colonized*; Cheng, *The Melancholy of Race*; Eng, Kazanjian, and Butler, *Loss*.
53 Luciano, *Arranging Grief*, 12.
54 Ferguson, *The Reorder of Things*, 6.
55 Ibid., 34.
56 Musser, "Specimen Days: Diversity, Labor, and the University."

CHAPTER 1. EATING OUT
 1 *The Dinner Party*, which had been in the making since 1974, was bankrolled largely by Chicago and various feminist fundraising efforts, which asked

contributors to "give the world women's history for the new year." It opened on March 14, 1979, at the San Francisco Museum of Modern Art. Despite being a popular attraction, other museums were unwilling to host the installation, so feminist community organizations stepped in to organize a grassroots tour. As Jane Gerhard writes in her history of the installation, "The unexpected success of its non-museum tour spoke unmistakably of the appeal of *The Dinner Party* and its feminist messages to audiences. One explanation for *The Dinner Party*'s success despite its across-the-board rejection by elite cultural institutions can be attributed to its translation of feminism—specifically, women's right to a heroic past—into an engaging message that spoke to a range of women not typically found under the banner of feminism" (*The Dinner Party*, 181).
2 Tompkins, *Racial Indigestion*, 5.
3 Ibid., 3.
4 Irigaray, "When Our Lips Speak Together," 209.
5 Ibid., 215–216.
6 Jagose, *Lesbian Utopics*, 30.
7 In "Irigaray's Body Symbolic," Margaret Whitford outlines the different stances on Irigaray's essay. Irigaray has been critiqued for morphological essentialism because the lips suggest that she is "positing a real body, unmediated by the symbolic order, which women might recognize as their own" (99). Elizabeth Grosz, however, argues that Irigaray is creating a new form of language: "She is creating a discourse to contest or combat other, prevailing discourses" (quoted in Whitford, 9). Taking both of these stances into account, Whitford writes that it is precisely this indecipherability that gives the essay its power: "What is important about the two lips is not only their literalness, but, above all, *the fact that no one can agree on exactly what they mean*" (98).
8 Huffer, *Are the Lips a Grave?*, 43.
9 Ibid., 45.
10 Ahmed, *Queer Phenomenology*.
11 "Frequently Asked Questions."
12 Gerhard, *The Dinner Party*, 174.
13 Spillers, "Interstices," 78.
14 Rooney and Walker, "A Sonorous Subtlety."
15 In taking on the task of feeding and nurturing children, mammies are *like* mothers, but owing to racial difference and the dynamics of slavery, there is no fear that a mammy could actually replace or be mistaken for the white mother. Instead, the mammy presents an altogether different version of the mother, especially since her servitude often rendered her unavailable to actually care for her own children. Christina Sharpe describes the contradiction of having the mammy serve as a mother figure while also being embedded within a legal circuit of black motherlessness since mammies were property of the white family: "In relation to the 'big black mammy of old' the parental function is repeatedly displaced as the fate of the black child is legally bound to the condition of the enslaved mother, as the

ability to mother that child is denied her, *or can always be denied her*, and as the woman legally denied the rights and functions of mother is made to do with the mothering of the white children" (*Monstrous Intimacies*, 165).

16 Micki McElya writes, "The myth of the faithful slave lingers because so many white Americans have wished to live in a world in which African Americans are not angry over past and present injustices, a world in which white people were and are not complicit, in which the injustices themselves—of slavery, Jim Crow, and ongoing structural racism—seem not to exist at all" (*Clinging to Mammy*, 3).

17 In her analysis of the interviews with former slaves conducted by the Federal Writers' Project of the Works Progress Administration, Cheryl Thurber discusses the absence of mammies and the actual dynamics of care-giving in the antebellum South:

> Very few former slaves mentioned any older relatives who had the role of mammy in antebellum times. In fact, they more commonly mentioned former slaves as having been raised by the white mistress as opposed to the adult black women who took care of the white children. The few references to mammy by former slaves usually include a story about the special protection the role provided, or the continued concern shown by the white folks toward their former mammy. . . . It is likely, however, that mammies did exist in the antebellum period, but in much smaller numbers than the mythology would indicate. ("The Development of the Mammy Image and Mythology," 91–92)

Patricia Turner describes this fictional selflessness as enabling an imagined form of happiness in slavery: "Like Aunt Jemima and her turn-of-the-century literary counterparts, these mammies were happily ensconced in the households of white employers. Implicit in each rendition was the notion that these thick-waisted black women were happy with their lot, honored to spend their days and nights caring for white benefactors" (*Ceramic Uncles & Celluloid Mammies*, 51).

18 This frames the affective work that mammies perform for white children as a form of mothering while triangulating the relationship between black mothers and their children with slavery. McElya describes the legacy of this division of naturalizing black maternal labor as love rather than work, writing: "The system of slavery placed a monetary and labor value on black women's production of more laboring black bodies. When black women's work was appropriated by the white household, their care-giving labor was reframed as motherly instinct and love in the figure of the mammy, thus not as work at all" (*Clinging to Mammy*, 82).

19 In her analysis of Harriet Beecher Stowe's *Uncle Tom's Cabin*, which contains one of the first literary representations of the mammy, Kyla Wazana Tompkins argues that the kitchen is central to understanding the forms of interracial intimacy encoded into the figure of the mammy. The kitchen symbolizes the "material life of the body as it is represented in food culture, where, as Gillian Brown has argued, the affective life (the woman's 'domestic sphere') is most closely integrated with

economic life (where the slave labor of producing and processing food occurs)" (*Racial Indigestion*, 107).

20. In addition to Walker, the figure of the mammy has a long history within black feminist art. Kimberly Wallace-Sanders describes her uptake in the 1960s as a type of subversive icon, writing that "the Aunt Jemima image signaled a particular kind of insult for African Americans during the 1960s, one that inspired artists to juxtapose the trademark from the 1890s with the new attitudes and agenda of the 1960s. . . . Essentially they were challenging people to reconsider what might be behind or beneath Aunt Jemima's smile"(*Mammy*, 142).
21. Rooney and Walker, "Sonorous Subtlety."
22. Gopnik "Rarely One for Sugarcoating."
23. Ibid.
24. Smith, "Sugar? Sure, but Salted with Meaning."
25. For an in-depth analysis of the controversy stirred up by the sugar sphinx, see Musser "Queering Sugar."
26. Powers, "Why I Yelled at the Kara Walker Exhibit."
27. Watts, "The Audacity of No Chill."
28. Malone, "What Kara Walker's 'Sugar Baby' Showed Us."
29. Callahan, "Reactions to Kara Walker's *A Subtlety*."
30. Lorde, "Uses of the Erotic," 58.
31. Thompson, "Kara Walker's Desecrated Cemetery for Blackness"; emphasis in original.
32. Sianne Ngai discusses the relationship between animatedness and blackness in *Ugly Feelings*.
33. Musser, *Sensational Flesh*, 102.
34. Pérez, *A Taste for Brown Bodies*, 104.
35. Woodward, *The Delectable Negro*, 9.
36. Ibid., 14.
37. Takagi, "Maiden Voyage," 98.
38. Puar, "Bodies with New Organs," 62.
39. We should note that there are many different arguments about what constitutes the limit of the human. Some position blackness, gender, indigeneity, disability. My point is that this limit is defined in terms of the capacity to choose.
40. Lindsey and Johnson, "Searching for Climax," 185.
41. Ibid., 190.
42. Weheliye, *Habeaus Viscus*, 124.
43. Thompson, "Curatorial Statement."
44. Mintz, *Sweetness and Power*.
45. Nyong'o, "Subtleties of Resistance," 114. For a further critique, see Diehl, "Walker's Dubious Alliance with Domino."
46. Lowe, *The Intimacies of Four Continents*, 1.
47. Ibid.
48. Schuller, "Biopower below and before the Individual."

49 Ibid., 636.
50 Walker and Abumrad, "Live Stream Kara Walker and Jad Abumrad's NYPL Talk."
51 Lowe, *Intimacy of Four Continents*, 18.
52 Nyong'o, "Subtleties of Resistance."
53 Gopnik, "Rarely One for Sugarcoating."
54 Silver, "Kara Walker's 'A Sublety' Proves that Sugar Isn't Always Sweet."
55 Manalasan, "Field Notes."
56 Stallings, *Funk the Erotic*, 6; emphasis in original.

CHAPTER 2. SURFACE PLAY

1 Jennifer Tyburczy has an extended discussion of the history and controversy surrounding Courbet's *The Origin of the World* in *Sex Museums*.
2 Ibid.
3 Williams, *Hardcore*, 49.
4 Smith, "Loud, Proud, and Painted."
5 Cheng, *Second Skin*, 1.
6 Ibid., 11.
7 Ibid., 29.
8 Dailey, "Mickalene Thomas."
9 Thompson, *Shine*.
10 Ibid., 24.
11 Ibid., 33.
12 One might also profitably, but perhaps controversially, discuss the relationship between Thomas's deployment of rhinestones and the early 2000s trend of vajazzling, in which crystals or glitter are affixed to the vulval area for decoration. This trend is more in keeping with particular consumerist ideologists of celebrating particular forms of female sexuality and differs from my reading of Thomas's use of rhinestones as critique, but further work could be done to analyze the differences between the instantiations of bejeweled vulvas.
13 Stallings, *Funk the Erotic*, xii.
14 Ibid., xv.
15 Cheng, *Second Skin*, 13.
16 Ibid., 166.
17 Bradley, "Introduction," 129.
18 For more on surface reading, see Best and Marcus, "Surface Reading."
19 Stockton, "Surfacing (in the Heat of Reading)," 8.
20 Stockton, "Reading as Kissing, Sex with Ideas." Here and elsewhere, emphasis in original unless otherwise noted.
21 Ibid.
22 Walker, "Mickalene Thomas."
23 From Dailey, "Mickalene Thomas."
24 Ibid.
25 Thomas, "A Different Type of Beauty."

26 Rosenberg, "Mickalene Thomas Rediscovers Her Mother—and Her Muse."
27 Ibid.
28 Landers, Interviews Mickalene Thomas.
29 Lorde, *Zami*, 7.
30 Freeman, *Time Binds*, 62.
31 Ibid., 64.
32 Garber describes her as "a pivotal character connecting lesbian feminism and queer theory; in her multiple self-positioning as 'Black lesbian feminist warrior poet mother,' she stands historically and rhetorically at the crux of the so-called generation gap between lesbian-feminist and queer theoretical notions of identity" (*Identity Poetics*, 97). See also Musser, "Re-Membering Lorde."
33 Alice Walker's definition of a "Womanist" from *In Search of Our Mothers' Gardens*, xi.
34 Hemmings, *Why Stories Matter*, 39.
35 Ibid., 54.
36 Holland, *The Erotic Life of Racism*, 59.
37 For more on the confounding history of the female orgasm, see Lloyd, *The Case of the Female Orgasm*.
38 Koedt, "Myth of the Vaginal Orgasm," 424.
39 Gerhard, *Desiring Revolution*, 2.
40 Koedt, "Myth of the Vaginal Orgasm," 423.
41 Gerhard, *Desiring Revolution*, 99.
42 Wittig, "The Straight Mind," 32. For a more in-depth elaboration of the construction of female sexual difference vis-à-vis orgasm, see Musser "On the Orgasm of the Species." Some of the material from that essay is reprinted here.
43 Walker, "Coming Apart."
44 Nash, *The Black Body in Ecstasy*, 131.
45 Sharpley-Whiting, *Black Venus*; Somerville *Queering the Color Line*.
46 Gibson "Clitoral Corruption."
47 Somerville, "Scientific Racism," 253–254.
48 Ibid., 256.
49 Ibid., 262. Somerville expands on this in *Queering the Color Line*.
50 We can also think about the history of black and brown clitorises as the object of debates within anthropological circles in relation to rituals of genital cutting. Those in opposition to the practice argue that it should be considered a mutilation of the female body and an attempt by patriarchal societies to control female sexuality. Others, however, argue that criticisms of the practice are not actually manifestations of concern for women, but attempts to further portray countries where this takes place as barbaric and backward. Though these discussions foreground the difficulty of understanding "universal" rights and norms while also bringing attention to the epistemological violences of colonialism, they also persist in objectifying black and brown women's sexuality. They are objects of study, rather than agents of action. See Hayes, "Female Genital Mutilation": Kirby, "Out of Africa."

51 Traub, "Psychomorphology of the Clitoris," and Halberstam, *Female Masculinity*.
52 Halberstam, *Female Masculinity*, 59.
53 Williams, "Cinema's Sex Acts," 10.
54 Chinn, "Feeling Her Way," 181.
55 Lorde, "Uses of the Erotic."
56 Lorde "Eye to Eye," 174.
57 Nash, "Practicing Love."
58 Ibid., 3.
59 Ibid., 10.
60 Ibid., 10, 11.
61 This is from *Our Bodies, Ourselves*, quoted in Musser "From Our Body to Your Selves," 95.
62 Lorde, *The Cancer Journals*, 25.
63 Bersani and Phillips, *Intimacies*.
64 Ibid., 85.
65 Ibid., 86.
66 Lorde, "Uses of the Erotic," 55.
67 Ibid., 56.
68 Ibid., 55.
69 Landers, Interview.
70 Wyma, "Mickalene Thomas."
71 Walker, "Womanism."
72 Nash, "Practicing Love," 9.

CHAPTER 3. DEEP LISTENING, BELONGING, AND THE PLEASURES OF BROWN JOUISSANCE

1 Rodríguez, "Viscous Pleasures and Unruly Feminisms," 10; Ramos, "Spic(y) Appropriations."
2 Ramos, "Spic(y) Appropriations," 2.
3 Ibid.
4 Ibid., 5.
5 Ibid., 17.
6 Rodríguez," Viscous Pleasures," 10; Ramos, "Spic(y) Appropriations," 15.
7 Rodríguez, "Viscous Pleasures," 10.
8 Ibid., 11.
9 Hollibaugh and Moraga, "What We're Rolling Around in Bed With," 58.
10 Ibid., 59.
11 Ibid.
12 Ibid., 60.
13 Swanson and Ibarra, artist's statement for *Untitled Fucking*.
14 Bersani, "Is the Rectum a Grave?" 212.
15 Ibid., 212. Here and elsewhere, emphasis in original unless otherwise noted.
16 Ibid., 222.

17 Butler, *Gender Trouble*, 97.
18 Braunstein, "Desire and Jouissance in the Teachings of Lacan," 110.
19 Butler, "The Body Politics of Julia Kristeva," 108.
20 Silverman, "Girl Love," 8.
21 De Lauretis, *The Practice of Love*, 190.
22 The fervor over Rich's essay led to a move to separate lesbianism from feminism in deep ways. We see this desire for separation in both Butler's and Sedgwick's work. In her later reflections, Butler situates the text as part of a tradition of critique—a critique of the heterosexist assumptions of feminist theory and an attempt to reconcile gay and lesbian studies with feminism. In "Against Proper Objects," Butler writes that the text was "the acerbic culmination of that history of unease and anger within feminism" (2). Feminism, according to Butler, was most concerned with elaborating the binary between "men" and "women." This binary, which was presented as irreversible, rested on "the implicit and compulsory presumption of heterosexuality," and it "posited relations of complementarity or asymmetry between its terms in ways that only shored up, without marking, the heterosexist assumptions of the paradigm" (2). On the other hand, Eve Sedgwick's introduction to *Between Men* describes the book as an intervention into feminist scholarship, a "feminist restructuring of a whole range of disciplines according to a relatively small number of powerful axioms. . . . I found oppressive the hygienic way in which a variety of different institutional, conceptual, political, ethical, and emotional contingencies promised (threatened?) to line up together so neatly in the development of a femiocentric field of women's studies in which subjects, paradigms, and political thrust of research, as well as the researchers themselves, might all be identified with the female" (vii).
23 Vannier, Currie, and O'Sullivan write:
    Part of the popularity of MILF videos is the appeal of female actors who demonstrate more sexual confidence and agency. As women in MILF videos are older than women in Teen videos and likely more sexually experienced, it is possible that they engage in more dominant or powerful behavior in relation to men than do their younger counterparts. By contrast, female actors in the Teen videos may be more likely to be portrayed as naïve, hesitant, and sexually passive as a result of their inexperience, and thus are depicted as having less power in a sexual encounter than their male partners and compared to female actors in the MILF category. ("Schoolgirls and Soccer Moms," 265)
24 Taormino writes:
    In theory, Mommy may have different qualities and a unique history compared to Daddy, but she's just as significant a figure (if not actually *more* significant) in everyone's life. No matter what your sexual orientation is, Mommy is every child's first love, first object of devotion, and the center of its universe. We are often at our most vulnerable and needy with our mothers. . . . So why do so many choose to do all that with Daddy? It can't be that

we've resolved all our issues with Mommy. Is she too intimate, too strong, too powerful an archetype to play with, to embody, to desire? ("The Rise of MILFs and Mommies in Sexual Fantasy Material," n.p.)

Taormino goes on to hypothesize that misogyny might be underlying our generally collective rejection of the mother. If the father represents power and the state, what does the mother represent? Taormino ends her essay with a suggestion that we think the mommy in multiple forms: "That's the great thing about a mommy: She can be a gentle, loving mentor or a stern spank-you-over-her-knee disciplinarian. Mommy's complex like that. So isn't it about time that Mommy got her moment in the spotlight?"

25 Doerr, "Making Space around the Beloved."
26 Sedgwick, "Anality: Notes from the Front."
27 We might think about Coxx's use of *mamí* in relation to Rodríguez's discussion of "sexual archives flavored by attachments and memory" (*Sexual Futures*, 131).
28 Braunstein, "Desire and Jouissance," 111.
29 Nancy, *Coming*, 21.
30 Kheshti, *Modernity's Ear*, 66.
31 Nancy, *Listening*, 9.
32 Ibid., 14.
33 Hart, "That Was Then."
34 Butler, *Bodies that Matter*, 88.
35 Scott articulates this as the rape of the black woman and the castration of the black man, but I think that we can position the rape of the white woman within this lexicon (*Extravagant Abjection*, 131). Following Fanon, we see that the idea of a black man raping a white woman is the frequent motivator for castration and lynching.
36 Ibid., 129.
37 Declue, "Let's Play," 224.
38 Ibid.
39 Ibid., 228.
40 Hoang, *View from the Bottom*, 17.
41 Ibid., 113.
42 Ibid., 9.
43 Rodríguez, *Sexual Futures*, 54.
44 Ibid., 55.
45 Ibid., 59.
46 Ibid., 56.
47 Scott, *Extravagant Abjection*, 166.
48 Rodríguez, *Sexual Futures*, 60.
49 Scott, *Extravagant Abjection*, 163.
50 Kristeva, *Powers of Horror*, 8.
51 Scott, *Extravagant Abjection*, 9.
52 Ibid., 8.

53 McMillan, *Embodied Avatars*, 7.
54 Ibid. 9.
55 Rodríguez, *Sexual Futures*, 131.
56 Rodríguez, *Sexual Futures*, 131.
57 Ramos, "Spic(y) Appropriations," 12.
58 Cvetkovich, "Recasting Receptivity," 134.
59 Ibid., 140.
60 For more on Bustamante's performance, see Arrizón, *Latina Performance*.
61 Anzaldúa, "Borderlands / La Frontera," 75.
62 Ibid., 81.
63 Ibarra, "Tapatío Cock and Strap-On."
64 In her reading of Ibarra's oeuvre in "Forms of Opacity," Christina Léon highlights moments when these performances "fail," which is to say that they register as imagined forms of transparency, rather than transgression. Despite Ibarra's play with opacity, the physical presence of her body has prevented some from reading her otherwise.

CHAPTER 4. PERFORMING WITNESS

1 Weems's use of these images was very controversial. Harvard gave Weems permission to use the archive, but did not want the images displayed without permission. They threatened to sue Weems, but settled on getting a fee each time the images are displayed. We might, however, also think about the ways in which this question about the images of black people is a further instantiation of the problem of commodification. See Murray, "From Here I Saw What Happened and I Cried."
2 Braunstein, "Desire and Jouissance," 112.
3 Wilson, *Hidden Witness*, 2.
4 Fleetwood, *Troubling Vision*, 7.
5 Ibid., 13.
6 Browne, *Dark Matters*.
7 Thinking expansively about this, we might position this representational conundrum of blackness in relation to slavery as explored in Colbert, Patterson, and Levy-Hussen, *The Psychic Hold of Slavery*, and Tillet, *Sites of Slavery*.
8 Spillers, "Mama's Baby, Papa's Maybe," 67.
9 Musser, *Sensational Flesh*.
10 Bernstein, *Racial Innocence*, 188.
11 Nash, *The Black Body in Ecstasy*, 25.
12 In *The Suffering Will Not Be Televised* Rebecca Wanzo discusses these narratives of racial sentimentality to show whose suffering holds cultural weight and whose does not.
13 Doyle, *Hold It against Me*, 120.
14 Ibid., 116.
15 Weems, audio interview.
16 Moten, *In the Break*, 104.

17 Barthes, "The Grain of the Voice," 182, 183.
18 Moten, *In the Break*, 103.
19 Ibid., 197.
20 Wallis, "Black Bodies, White Science," 59.
21 See Sharpe, *In the Wake*, for an analysis of the expressiveness and opacity of the eyes in these portraits in relation to her discussion of redaction.
22 Barthes, *Camera Lucida*.
23 Campt, *Listening to Images*, 4.
24 Ibid.
25 Quashie, *The Sovereignty of Quiet*, 6.
26 Spillers, "All the Things You Could Be by Now," 383.
27 Ibid., 400. Here and elsewhere, emphasis in original unless otherwise noted.
28 Campt, *Listening to Images*, 6.
29 Stephens, *Skin Acts*, 162.
30 I am thinking here of Richard Powell's work in *Cutting a Figure*, where he argues for a history of black portraiture that centers on various modes of self-fashioning. While this is a profitable line of inquiry, I am interested in how Weems's work differs in its investment in thinking collectively.
31 Hartman, *Scenes of Subjection*.
32 Spillers, "Mama's Baby, Papa's Maybe," 66.
33 Ibid., 67.
34 Butler, *Gender Trouble*, 96.
35 Moten, *In the Break*, 104.
36 Marder, *The Mother in the Age of Mechanical Reproduction*, 2.
37 Ibid., 7.
38 Murray, "From Here I Saw," 7.
39 Lorde, "Open Letter to Mary Daly," 95; my emphasis.
40 For an extended discussion of *Zami* in relation to Lorde's theorization of the maternal, see Musser, "Re-Membering Lorde" and "Reading Lorde after Queer."
41 De Veaux, *Warrior Poet*, 151.
42 Lorde, "Dahomey," 10.
43 Wright, *Becoming Black*, 142.
44 Eng, *The Feeling of Kinship*, 13–14.
45 Gopinath, *Impossible Desires*, 11.
46 Ellis, *Territories of the Soul*, 4.
47 Moten, *In the Break*, 203.
48 Ibid., 205.
49 Gumbs, "We Can Learn to Mother Ourselves," 51.
50 Campt, *Listening to Images*, 17; emphases in original.
51 Brewer Ball, "The Veering Escapology of Sharon Hayes and Patty Hearst," 39.
52 Barthes, "Grain of the Voice," 183.
53 Ibid.
54 Moten, *In the Break*, 13.

55 Irigaray, "The Mechanics of Fluids," 109.
56 Crawley, *Blackpentecostal Breath*.
57 Josef Sorrett provides a useful exploration of the presumed relationship between blackness and spirituality in *Spirit in the Dark*.
58 This spirituality also brings us back to Lorde and the erotic. In his theorization of erotic subjectivity, Lyndon Gill draws on the spiritual dimensions of the erotic to argue for an analytic frame that "encourages a recognition of the fact that systems of colonial (as well as neocolonial/imperial) domination depend partly on a tripartite strategy of coercion based on a politics of ontological racial difference, a hierarchy of spiritual rectitude, and a Victorian sense of (sexual) respectability—erotic *subjugation*, as it were. Erotic subjectivity is tasked with providing a postcolonial theoretical response to this mechanism of subjugation" ("Chatting Back an Epidemic," 280). Gill argues that we think the spiritual as a form of critique of prevailing epistemologies. In this way it cannot be reduced to a formation of religion or religiosity. In this I take my cue from Gill, but move away from thinking about individual attachments to spirituality to thinking through spirituality as a connective tissue that brings people together. In parsing Lorde's understanding of the erotic, Sharon Holland writes, "The erotic, to echo Lorde, refers to women's power—a power located not just in an aroused body, but through a body made whole in connection with physical, spiritual, and discursive selves" ("To Touch the Mother's C(o)untry," 212).
59 Pethes, "Psychicones."

CHAPTER 5. WEEPING MACHINES

1 Muñoz, "Feeling Brown, Feeling Down," 676.
2 Ibid., 679.
3 Luciano, *Arranging Grief*, 11.
4 Da Silva, *Toward a Global Idea of Race*, 31.
5 Riskin, "The Defecating Duck," 604.
6 Roach, *The Player's Passion*, 130.
7 Ibid., 133.
8 Westbrook, "Review," 14.
9 Muñoz, "Feeling Brown, Feeling Down," 687.
10 Schuller, "Taxonomies of Feeling," 292. Here and elsewhere, emphasis in original unless otherwise noted.
11 Muñoz, "Feeling Brown: Ethnicity and Affect," 70.
12 Viego, "The Unconscious of Latino/a Studies."
13 Luciano, *Arranging Grief*, 20.
14 For more on pathologies of temporality, see Musser, "Consent, Capacity, and the Non-Narrative."
15 Bustamante, *Neapolitan*.
16 Ibid.
17 Parisi, "Introduction: Abstract Sex," 1.

18 Galison, "Judgment against Objectivity," 332.
19 Masters and Johnson, *Human Sexual Response*, 21–22.
20 Berlant, "On Persistence," 35.
21 Ibid.
22 Rachel Maines argues in *The Technology of Orgasm* that physicians invented the vibrator in order to facilitate the production of orgasm in hysterical women, since orgasm was believed to be one of the ways to calm hysteria.
23 Through this discourse of hysteria, however, we also see a moment of fracturing in the discourses of the brown female body as existing within the realm of sensation. Hysteria produced the black and brown female body as "insensate," which is to say not reactive to pain. Briggs writes, "This ideology had material effects, rendering the ostensibly insensate 'savage' woman fit material for medical experimentation. Hence, African American, immigrant, and poor women played a role in the professional consolidation of obstetrics and gynecology" ("The Race of Hysteria," 262).
24 Ibid., 249.
25 Ibid., 250.
26 Micale, *Approaching Hysteria*.
27 Doyle, *Hold It against Me*, 86.
28 Ibid., 86.
29 Muñoz, *Disidentifications*.
30 Vaccaro, "Handmade," 96–97.
31 Roberts, "Put Your Thing Down," 183.
32 Wilson Bryan, "What's Contemporary about Craft," 8.
33 Vaccaro, "Handmade."
34 Muñoz, "Feeling Brown, Feeling Down," 684.
35 Quiroga, *Tropics of Desire*.
36 Anker writes:
   What I call *melodramatic political discourse* casts politics, policies, and practices of citizenship within a moral economy that identifies the nation state as a virtuous and innocent victim of villainous action. It locates goodness in the suffering of the nation, evil in its antagonists, and heroism in sovereign acts of war and global control coded as expressions of virtue. By evoking intense visceral responses to wrenching injustices imposed upon the nation-state, melodramatic discourse solicits affective states of astonishment, sorrow, and pathos through the scenes it shows of persecuted citizens. It suggests that the redemption of virtue obligates state power to exercise heroic retribution on the forces responsible for national injury. Melodrama depicts the United States as both the feminized, virginal victim and the aggressive, masculinized hero in the story of freedom, as the victim-hero of geopolitics. (*Orgies of Feeling*, 2–3)
37 Doyle, *Hold It against Me*, 86.
38 Mulvey, "Notes on Sirk and Melodrama," 43.

39 Ang, *Watching Dallas*, 79–80.
40 Modleski, "Time and Desire," 24.
41 Alexander, "Modes of Incorporation," 243.
42 Cheng, *The Melancholy of Race*; Eng, Kazanjian, and Butler, *Loss*.
43 Shimizu, *The Hypersexuality of Race*, 18.
44 Ibid., 6.
45 Ibid.
46 Kim, *The Racial Mundane*, 4.
47 Ibid., 179.
48 Hayot, "Chinese Bodies, Chinese Futures," 102–103.
49 Lee, *The Exquisite Corpse of Asian America*, 13.
50 Brintnall, *Ecco Homo*, 36.
51 Doyle, *Hold It against Me*, 85.
52 Ibid., 86.
53 Oishi, "Interview with Patty Chang," 125.
54 Harkins, *Everybody's Family Romance*, 69.
55 Ibid., 8.
56 Ibid., 74.
57 Chang, *In Love*, 2001.
58 Kim, *The Racial Mundane*, 31.
59 Shimikawa, *National Abjection*, 3.
60 Ibid.
61 Berlant, "Lauren Berlant Discusses 'Reading With.'"

CHAPTER 6. FEMME AGGRESSION AND THE VALUE OF LABOR

1 For more on the cinema of distraction, see Gunning, "An Aesthetic of Astonishment."
2 Sontag, "Notes on Camp," 54.
3 Riviere, "Womanliness as Masquerade," 305.
4 Heath, *Joan Riviere and the Masquerade*.
5 Butler, *Gender Trouble*, 174.
6 In her ethnography of drag performers completed in the 1960s, *Mother Camp*, Esther Newton writes, "At the most complex, [drag] is a double inversion that says, 'appearance is an illusion.' Drag says "my 'outside' appearance is feminine, but my essence 'inside' [the body] is masculine." At the same time it symbolizes the opposite inversion; "my appearance 'outside' [my body, my gender] is masculine but my essence 'inside' [myself] is feminine" (103).
7 Ibid., 175. Here and elsewhere, emphasis in original unless otherwise noted.
8 Ibid., 64.
9 Riviere, "Womanliness as Masquerade," 303.
10 Ibid., 306.
11 Ibid.
12 Butler, *Gender Trouble*, 68.

13　Doane, "Masquerade Reconsidered," 33.
14　Ahmed, *The Promise of Happiness*, 66.
15　Pellegrini, *Performance Anxieties*; Walton, *Fair Sex, Savage Dreams*.
16　Wilson, *Gut Feminism*.
17　Halperin, *How to Be Gay*; Muñoz, *Disidentifications*.
18　Muñoz, *Disidentifications*, 128.
19　Butler, *Gender Trouble*, 157.
20　Davis, "Epilogue, Nine Years Later," 270.
21　Duggan and McHugh, "A Fem(me)inist Manifesto," 155.
22　Freeman, *Time Binds*, 63.
23　Keller, "'Was It Right to Love Her Brother's Wife So Passionately?,'" 402.
24　Ibid., 393.
25　Worley, "The Mid-Century Pulp Novel," 120.
26　Catbagan, "Crush."
27　Freud, *Three Essays on the Theory of Sexuality*.
28　Freud, "Fetishism," 152–153.
29　Marriot, "On Racial Fetishism," 215.
30　Apter, *Feminizing the Fetish*, 13.
31　Ibid., 14.
32　One could imagine thinking profitably with Kadji Amin's discussion of racial fetishism in relation to temporality, specifically vis-à-vis the multiple temporalities that race entails. Amin writes, "Racial fetishism is *always* a form of what Elizabeth Freeman has termed *erotohistoriography*, a method of using bodily pleasure to access residues of the past within the present. . . . Racial fetishism demonstrates that the history into which the erotic throws us is as likely to be predictably oppressive as surprisingly counternormative" (*Disturbing Attachments*, 101).
33　Fanon, *Black Skin, White Masks*.
34　Marriot, "On Racial Fetishism," 218.
35　Cheng, "Skin Deep," 39.
36　Marx, *Capital*, 1:163.
37　Ibid., 187.
38　Weeks, *The Problem with Work*, 24.
39　Parreñas, *Servants of Globalization*, 1.
40　Ibid., 61.
41　Ibid., 62.
42　Parreñas uses this term as a framework for her analysis, citing four primary axes of dislocation: partial citizenship, pain of family separation, contradictory class mobility, and non-belonging.
43　Da Silva, "To Be Announced," 49–50.
44　Ibid., 47.
45　Ibid., 53.
46　Ahmed, "Creating Disturbance," 36.
47　See, *The Decolonized Eye*, 116.

48 Balance, "How It Feels to Be Viral Me," 147.
49 Ibid.
50 Ibid, 148.
51 Tadiar, *Things Fall Away*, 234.
52 Ibid.
53 Hong, "Existentially Surplus Women of Color Feminism," 90.
54 Cacho, *Slow Death*, 13.
55 Barrett, *Blackness and Value*, 5.
56 Hong, "Existentially Surplus," 92.
57 San Pablo Burns, *Puro Arte*, 119.
58 Ibid., 119.
59 See, *Decolonized Eye*, xv.
60 Balance, "How It Feels to Be Viral Me," 143.
61 Ibid., 145–146.
62 Ibid., 145.
63 Tadiar, "Remaindered Life," 484.
64 Wesling, "Queer Value," 107.
65 Gayatri Chokravorty Spivak writes, "I say above that 'the full implications of the question of Value posed within the "materialist" predication of the subject cannot yet be realized.' I must now admit what many Marxist theoreticians admit today: that in any theoretical formulation, the horizon of full realization must be indefinitely and irreducibly postponed" ("Scattered Speculations," 92).
66 Moten, *In the Break: The Aesthetics of the Black Radical Tradition*, 9.
67 Ibid., 12.

CODA

1 Spillers, "Mama's Baby, Papa's Maybe," 229.
2 Firestone, *The Dialectic of Sex*, 65.
3 Huffer, *Maternal Pasts, Feminist Futures*, 10.
4 Elissa Marder writes, "Although the physical act of bearing children may be construed (and experienced) as a 'natural act,' the place accorded to the mother in culture and history, and the philosophical, political, and psychological *meaning* of what I shall call 'the maternal function' is anything but natural. . . . I have chosen to use the term 'maternal function' here in order to highlight the technological, and non-anthropomorphic aspects that are often latently inscribed within the concept of birth" (*The Mother in the Age of Mechanical Reproduction*, 2).
5 Johnson, *Mother Tongues*, 4–5.
6 Klein, "Notes on Some Schizoid Mechanisms," 99.
7 Likierman, *Melanie Klein*, 65.
8 Zaretsky, "'One Large Secure, Solid Background,'" 143.
9 Spivak, "Translation as Culture," 13.
10 Spillers, "Mama's Baby, Papa's Maybe," 229.

11 Moten, *In the Break*, 16; emphasis in original.
12 Hartman, "Belly of the World," 167. See also Spillers, "Mama's Baby, Papa's Maybe"; Jennifer Morgan, *Laboring Women*; Weinbaum, *Wayward Reproductions*; Tadiar, *Things Fall Away*.
13 Chambers-Letson, "The Queer of Color's Mother," 49.
14 Johnson, *Appropriating Blackness*, 77.
15 Butler, *Gender Trouble*, 97.
16 Cheng, *The Melancholy of Race*, xi.
17 Moten, *In the Break*, 18.
18 I am indebted to Jacqueline Feldman for pointing out the resonances of thinking with the formation of elsewhere in relation to queerness.
19 Hoang, *A View from the Bottom*, 28.
20 Muñoz, *Cruising Utopia*, 1.
21 Lorde, *Zami*, 7.
22 Ibid.
23 Ibid., 9.
24 Ibid., 78.
25 Ibid., 256.
26 Campt, *Listening to Images*.
27 Though I do not dwell on it in here. We might also think about Cherríe Moraga's writings in the 1980s, collected in both *A Bridge Called My Back* and *Loving in the War Years*, which illustrate the difficulties of being a daughter. Growing up in 1950s and 1960s California as the daughter of a white man and Chicana woman, Moraga narrates an early estrangement from her mother's Mexican heritage and her mother, an estrangement that she comes to recognize through her feminism and lesbianism. *Loving in the War Years*, published in 1983, becomes a love letter to her mother, to Chicanidad, and to lesbianism. In this text, Moraga gives us a way to nuance our understanding of the reparative and its importance to theorizing the mother and difference.
28 Lorde, *Zami*, 15.
29 Nixon, *Resisting Paradise*, 76.
30 Ibid., 77.
31 Hammonds, "Black (W)holes and the Geometry of Black Sexual Difference"; Spillers, "Interstices."
32 Lorde, "Woman," 82.
33 Lorde, "Meet," 33–34.
34 Chinn, "Feeling Her Way," 188.
35 Lorde, "Meet," 33.
36 Da Silva, "To Be Announced," 55–56.
37 Chambers-Letson, *After the Party*, 71.
38 Johnson, "Quare Studies," 2.
39 Tompkins, "You Make Me Feel Right Quare," 61.
40 I am indebted to Maureen Catbagan for pointing this out to me.

41 Lorde, *Zami*, 33.
42 This is an argument that scholars working within queer of color critique have been making for years. See, for example, Eng, *The Feeling of Kinship*; Ferguson, *Aberrations in Black*; Musser, *Sensational Flesh*; Puar, *Terrorist Assemblages*; Reddy, *Freedom with Violence*.
43 Harkins, *Everybody's Family Romance*.
44 Chow, *The Protestant Ethnic and the Spirit of Capitalism*.
45 Rusert, *Fugitive Science*, 20.

BIBLIOGRAPHY

Ahmed, Sara. *The Promise of Happiness*. Durham, NC: Duke University Press, 2010.
———. "Creating Disturbance: Feminism, Happiness, and Affective Differences." In *Working with Affect in Feminist Readings: Disturbing Differences*, edited by Marianne Liljeström and Susanna Paasonen, 31–44. London: Routledge, 2010.
———. *Queer Phenomenology: Orientations, Objects, Others*. Durham, NC: Duke University Press, 2006.
Alexander, Jeffrey. "Modes of Incorporation: Assimilation, Hyphenation, and Multiculturalism as Varieties of Civil Participation." *Sociological Theory* 15, no. 3 (2001): 237–249.
Amin, Kadji. *Disturbing Attachments: Genet, Modern Pederasty, and Queer History*. Durham, NC: Duke University Press, 2017.
Amin, Kadji, Amber Jamilla Musser, and Roy Pérez. "Queer Form: Aesthetics, Race, and the Violences of the Social." *ASAP/Journal* 2, no. 2 (2017): 227–239.
Ang, Ien. *Watching Dallas: Soap Opera and the Melodramatic Imagination*. London: Routledge, 1985.
Anker, Elisabeth Robin. *Orgies of Feeling: Melodrama and the Politics of Freedom*. Durham, NC: Duke University Press, 2014.
Anzaldúa, Gloria. *Borderlands / La Frontera*, 2nd ed. San Francisco: Aunt Lute Books, 1987.
Apter, Emily. *Feminizing the Fetish: Psychoanalysis and Narrative Obsession in Turn-of-the-Century France*. Ithaca, NY: Cornell University Press, 1991.
Arrizón, Alicia. *Latina Performance: Traversing the Stage*. Bloomington: Indiana University Press, 1999.
Balance, Christine Bacareza. "How It Feels to Be Viral Me: Affective Labor and Asian American Youtube Performance." *WSQ: Women's Studies Quarterly* 40, no.1 (2012): 138–152.
Barrett, Lindon. *Blackness and Value: Seeing Double*. Cambridge: Cambridge University Press, 1999.
Barthes, Roland. *Camera Lucida: Reflections on Photography*. Translated by Richard Howard. New York: Hill and Wang, 1981.
———. "The Grain of the Voice." In *Image—Music—Text*, edited and translated by Stephen Heath, 179–189. London: Fontana Press, 1977.
Baudrillard, Jean. *America*. Translated by Chris Turner. London: Verso, 1988.
Berlant, Lauren. "On Persistence." *Social Text* 32, no. 4 (2014): 33–37.

———. "Lauren Berlant Discusses 'Reading With' and Her Recent Work." *Art Forum*, January 30, 2014. http://artforum.com.
———. *Cruel Optimism*. Durham, NC: Duke University Press, 2011.
Bernstein, Robin. *Racial Innocence: Performing American Childhood from Slavery to Civil Rights*. New York: New York University Press, 2012.
Bersani, Leo. "Is the Rectum A Grave?" *October* 43 (Winter 1987): 197–222.
Bersani, Leo, and Adam Phillips. *Intimacies*. Chicago: University of Chicago Press, 2008.
Best, Stephen, and Sharon Marcus. "Surface Reading: An Introduction." *Representations* 108, no. 1 (2009): 1–21.
Boyarin, Daniel. "What Does the Jew Want? Or, the Political Meaning of the Phallus." In *Psychoanalysis of Race*, edited by Christopher Lane, 211–240. New York: Columbia University Press, 1998.
Bradley, Rizvana. "Other Sensualities." Introduction to "The Haptic: Textures of Performance." Special issue, *Women and Performance*, edited by Rizvana Bradley, 24, nos. 2–3 (2015): 129–133.
Braunstein, Néstor. "Desire and Jouissance in the Teachings of Lacan." In *The Cambridge Companion to Lacan*, edited by Jean-Michel Rabaté, 102–115. Cambridge: Cambridge University Press, 2003.
Brewer Ball, Katherine "The Veering Escapology of Sharon Hayes and Patty Hearst." *WSQ: Women's Studies Quarterly* 44, nos. 1–2 (2016): 35–51.
Briggs, Laura. "The Race of Hysteria: 'Overcivilization' and the 'Savage' in Nineteenth-Century Obstetrics and Gynecology." *American Quarterly* 52, no. 2 (2000): 246–273.
Brintnall, Kent. *Ecco Homo: The Male Body in Pain as Redemptive Figure*. Chicago: University of Chicago Press, 2012.
Browne, Simone. *Dark Matters: On the Surveillance of Blackness*. Durham, NC: Duke University Press, 2015.
Buse, Peter. "Photography Degree Zero: Cultural History of the Polaroid Image." *New Formations* 62 (2007): 29–44.
Bustamante, Nao. *Neapolitan*. 2003. www.naobustamante.com.
Butler, Judith. "Against Proper Objects." *differences: A Journal of Feminist Cultural Studies* 6 nos. 2–3 (1994): 1–27.
———. *Bodies That Matter: On the Discursive Limits of "Sex."* London: Routledge, 1993.
———. "Imitation and Gender Insubordination." In *Inside/Out: Lesbian Theories, Gay Theories*, edited by Diana Fuss, 13–31. New York: Routledge, 1991.
———. *Gender Trouble: Feminism and the Subversion of Identity*. New York: Routledge, 1990.
———. "The Body Politics of Julia Kristeva." *Hypatia* 3, no. 3 (1988): 104–118.
Cacho, Lisa Marie. *Slow Death: Racialized Rightlessness and the Criminalization of the Unprotected*. New York: New York University Press, 2012.
Callahan, Yesha. "Reactions to Kara Walker's *A Subtlety* Prove a Black Woman Will Be Sexualized Even in Art." *Root*, May 28, 2014. www.theroot.com.
Campt, Tina. *Listening to Images*. Durham, NC: Duke University Press, 2017.

Catbagan, Maureen. *Crush*. 2010–2012. www.maureencatbagan.com.
Chambers-Letson, Joshua. *After the Party*. New York: New York University Press, 2018.
———. "The Queer of Color's Mother: Ryan Rivera, Audre Lorde, Martin Wong, Danh Võ." *TDR: The Drama Review* 62, no. 1 (2018): 46-59.
Chang, Patty. *In Love*, two-channel video installation, 3 min., 28 sec. New York: Solomon R. Guggenheim Museum, 2001. www.guggenhiem.org.
Chen, Mel. *Animacies: Biopolitics, Racial Mattering, and Queer Affect*. Durham, NC: Duke University Press, 2012.
Cheng, Anne Anlin. *Second Skin: Josephine Baker and the Modern Surface*. Oxford: Oxford University Press, 2011.
———. "Skin Deep: Josephine Baker and the Colonial Fetish." *Camera Obscura* 23, no. 3 (2008): 35-79.
———. *The Melancholy of Race: Psychoanalysis, Assimilation, and Hidden Grief*. Oxford: Oxford University Press, 2001.
Chinn, Sarah E. "Feeling Her Way: Audre Lorde and the Power of Touch." *GLQ: A Journal of Lesbian and Gay Studies* 9, nos. 1-2 (2003): 181-204.
Chow, Rey. *The Protestant Ethnic and the Spirit of Capitalism*. New York: Columbia University Press, 2002.
Colbert, Soyica Diggs, Robert J. Patterson, and Aida Levy-Hussen, eds. *The Psychic Hold of Slavery: Legacies in American Expressive Culture*. New Brunswick, NJ: Rutgers University Press, 2016.
Crawley, Ashon. *Blackpentecostal Breath: The Aesthetics of Possibility*. Durham, NC: Duke University Press, 2016.
Cruz, Ariane. *The Color of Kink: Black Women, BDSM, and Pornography*. New York: New York University Press, 2016.
Cvetkovich, Ann. "Recasting Receptivity: Female Sexualities." In *Lesbian Erotics*, edited by Karla Jay, 125-146. New York: New York University Press, 1995.
Da Silva, Denise Ferreira. "To Be Announced: Radical Praxis or Knowing at the Limits of Justice." *Social Text* 31, no. 1 (2013): 43-62.
———. *Toward A Global Idea of Race*. Minneapolis: University of Minnesota Press, 2007.
Dailey, Meghan. "Mickalene Thomas: Art + Auction: In the Studio." Lehmann Maupin Gallery website, February 28, 2009. www.lehmannmaupin.com.
Davis, Madeline. "Epilogue, Nine Years Later." In *The Persistent Desire: A Femme-Butch Reader*, edited by Joan Nestle, 270-271. Boston: Alyson, 1992.
Declue, Jennifer. "Let's Play: Exploring Cinematic Black Lesbian Fantasy, Pleasure, and Pain." In *No Tea, No Shade: New Writings in Black Queer Studies*, edited by E. Patrick Johnson, 216-238. Durham, NC: Duke University Press, 2016.
De Lauretis, Teresa. *The Practice of Love: Lesbian Sexuality and Perverse Desire*. Bloomington: Indiana University Press, 1994.
De Veaux, Alexis. *Warrior Poet: A Biography of Audre Lorde*. New York: W. W. Norton, 2004.
Deavere Smith, Anna. *Lyle Ashton Harris*. New York: George Miller, 2004.

Deleuze, Gilles, and Félix Guattari. *A Thousand Plateaus: Capitalism and Schizophrenia*. London: Bloomsbury, 1988.
Diehl, Carol. "Dirty Sugar: Kara Walker's Dubious Alliance with Domino." *Carol Diehl's Art Vent*, June 16, 2014. http://artvent.blogspot.com.
Doane, Mary Ann. "Masquerade Reconsidered: Further Thoughts on the Female Spectator." *Discourse* 11, no. 1 (1988): 42–54.
Doerr, Jennifer. "Making Space around the Beloved," interview with Maggie Nelson for *Brooklyn Quarterly*, October 26, 2015. http://brooklynquarterly.org.
Doyle, Jennifer. *Hold It Against Me: Difficulty and Emotion in Contemporary Art*. Durham, NC: Duke University Press, 2013.
Doyle Jennifer, and David Getsy. "Queer Formalisms: Jennifer Doyle and David Getsy in Conversation." *Art Journal*, March 31, 2013. http://artjournal.collegeart.org.
Duggan, Lisa, and Kathleen McHugh, "A Fem(me)inist Manifesto." *Women and Performance* 8, no. 2 (2002): 153–159.
Ellis, Nadia. *Territories of the Soul: Queered Belonging in the Black Diaspora*. Durham, NC: Duke University Press, 2015.
Eng, David, David Kazanjian, and Judith Butler, eds. *Loss: The Politics of Mourning*. Berkeley: University of California Press, 2002.
Eng, David L. *The Feeling of Kinship: Queer Liberalism and the Racialization of Intimacy*. Durham, NC: Duke University Press, 2010.
Fanon, Frantz. *Black Skin, White Masks*. Translated by Charles Lamm Markmann. New York: Grove Press, 1967.
Farley, Anthony Paul. "The Black Body as Fetish Object." *Oregon Law Review* 76, no. 3 (1997): 457–535.
Ferguson, Roderick. *The Reorder of Things: The University and Its Pedagogies of Minority Difference*. Minneapolis: University of Minnesota Press, 2012.
———. *Aberrations in Black: Toward a Queer of Color Critique*. Minneapolis: University of Minnesota Press, 2004.
Firestone, Shulamith. *The Dialectic of Sex: The Case for Feminist Revolution*. New York: Farrar, Straus and Giroux, 2003.
Fleetwood, Nicole. *Troubling Vision: Performance, Visuality, and Blackness*. Chicago: University of Chicago Press, 2011.
Freeman, Elizabeth. *Time Binds: Queer Temporalities, Queer Histories*. Durham, NC: Duke University Press, 2010.
"Frequently Asked Questions." *Judy Chicago*, n.d. www.judychicago.com (accessed February 1, 2016).
Freud, Sigmund. *Three Essays on the Theory of Sexuality*. Translated and edited by James Strachey. New York: Basic Books, 2000.
———. "Fetishism." In *The Complete Psychological Works of Sigmund Freud*, translated and edited by James Strachey, 21:147–157. London: Hogarth Press and the Institute of Psychoanalysis, 1927.
Fuss, Diana. *Identification Papers: Readings on Psychoanalysis, Sexuality, and Culture*. New York: Routledge, 1995.

Galison, Peter. "Judgment against Objectivity." In *Picturing Science: Producing Art*, edited by Peter Galison and Caroline Jones, 327–359. New York; London: Routledge, 1998.

Garber, Linda. *Identity Poetics: Race, Class and the Lesbian-Feminist Roots of Queer Theory*. New York: Columbia University Press, 2001.

Gerhard, Jane. *The Dinner Party: Judy Chicago and the Power of Popular Feminism, 1970–2007*. Atlanta: University of Georgia Press, 2013.

———. *Desiring Revolution: Second-Wave Feminism and the Rewriting of American Sexual Thought, 1920 to 1982*. New York: Columbia University Press, 2001.

Gibson, Margaret. "Clitoral Corruption: Body Metaphors and American Doctors' Constructions of Female Homosexuality, 1870–1900." In *Science and Homosexualities*, edited by Vernon Rosario, 108–132. New York: Routledge, 1997.

Gill, Lyndon. "Chatting Back an Epidemic: Caribbean Gay Men, HIV/AIDS, and the Uses of Erotic Subjectivity." *GLQ: A Journal of Lesbian and Gay Studies* 18, nos. 2–3 (2012): 277–295.

Glissant, Edouard. *Poetics of Relation*. Translated by Betsey Wing. Ann Arbor: University of Michigan Press, 1997.

Gopinath, Gayatri. *Impossible Desires: Queer Diasporas and South Asian Public Cultures*. Durham, NC: Duke University Press, 2005.

Gopnik, Blake. "Rarely One for Sugarcoating: Kara Walker Creates a Confection at the Domino Refinery." *New York Times*, April 25, 2014. www.nytimes.com.

Griffin, Farah Jasmine. *If You Can't Be Free, Be a Mystery: In Search of Billie Holiday*. New York: Simon and Schuster, 2002.

Gumbs, Alexis Pauline. "We Can Learn to Mother Ourselves: The Queer Survival of Black Feminism, 1968–1996." PhD diss., Duke University, 2010.

Gunning, Tom. "An Aesthetic of Astonishment: Early Film and the (In)Credulous Spectator." In *Film Theory: Critical Concepts in Media and Cultural Studies*, edited by KJ Shepherdson, Philip Simpson, and Andrew Utterson, 114–133 London: Routledge, 2003.

Halberstam, Jack. *Female Masculinity*. Durham, NC: Duke University Press, 1998.

Halperin, David. *How to Be Gay*. Cambridge, MA: Harvard University Press, 2012.

Hammonds, Evelynn. "Black (W)holes and the Geometry of Black Female Sexuality." *differences: A Journal of Feminist Cultural Studies* 6, nos. 2–3 (1994): 127–145.

Harkins, Gillian. *Everybody's Family Romance: Reading Incest in Neoliberal America*. Minneapolis: University of Minnesota Press, 2009.

Hart, L. "That Was Then: This Is Now: Ex-Changing the Phallus." *Postmodern Culture* 4 no. 1 (1993): n.p. Project MUSE, doi:10.1353/pmc.1993.0039.

Hartman, Saidiya V. "Belly of the World: A Note on Black Women's Labors." *Souls* 18, no. 1 (2016): 166–173.

———. *Scenes of Subjection: Terror, Slavery, and Self-Making in Nineteenth-Century America*. New York: Oxford University Press, 1997.

Hawk Swanson, Amber, and Xandra Ibarra. Artists' statement for *Untitled Fucking*. www.amberhawkswanson.com (accessed May 2, 2017).

Hayes, Rose Oldfield. "Female Genital Mutilation, Fertility Control, Women's Roles, and the Patrilineage in Modern Sudan: A Functional Analysis." *American Ethnologist* 2, no. 4 (1975): 617–633.

Hayot, Eric. "Chinese Bodies, Chinese Futures." *Representations* 99, no. 1 (Summer 2007): 99–129.

Heath, Stephen. "Joan Riviere and the Masquerade." In *Formations of Fantasy*, edited by Victor Burgin, James Donald, and Cora Kaplan, 45–61. New York: Methuen, 1986.

Hemmings, Clare. *Why Stories Matter: The Political Grammar of Feminist Theory*. Durham, NC: Duke University Press, 2012.

Hoang, Nguyen Tan. *A View from the Bottom: Asian American Masculinity and Sexual Representation*. Durham, NC: Duke University Press, 2014.

Holland, Sharon. *The Erotic Life of Racism*. Durham, NC: Duke University Press, 2011.

———. "To Touch the Mother's C(o)untry: Siting Audre Lorde's Erotics." In *Lesbian Erotics*, edited by Karla Jay, 212–226. New York: New York University Press, 1995.

Holland, Sharon Patricia, Marcía Ochoa, and Kyla Wazana Tompkins. "On the Visceral." *GLQ: A Journal of Lesbian and Gay Studies* 20, no. 4 (2014): 391–406.

Hollibaugh, Amber, and Cherrie Moraga. "What We're Rolling Around in Bed With: Sexual Silences in Feminism: A Conversation toward Ending Them." *Freedom Archives* (1981): 58–62. http://freedomarchives.org.

Hong, Grace Kyungwon. "Existentially Surplus Women of Color Feminism and the New Crises of Capitalism." *GLQ: A Journal of Lesbian and Gay Studies* 18, no. 1 (2012): 87–106.

Huffer, Lynne. *Are the Lips a Grave? A Queer Feminist on the Ethics of Sex*. New York: Columbia University Press, 2013.

———. *Maternal Pasts, Feminist Futures: Nostalgia, Ethics, and the Question of Difference*. Palo Alto, CA: Stanford University Press, 2003.

Ibarra, Xandra. "Tapatío Cock and Strap-On Harness." www.xandraibarra.com (accessed November 5, 2017).

Irigaray, Luce. "When Our Lips Speak Together." In *The Sex Which Is Not One*, translated by Catherine Porter with Carolyn Burke, 205–218. Ithaca, NY: Cornell University Press, 1985.

———. "The Mechanics of Fluids." *This Sex Which Is Not One*, translated by Catherine Porter with Carolyn Burke, 106–118. Ithaca, NY: Cornell University Press: 1985.

Jagose, Annemarie. *Orgasmology*. Durham, NC: Duke University Press, 2012.

———. *Lesbian Utopics*. London: New York: Taylor & Francis, 1994.

Jardine, Alice. "Woman in Limbo: Deleuze and His Br(others)." *Substance* 13, nos. 3–4 (1984): 46–60.

Johnson, Barbara. *Mother Tongues: Sexuality, Trials, Motherhood, Translation*. Cambridge, MA: Harvard University Press, 2003.

Johnson, E Patrick. *Appropriating Blackness: Performance and the Politics of Authenticity*. Durham, NC: Duke University Press, 2003.

———. "'Quare' Studies, or (Almost) Everything I Know about Queer Studies I Learned from My Grandmother." *Text and Performance Quarterly* 12, no. 1 (2001): 1–25.

Johnson, Jessica Marie, and Treva B. Lindsey. "Searching for Climax: Black Erotic Lives in Slavery and Freedom." *Meridians: Feminism, Race, Transnationalism* 12, no. 2 (2014): 169–195.
Jones, Amelia. "The 'Eternal Return': Self-Portrait Photography as a Technology of Embodiment." *Signs* 27, no. 4 (2002): 947–978.
Keller, Yvonne. "'Was It Right to Love Her Brother's Wife So Passionately?': Lesbian Pulp Novels and US Lesbian Identity, 1950–1965." *American Quarterly* 57, no. 2 (2005): 385–410.
Kheshti, Roshanak. *Modernity's Ear: Listening to Race and Gender in World Music*. New York: New York University Press, 2015.
Kim, Ju Yon. *The Racial Mundane: Asian American Performance and the Embodied Everyday*. New York: New York University Press, 2015.
King, Tiffany Lethabo. "Interview with Dr. Tiffany Lethabo King." *Feral Feminisms* 4 (Summer 2015): n.p. www.feralfeminisms.com.
Kirby, Vicky. "Out of Africa: 'Our Bodies Ourselves?.'" In *Female Circumcision and the Politics of Knowledge: African Women in Imperialist Discourses*, edited by Obioma Nnaemeka, 81–96. Westport, CT: Praeger, 2005.
Klein, Melanie. "Notes on Some Schizoid Mechanisms." *International Journal of Psychoanalysis* 27 (1946): 99–110.
Kristeva, Julia. *Powers of Horror*. Translated by L. Roudiez. New York: Columbia University Press, 1982.
Koedt, Anne. "'Myth of the Vaginal Orgasm': Notes from the First Year." In *'Takin' It to the Streets': A Sixties Reader*, 2nd ed., edited by A. Bloom and W. Breines, 422–428. Oxford: Oxford University Press, 2002.
Landers, Sean. Interview with Mickalene Thomas. *Bomb Magazine*, Summer 2011. http://bombmagazine.org.
Lee, Rachel C. *The Exquisite Corpse of Asian America: Biopolitics, Biosociality, and Posthuman Ecologies*. New York: New York University Press, 2014.
León, Christina. "Forms of Opacity: Roaches, Blood, and Being Stuck in Xandra Ibarra's Corpus." *ASAP/Journal* 2, no. 2 (2017): 369–394.
Lloyd, Elisabeth. *The Case of the Female Orgasm: Bias in the Science of Evolution*. Cambridge, MA: Harvard University Press, 2009.
Likierman, Meira. *Melanie Klein: Her Work in Context*. London: A&C Black, 2001.
Lorde, Audre. "There Is No Hierarchy of Oppression." In *I Am Your Sister: Collected and Unpublished Writings of Audre Lorde*, edited by Rudolph P. Byrd, Johnnetta Betsch Cole, and Beverly Guy-Sheftall, 219–220. Oxford, UK: Oxford University Press, 2009.
———. "Uses of the Erotic: The Erotic as Power." In *Sister Outsider: Essays and Speeches*, 53–59, Berkeley, CA: Crossing Press, 2007.
———. "Open Letter to Mary Daly." In *Sister Outsider: Essays and Speeches*, 66–71. Berkeley, CA: Crossing Press, 2007.
———. "Sexism: An American Disease in Blackface." In *Sister Outsider: Essays and Speeches*, 60–65. Berkeley, CA: Crossing Press, 1984.

———. "Eye to Eye: Black Women, Hatred, and Anger." In *Sister Outsider: Essays and Speeches*, 145–175. Berkeley, CA: Crossing Press, 1984.

———. "An Interview: Audre Lorde with Adrienne Rich." In *Sister Outsider: Essays and Speeches*, 81–109. Berkeley, CA: Crossing Press, 1984.

———. "Scratching the Surface: Some Notes on Barriers to Women and Loving." In *Sister Outsider: Essays and Speeches*, 45–52. Berkeley, CA: Crossing Press, 1984.

———. *Zami: A New Spelling of My Name*. Freedom, CA: Crossing Press, 1982.

———. *The Cancer Journals*. Argyle, NY: Spinsters Ink, 1980.

———. "Dahomey." In *The Black Unicorn*, 10. New York: Norton, 1978.

———. "Woman." In *The Black Unicorn*, 82. New York: Norton, 1978.

———. "Meet." In *The Black Unicorn*, 33–34. New York: Norton, 1978.

Lowe, Lisa. *The Intimacies of Four Continents*. Durham, NC: Duke University Press, 2015.

Luciano, Dana. *Arranging Grief: Sacred Time and the Body in Nineteenth-Century America*. New York: New York University Press, 2007.

Malone, Gloria. "What Kara Walker's 'Sugar Baby' Showed Us." *RH Reality Check: Reproductive & Sexual Health and Justice News, Analysis & Commentary*, July 21, 2014. http://rhrealitycheck.org.

Maines, Rachel. *The Technology of Orgasm*. Baltimore, MD: Johns Hopkins University Press, 2001.

Manalansan, Martin F. "The Messy Itineraries of Queerness." *Cultural Anthropology*, July 21, 2015. www.culanth.org.

———. "Immigrant Domesticity and the Politics of Olfaction in the Global City." In *The Smell Culture Reader*, edited by Jim Drobnick, 41–52. New York: Berg, 2006.

Marder, Elissa. *The Mother in the Age of Mechanical Reproduction: Psychoanalysis, Photography, Deconstruction*. New York: Fordham University Press, 2012.

Marriot, David. "On Racial Fetishism." *Qui Parle* 18, no. 2 (2010): 215–248.

Marx, Karl. *Capital: A Critique of Political Economy*. Volume 1. Translated by Ben Fowkes. New York: Penguin, 1990.

Masters, William, and Virginia Johnson. *Human Sexual Response*. Boston: Brown and Little, 1966.

McElya, Micki. *Clinging to Mammy: The Faithful Slave in Twentieth-Century America*. Cambridge, MA: Harvard University Press, 2007.

McMillan, Uri. *Embodied Avatars: Genealogies of Black Feminist Art and Performance*. New York: New York University Press, 2015.

Memmi, Albert. *The Colonizer and the Colonized*. New York: Routledge, 2013.

Micale, Mark S. *Approaching Hysteria: Disease and Its Interpretations*. Princeton, NJ: Princeton University Press, 1995.

Mintz, Sidney. *Sweetness and Power: The Place of Sugar in World History*. New York: Vintage, 1985.

Modleski, Tania. "Time and Desire in the Woman's Films," *Cinema Journal* 23 (Spring 1984): 19–30.

Morgan, Jennifer. *Laboring Women*. Philadelphia: University of Pennsylvania Press, 2004.

Morgensen, Scott Lauria. *Spaces between Us: Queer Settler Colonialism and Indigenous Decolonization*. Minneapolis: University of Minnesota Press, 2011.

Moten, Fred. *In the Break: The Aesthetics of the Black Radical Tradition*. Durham, NC: Duke University Press, 2003.

Mulvey, Laura. "Notes on Sirk and Melodrama." In *Visual and Other Pleasures*, 39–44. London: Palgrave Macmillan, 1989.

Muñoz, José Esteban. *Cruising Utopia: The Then and There of Queer Futurity*. New York: New York University Press, 2009.

———. "Feeling Brown, Feeling Down: Latina Affect, the Performativity of Race, and the Depressive Position." *Signs* 31, no. 3 (2006): 675–688.

———. "Feeling Brown: Ethnicity and Affect in Ricardo Bracho's 'The Sweetest Hangover (and Other STDs).'" *Theatre Journal* 52, no. 1 (2000): 67–79.

———. *Disidentifications: Queers of Color and the Performance of Politics*. Minneapolis: University of Minnesota Press, 1999.

Murray, Yxta Maya. "From Here I Saw What Happened and I Cried: Carrie Mae Weems' Challenge to the Harvard Archive." *Unbound: Harvard Journal of the Legal Left* 1 (2013). Loyola-LA Legal Studies Paper No. 2013-31. http://ssrn.com.

Musser, Amber Jamilla. "Consent, Capacity, and the Non-Narrative." In *Queer Feminist Science Studies*, edited by Kristina Gupta, Angela Wiley, and Cyd Cipolla, 221–233. Seattle: University of Washington Press, 2017.

———. "Queering Sugar: Kara Walker's Sugar Sphinx and the Intractability of Black Female Sexuality." *Signs: Journal of Women and Culture* 42, no. 1 (2016): 1–22.

———. "Re-Membering Lorde." In *No Tea, No Shade: New Writings on Black Queer Studies*, edited by E Patrick Johnson, 346–361. Durham, NC: Duke University Press, 2016.

———. "Specimen Days: Diversity, Labor, and the University." *Feminist Formations* 27, no. 3 (2015): 1–20.

———. *Sensational Flesh: Race, Power, and Masochism*. New York: New York University Press, 2014.

———. "On the Orgasm of the Species: Female Sexuality, Science, and Sexual Difference." *Feminist Review* 102 (2012): 1–20.

———. "From Our Body to Your Selves: The Boston Women's Health Book Collective and Changing Notions of Subjectivity, 1969–1973," *WSQ: Women's Studies Quarterly* 35, nos. 1–2 (2007): 93–109.

———. "Reading Lorde after Queer." In *After Queer Studies: Literary Theory and Critical Interpretation*. Edited by Tyler Bradway and E. L. McCallum. Cambridge: Cambridge University Press, forthcoming.

Nancy, Jean Luc. *Coming*. Translated by Charlotte Mandell with Adele Van Reeth. New York: Fordham University Press, 2016.

———. *Listening*. Translated by Charlotte Mandell. New York: Fordham University Press, 2007.

Nash, Jennifer. *The Black Body in Ecstasy: Reading Race, Reading Pornography*. Durham, NC: Duke University Press, 2014.

———. "Practicing Love: Black Feminism, Love-Politics, and Post-Intersectionality." *Meridians* 11, no. 2 (2011): 1–24.

———. "Black Anality." *GLQ: A Journal of Lesbian and Gay Studies* 20, no. 4 (2014): 439–460.

Newton, Esther. *Mother Camp: Female Impersonators in America*. Chicago: University of Chicago Press, 1972.

Ngai, Sianne. *Ugly Feelings*. Cambridge, MA: Harvard University Press, 2009.

Nixon, Angelique. *Resisting Paradise: Tourism, Diaspora, and Sexuality in Caribbean Culture*. Jackson: University of Mississippi Press, 2015.

Nyong'o, Tavia. "Subtleties of Resistance: Sweetness and Violence in Kara Walker's *A Subtlety*." In *Giving Contours to Shadows*, edited by Marius Babias, 113–121. Berlin, DE: Neuer Berliner Kunstverein, 2014.

Oishi, Eve. "Interview with Patty Chang." *Camera Obscura* 18, no. 3 (2003): 118–129.

Parisi, Luciana. *Abstract Sex: Philosophy, Bio-Technology and the Mutations of Desire*. New York: Continuum, 2004.

Parreñas, Rhacel Salazar. *Servants of Globalization: Women, Migration and Domestic Work*. Palo Alto, CA: Stanford University Press, 2001.

Parreñas Shimizu, Celine. *The Hypersexuality of Race: Performing Asian/American Women on Screen and Stage*. Durham, NC: Duke University Press, 2007.

Pellegrini, Ann. *Performance Anxieties: Staging Psychoanalysis, Staging Race*. New York: Routledge, 1997.

Pérez, Hiram. *A Taste for Brown Bodies: Gay Modernity and Cosmopolitan Desire*. New York: New York University Press, 2015.

Pethes, Nicolas. "Psychicones: Visual Traces of the Soul in Late Nineteenth-Century Fluidic Photography." *Journal of Medical History* 60, no. 3 (2016): 325–341. www.ncbi.nlm.nih.gov.

Powell, Richard. *Cutting a Figure: Fashioning Black Portraiture*. Chicago: University of Chicago Press, 2009.

Powers, Nicholas. "Why I Yelled at the Kara Walker Exhibit." *Indypendent*, June 30, 2014. https://indypendent.org.

Puar, Jasbir. "Bodies with New Organs: Becoming Trans, Becoming Disabled." *Social Text* 33 no. 3 (2015): 45–73.

———. *Terrorist Assemblages: Homonationalism in Queer Times*. Durham, NC: Duke University Press, 2007.

Quashie, Kevin. *The Sovereignty of Quiet*. Rutgers, NJ: Rutgers University Press, 2012.

Quiroga, José. *Tropics of Desire: Interventions from Queer Latino America*. New York: New York University Press, 2000.

Ramos, Iván A. "Spic(y) Appropriations: The Gustatory Aesthetics of Xandra Ibarra (aka La Chica Boom)." *ARARA: Art and Architecture in the Americas* 12 (2016): 1–18.

Reddy, Chandan. *Freedom with Violence: Race, Sexuality, and the US State*. Durham, NC: Duke University Press, 2011.

Riskin, Jessica. "The Defecating Duck, or the Ambiguous Origins of Artificial Life." *Critical Inquiry* 29, no. 4 (2003): 599–633.

Riviere, Joan. "Womanliness as Masquerade." *International Journal of Psychoanalysis* 10 (1929): 303–313.

Roach, Joseph. *The Player's Passion: Studies in the Science of Acting.* Newark, NJ: University of Delaware Press, 1986.

Roberts, Lacey Jane. "Put Your Thing Down, Flip It, and Reverse It: Re-Imagining Craft Identities Using Queer Theory." In *Extra/Ordinary: Craft and Contemporary Art,* edited by Maria Elena Buszek, 243–259. Durham, NC: Duke University Press, 2011.

Rodríguez, Juana María. "Viscous Pleasures and Unruly Feminisms." *GLQ: A Journal of Lesbian and Gay Studies* 21, no. 1 (2015): 10–12.

———. *Sexual Futures, Queer Gestures, and Other Latina Longings.* New York: New York University Press, 2014.

Roof, Judith. *A Lure of Knowledge: Lesbian Sexuality and Theory.* New York: Columbia University Press, 1991.

Rooney, Kara, and Kara Walker. "A Sonorous Subtlety: Kara Walker with Kara Rooney." *Brooklyn Rail: Critical Perspectives on Art, Politics, and Culture,* May 6, 2014, www.brooklynrail.org.

Rosenberg, Karen. "Mickalene Thomas Rediscovers Her Mother—and Her Muse." *New York Times Magazine,* September 27, 2012. www.nytimes.com.

Rusert, Britt. *Fugitive Science: Empiricism and Freedom in Early African American Culture.* New York: New York University Press, 2017.

Salamon, Gayle. *Assuming a Body: Transgender and Rhetorics of Materiality.* New York: Columbia University Press, 2010.

San Pablo Burns, Lucy Mae. *Puro Arte: Filipinos on the Stages of Empire.* New York: New York University Press, 2012.

Schuller, Kyla. "Biopower below and before the Individual." *GLQ: A Journal of Lesbian and Gay Studies* 22, no. 4 (2016): 629–636.

———. "Taxonomies of Feeling: The Epistemology of Sentimentalism in Late Nineteenth-Century Racial and Sexual Science." *American Quarterly* 64, no. 2 (June 2012): 277–299.

Scott, Darieck. *Extravagant Abjection: Blackness, Power, and Sexuality in the African American Literary Imagination.* New York: New York University Press, 2010.

Sedgwick, Eve. "Anality: Notes from the Front." In *The Weather in Proust,* edited by Jason Goldberg, 166–182. Durham, NC: Duke University Press, 2011.

———. *Between Men: English Literature and Homosexual Desire.* New York: Columbia University Press, 1985.

See, Sarita. *The Decolonized Eye: Filipino Art and Performance.* Minneapolis: University of Minnesota Press, 2009.

Sexton, Jared. "The Social Life of Social Death: On Afro-Pessimism and Black Optimism." *InTensions* 5 (Fall/Winter 2011): 1–47.

Sharpe, Christina. *In the Wake: On Blackness and Being.* Durham, NC: Duke University Press, 2016.

———. *Monstrous Intimacies: Making Post-Slavery Subjects.* Durham, NC: Duke University Press, 2009.

Sharpley-Whiting, T. Deenan. *Black Venus: Sexualized Savages, Primal Fears, and Primitive Narratives in French*. Durham, NC: Duke University Press, 1999.

Shimikawa, Karen. *National Abjection*. Durham, NC: Duke University Press, 2002.

Silver, Leigh. "Kara Walker's 'A Sublety' Proves that Sugar Isn't Always Sweet." *Complex*, May 13, 2014. www.complex.com.

Silverman, Kaja. *The Miracle of Analogy: Or, The History of Photography*. Palo Alto, CA: Stanford University Press, 2015.

———. "Girl Love." *October* 104 (Spring 2003): 4–27.

Smith, Roberta. "Sugar? Sure, but Salted with Meaning: 'A Subtlety, or the Marvelous Sugar Baby' at the Domino Plant." *New York Times*, May 11, 2014. www.nytimes.com.

———. "Loud, Proud, and Painted." *New York Times*, September 27, 2012. www.nytimes.com.

Somerville, Siobhan. *Queering the Color Line: Race and the Invention of Homosexuality in American Culture*. Durham, NC: Duke University Press, 2000.

———. "Scientific Racism and the Emergence of the Homosexual Body." *Journal of the History of Sexuality* 5, no. 2 (1994): 243–266.

Sontag, Susan. "Notes on Camp." In *Camp: Queer Aesthetics and the Performing Subject: A Reader*, edited by Fabio Cleto, 53–65. Edinburgh: Edinburgh University Press, 1999.

Sorrett, Josef. *Spirit in the Dark: A Religious History of Racial Aesthetics*. Oxford: Oxford University Press, 2016.

Spillers, Hortense. "Mama's Baby, Papa's Maybe: An American Grammar Book." In *Black, White, and in Color: Essays on American Literature and Culture*, 203–229. Chicago: University of Chicago Press, 2003.

———. "'All the Things You Could Be by Now If Sigmund Freud's Wife Was Your Mother': Psychoanalysis and Race." In *Black, White, and In Color: Essays on American Literature and Culture*, 376–427. Chicago: University of Chicago Press, 2003.

———. "Interstices: A Small Drama of Words." In *Pleasure and Danger: Exploring Female Sexuality*, edited by Carole Vance, 73–100. New York: Routledge: 1984.

Spivak, Gayatri Chakravorty. "Translation as Culture." *Parallax* 6, no. 1 (2000): 13–24.

———. "Can the Subaltern Speak?" In *Marxism and the Interpretation of Culture*, edited by Cary Nelson and Larry Grossberg, 271–313. Chicago: University of Illinois Press, 1988.

———. Scattered Speculations on the Question of Value." *Diacritics* 15 no. 4 (1985): 73–93.

Stallings, L. H. *Funk the Erotic: Transaesthetics and Black Sexual Cultures*. Chicago: University of Illinois Press, 2015.

Stephens, Michelle. *Skin Acts: Race, Psychoanalysis, and the Black Male Performer*. Durham, NC: Duke University Press, 2014.

Stockton, Kathryn Bond. "Surfacing (in the Heat of Reading): Is It Like Kissing or Some Other Sex Acts?" *J19: The Journal of Nineteenth-Century Americanists* 3, no. 1 (2015): 7–13.

———. "Reading as Kissing, Sex with Ideas: 'Lesbian: Barebacking.'" *Los Angeles Review of Books*, March 8, 2015. https://lareviewofbooks.org.

Tadiar, Neferti XM. "Remaindered Life or Citizen-Man, Medium of Democracy." *Southeast Asian Studies* 49, no. 3 (2011): 464–495.

———. *Things Fall Away: Philippine Historical Experience and the Makings of Globalization*. Durham, NC: Duke University Press, 2009.

Takagi, Dana Y. "Maiden Voyage: Excursion into Sexuality and Identity Politics in Asian America." *Amerasia Journal* 20, no. 1 (1994): 1–17.

Taormino, Tristan. "The Rise of MILFs and Mommies in Sexual Fantasy Material." *Village Voice*, October 30, 2007. www.villagevoice.com.

Thomas, Mickalene, "A Different Type of Beauty: Painter Mickalene Thomas Eulogizes Her Late Mother." *Creative Time Reports*, February 24, 2014. http://creativetimereports.org.

Thompson, Krista. *Shine: The Visual Economy of Light in African Diasporic Aesthetics Practice*. Durham, NC: Duke University Press, 2015.

Thompson, Malik. "Kara Walker's Desecrated Cemetery for Blackness." Groundwork for Praxis, July 3, 2014. http://groundworkforpraxis.com.

Thompson, Nato. "Creative Time Presents Kara Walker: Curatorial Statement." Creative Time, March 5, 2018. http://creativetime.org/.

Thurber, Cheryl. "The Development of the Mammy Image and Mythology." In *Southern Women: Histories and Identities*, edited by Virginia Bernhard, Betty Brandon, Elizabeth Fox-Genovese, and Theda Perdue, 87–108. Columbia: University of Missouri Press, 1992.

Tillet, Shalamisha. *Sites of Slavery: Citizenship and Racial Democracy in the Post–Civil Rights Imagination*. Durham, NC: Duke University Press, 2012.

Tompkins, Kyla Wazana. "'You Make Me Feel Right Quare': Promiscuous Reading, Minoritarian Critique, and White Sovereign Entrepreneurial Terror." *Social Text* 35, no. 4 (2017): 53–86.

———. *Racial Indigestion: Eating Bodies in the Nineteenth Century*. New York: New York University Press, 2012.

Traub, Valerie. "The Psychomorphology of the Clitoris." *GLQ: A Journal of Lesbian and Gay Studies* 2, nos. 1–2 (1995): 81–113.

Turner, Patricia A. *Ceramic Uncles & Celluloid Mammies: Black Images and Their Influence on Culture*. Des Plaines, IL: Bantam-Doubleday-Dell, 1994.

Tyburczy, Jennifer. *Sex Museums: The Politics and Performance of Display*. Chicago: University of Chicago Press, 2016.

Vaccaro, Jeanne. "Handmade." *TSQ: Transgender Studies Quarterly* 1, nos. 1–2 (2014): 96–97.

Vannier, S. A., A. B. Currie, and L. F. O'Sullivan. "Schoolgirls and Soccer Moms: A Content Analysis of Free 'Teen' and 'MILF' Online Pornography." *Journal of Sex Research* 51, no. 3 (2014): 253–264. doi: 10.1080/00224499.2013.829795.

Viego, Antonio. "The Unconscious of Latino/a Studies." *Latino Studies* 1, no. 3 (2003): 333–362.

Walker, Alice. "Coming Apart." In *The Womanist Reader*, edited by Layli Phillips, 3–11. New York: Taylor and Francis, 2006.

———. *In Search of Our Mothers' Gardens: Womanist Prose*. San Diego, CA: Harcourt Brace Jovanovich, 1983.

Walker, Kara. "Mickalene Thomas." *Bomb Magazine*, April 1, 2009, http://bombmagazine.org.

Walker, Kara, and Jad Abumrad, "Live Stream Kara Walker and Jad Abumrad's NYPL Talk." Creative Time, May 20, 2014. http://creativetime.org.

Wallace-Sanders, Kimberly. *Mammy: A Century of Race, Gender, and Southern Memory*. Ann Arbor: University of Michigan Press, 2008.

Wallis, Brian. "Black Bodies, White Science: Louis Agassiz's Slave Daguerreotypes." *American Art* 9, no. 2 (1995): 38–61.

Walton, Jean. *Fair Sex, Savage Dreams: Race, Psychoanalysis, Sexual Difference*. Durham, NC: Duke University Press, 2001.

Wanzo, Rebecca. *The Suffering Will Not Be Televised: African American Women and Sentimental Political Storytelling*. Albany: State University of New York Press, 2009.

Watts, Stephanye. "The Audacity of No Chill: Kara Walker in the Instagram Capital." *Gawker*, June 4, 2014. http://gawker.com.

Weeks, Kathi. *The Problem with Work: Feminism, Marxism, Antiwork Policies, and Postwork Imaginaries*. Durham, NC: Duke University Press, 2011.

Weems, Carrie Mae. Audio interview for *MOMA 2000: Open Ends*. New York: The Museum of Modern Art and Acoustiguide, 2000. www.moma.org.

Weheliye, Alex. *Habeaus Viscus: Racializing Assemblages, Biopolitics, and Black Feminist Theories of the Human*. Durham, NC: Duke University Press, 2014.

Weinbaum, Alys. *Wayward Reproductions*. Durham, NC: Duke University Press, 2004.

Wesling, Meg. "Queer Value." *GLQ: A Journal of Lesbian and Gay Studies* 18, no. 1 (2012): 107–125.

Westbrook, Lindsey. "Review." *Artweek* 34, no. 10 (2003): 14.

Whitford, Margaret. "Irigaray's Body Symbolic," *Hypatia* 6, no. 3 (1991): 97–110.

Wiegman, Robyn. *Object Lessons*. Durham, NC: Duke University Press, 2012.

Wilderson, Frank B. *Red, White, and Black: Cinema and the Structure of U.S. Antagonisms*. Durham, NC: Duke University Press, 2010.

Williams, Linda. "Cinema's Sex Acts." *Film Quarterly* 67, no. 4 (2014): 9–25.

———. *Hardcore: Power, Pleasure, and "The Frenzy of the Visible."* Berkeley: University of California Press, 1999.

Wilson, Elizabeth. *Gut Feminism*. Durham, NC: Duke University Press, 2015.

Wilson, Jackie Napolean. *Hidden Witness: African American Photography from the Dawn of Photography to the Civil War*. New York: Saint Martin's Griffin, 2000.

Wilson Bryan, Julia. "Eleven Propositions in Response to the Question: 'What's Contemporary about Craft?.'" *Journal of Modern Craft* 6, no. 1 (2013): 7–10.

Wittig, Monique. "The Straight Mind." In *The Straight Mind and Other Essays*, 21–32. Boston: Beacon Press, 1992.

Woodward, Vincent. *The Delectable Negro: Human Consumption and Homoeroticism within US Slave Culture*. Edited by Dwight McBride. New York: New York University Press, 2014.
Worley, Jennifer. "The Mid-Century Pulp Novel and the Imagining of Lesbian Community." In *Invisible Suburbs: Recovering Protest Fiction in the 1950s United States*, edited by Josh Lukin, 104–123. Jackson: University of Mississippi Press, 2008.
Wright, Michelle. *Becoming Black: Creating Identity in the African Diaspora*. Durham, NC: Duke University Press, 2004.
Wyma, Chloe "Mickalene Thomas on Motherhood, the Mirror Stage, and Her Brooklyn Museum Show." Blouin Artinfo, September 27, 2012. www.blouinartinfo.com.
Zaretsky, Eli. "'One Large Secure, Solid Background': Melanie Klein and the Origins of the British Welfare State." *Psychoanalysis and History* 1, no. 2 (1999): 136–154.

INDEX

abandonment: in *Billie #21* (Harris), 1
abjection, 22; into agency (via objecthood), 88; bottoming and the joys of, 84–86; and care, 91–92; and consumption, 36; and the excess that blackness produces (Scott), 82, 87; and labor, 90, 162; in *The Onion* (Abramovic), 137
Abramovic, Marina: *The Onion* (1995), 137
abuse, 34–35
acting: vs. authenticity, 120–21
Afropessimism, 6–7; and "yes, and," 9
Agassiz, Louis, 95, 102, 105, 108, 111–12. See *From Here I Saw What Happened and I Cried* (Weems)
agency: as an activity of maintenance (Berlant), 5; and blackness, 6; and the loop, 126–27; through mediation, 148–49; of mothering, 110, 168; and objectification ("objecthood"), 87–88; and one's sexuality, 38, 85–86; stomping as a form of feminine, 151; of Thomas in *Origin of the Universe 1*, 48
aggression: and familiarity, 159–60; and mimesis, 162–63; and misery, 150, 153; and the model minority, 160; and waste, 164. See also *Crush* (Catbagan)
Ahmed, Sara: on feminist killjoys, 149; on orientation, 29; on racialized anger, 159
Alexander, Jeffrey: on assimilation, 133–34
alterity, 29, 78–79, 88
Amin, Kadji: on racial fetishism, 200n32; on relation and sensuality, 16

anal sex: Hoang on, 83–84; and jouissance (Bersani), 72; and the maternal body, 77. See also bottoming
Ang, Ien: on melodrama and everyday life, 132
Anker, Elizabeth: on melodrama as a form of national rhetoric, 131, 198n36
Anzaldúa, Gloria: on *la frontera* and a hybrid tongue, 92–93
apostrophe: Weems's use of, 100, 107
appetite, 29–30; for black performance, 43; for black sweetness, 32; and colonialism, 41; femininity with, 176; for Ibarra, 93; and penetration, 71; and Walker's *A Subtlety*, 36–37, 40–45
Apter, Emily: on Freud's fetishist and the realm of the simulacrum, 154
assimilation, 92–93, 133–35, 140–41, 160, 163, 171
Attack of the Fifty-Foot Woman (1958), 145–46, 149, 152
audience: affecting Walker's Sugar Baby, 43–44; and Billie Holiday (for Moten), 1–2, 9, 102
Aunt Hester: scream of, 165
Aunt Jemima, 188n17, 189n20. See also mammy
authenticity: vs. acting, 120–21; in *Billie #21* (Harris), 2; and lesbians, 60–61; and surface, 49; of tears, 121, 137–38; and the voice, 116
automaticity, 120–43

Baartman, Saartjie, 59
Bacon, Francis, 136

Balance, Christine Bacareza: on Asian American rage, 160; on viral videos, 163–64
Barrett, Lindon: on violence and value, 161
Barthes, Roland, 79; grain of the voice, 102, 116; photography and the mother, 109; punctum, 106
BDSM, 83
becoming-atomic, 165–66
becoming-material: and becoming-maternal (photography), 110
becoming-molecular, 42–45
becoming-object, 155
becoming-spectacle, 35
becoming-woman, 3, 72, 185n9
being-with, 177
Bentham, Jeremy: panopticon, 97
Berlant, Lauren: on agency, 5; on elliptical thinking, 143; on the loop in *Neapolitan* (Bustamante), 126–27
Bernstein, Robin: on black bodies and pain tolerance, 98
Bersani, Leo: impersonal narcissism, 65–66; jouissance and anal sex, 72–73; suicidal ecstasy, 72, 77
Billie #21 (Harris), x, 1–5, 9, 15, 18–19
black hypervisuality, 48
blackness: and abjection, 87; and brownness, 7–8; and enfleshment, 97; fungibility of (Hartman), 107; as (un)hidden witness, 105; and humanity, 6, 39, 96, 100; and pain, 35–36, 98–99; penetrated, 33; and the semiotic, 81; visual manifestation of, 97
black women: and abjection, 10; angry, 159; and consent, 34–37; as the fleshy limit of theory, 9; and gynecological experimentation, 46; as hyperfecund and hypersexual, 127–28; lesbian feminism, 22, 55–56, 61; and pain/pleasure, 2–3, 20
bling(-bling). *See* shine

Bluest Eye, The (Morrison), 139
body: and abjection, 87; as body, 77, 89; and breath, 166; and excess, 176; vs. flesh, 5–6, 97, 170; and food (Mexican), 70; and hygiene, 23; as ideal, 136; as an instrument of pleasure, 90; materiality of, 95; as mechanical, 120–21; of the mother, 169; and pain, 35–36, 98; as racial signifier, 90; and sensuality, 6, 9; strap-on as extension of, 81; as subject and object, 39, 48; and theory/knowledge, 9, 11, 17, 176–77
borderlands, 89, 92
bottoming, 83–84; Chong's, 134; in *Mommy is Coming* (Dunye), 83–86, 90; in *Untitled Fucking* (Hawk Swanson / Ibarra), 72, 91–92. *See also* topping
Bradley, Rizvana: on the haptic, 16, 52
Braunstein, Néstor: on jouissance, 13, 73, 78, 95, 115
Brewer Ball, Katherine: on the voice, 116
Briggs, Laura: on race and sexuality, 127–28
Brintnall, Kent: on tableaux of masculine suffering, 136
Browne, Simone: on blackness and surveillance, 97
brown femininity, 24, 26, 120, 176; as flesh, 137
brown jouissance, 3–5, 9, 16; and abjection, 88; and the aesthetic, 15–16; and belonging, 23; and *Billie #21* (Harris), 18–19; and the body as object/abject, 87; and "brown feeling" (Muñoz), 119; via citation, 15; and the commodity's scream, 165–66; in *Crush* (Catbagan), 144–45; in *From Here I Saw What Happened and I Cried* (Weems), 24, 115; and grief/joy, 115; in *In Love* (Chang), 140–41, 143; and kinship, 94; and (black and brown) labor, 158–59; and liquidity, 117; and the mobilization of flesh's liquidity, 60; in *Neapolitan*

(Bustamante), 141, 143; and opacity, 102; and *Origin of the Universe 1* (Thomas), 22, 48, 51, 53; and penetration, 71–72; as political, 11, 17; and queer femininity, 178; and selfhood, 13–14; and tactility, 52; and temporality, 127, 143; and voice, 95–96, 102; and witnessing, 95–96
brown paranoia, 122
burrito: as strap-on in *Indigurrito* (Bustamente), 91
Buse, Peter: on the Polaroid image, 18
Bush, Sandra, 54
Bustamante, Nao: *Indigurrito* (1992), 91; *Neapolitan* (2003), 23–24, 119–32, 141–43
butch/femme dynamic, 71–72, 90–91, 151
Butler, Judith: on desire for the mother, 171; on drag, 147; on gender, 73, 108; on lesbian femmes and subversion, 151; on the lesbian phallus, 81; on the libido-as-masculine, 148; on the semiotic, 74

Cacho, Lisa Marie: on value, 161
Caldwell, Molly, 144–45, 150–53, 156, 159–62. See *Crush* (Catbagan)
Califia, Pat: *Doing It for Daddy*, 84
Callahan, Yesha: on the black woman's body and Walker's Sugar Baby, 34
camp: as "a certain mode of aestheticism" (Sontag), 146; and femininity/gender, 147, 153; Ibarra's performances as, 11; as a strategy for minoritarian survival (Muñoz), 150; and upper middle-class gay male life, 150. See also pulp
Campt, Tina: on the conditional tense to speak of black feminist futurity, 174; on quiet, 106
cannibalism: in slave culture in the United States, 36
capitalism, global: and black and brown maternal absences, 170; and *Crush* (Catbagan), 156–166; and *A Subtlety* (Walker), 40
care: and the mammy, 32, 187n15, 188n17–18; and the mother, 168–69, 177; in *Neapolitan* (Bustamante), 128; self-care and pleasure, 63; in *Untitled Fucking* (Hawk Swanson / Ibarra), 22, 91–92; in Weems's work, 110, 114–16
castration: of the black man, 194; of the mother (fetish), 154
Catbagan, Maureen: *Crush* (2010–2012), 24–26, 144–45, 150–66
Chambers-Letson, Joshua: on black female flesh and possibility, 176; on black women and the name "mother," 170
Chang, Patty: *In Love* (2001), 23–24, 119–21, 133–43, 163
Chen, Mel, 14
Cheng, Anne Anlin, 22; on assimilation, 134, 171; on fetishism, 155; on the surface, 48–49, 51
Chicago, Judy: *The Dinner Party* (1979), 21, 27–31, 186n1
Chinn, Sarah: on Lorde, 62, 175
Chong, Annabel, 134, 137
Chow, Ray: on Foucault's *History of Sexuality*, 178
citation: and aggression, 163; and femmeness, 152; of Holiday by Harris, 2–5, 9, 15, 18–19
Clinton, George, 50
clitoris, 57–61; genital cutting, 191n50; myth of the black enlarged, 59–60
color: and emotion, 103, 110
Color Purple, The (Walker), 139
commodities: commodification of black pain, 33; commodity fetishism (Marx), 156; the commodity's scream (Moten), 165; people reduced to, 6, 107, 157; photographs from the Agassiz archive as, 111
consent, 34–36

consumption: in *The Dinner Party* (Chicago), 27–31; and mimesis, 164; in *A Subtlety* (Walker), 33–44
copyright: in Harvard's threatened suit against Weems, 111–12
Corregidora (Jones), 139
Courbet, Gustave: *The Origin of the World* (1866), 21
Coxx, Papi, 75. See also *Mommy is Coming* (Dunye)
crafting: 129–30
Crawley, Ashon: on voice and religion, 117
Crush (Catbagan), 24–26, 144–45, 150–66
crying. *See* weeping
Cuvier, Georges, 59

daddies, leather, 82–86; and whiteness, 84–85
Dailey, Meghan: on rhinestones in the work of Thomas, 49
Daly, Mary, 112
da Silva, Denise Ferreira: on the body as Thing, 158–59; on Irigaray's female lover, 176; on the subject and the Other, 13, 120
Davis, Betty, 50
Davis, Madeline: on femmes and subversion, 151
Deavere Smith, Anna: on *Billie #21* (Harris), 4; on Harris, 3
Declue, Jennifer: on the erotics of the bottom in *Mommy is Coming* (Dunye), 83
de Lauretis, Teresa: on lesbianism and the mother, 75
Deleuze, Gilles, 178: becoming-woman, 3; criticism of, 185n9
depression: as a strategy of minoritarian critique, 122
desire: and accumulation and exchange, 164; for black men, 36; diaspora as a queer horizon produced by (Ellis), 114; female, 74; and the fetish, 154; to hear the self, to hear the other, and to be heard as the other hears us, 107; for the mother, 73–75, 171; "repetition of suffocated desire" in Billie Holiday's singing (Moten), 1, 102; scopic, 10; space before, 74; and subjectivity, 7, 23; and Thingness (da Silva), 158
De Veaux, Alexis: on the spiritual voyages of Lorde, 112
deviance: and large clitorises, 59–60
Diderot, Denis: on acting and authenticity, 121
Dinner Party, The (Chicago), 21, 27–31, 186n1
diversity: as a tool to discipline subjects, 25
Doane, Mary Ann: on masquerade, 148
dolls: as eliciting racialized performances of violence, 98
domestic, the, 128–31; in *Attack of the Fifty-Foot Woman*, 146; in *Crush* (Catbagan), 152–58; in pulp, 146
Douglass, Frederick: Aunt Hester's scream, 165
Doyle, Jennifer: on *From Here I Saw What Happened and I Cried* (Weems), 99; on *Neapolitan* (Bustamante), 128–32; on *The Onion* (Abramovic), 137; on the sensuous relationship between artist, art, and viewer, 16–17
drag, 147, 199n6: temporal, 55
dualism: Cartesian, 11–12
Duggan, Lisa: on femme identity, 152
Dunye, Cheryl: *Mommy is Coming* (2012), 22, 75–89
Dworkin, Andrea: on penetration, 73
Dyer, Richard, 160

eating, 14; of an onion in *In Love* (Chang), 138–40; of an onion in *The Onion* (Abramovic), 137–38; Tompkins's analysis of, 28, 42
ecstasy: in *Billie #21* (Harris), 1; and subjectivity, 7; suicidal (Bersani), 72, 77

Ellington, Duke, 100
Ellis, Nadia: on diaspora as a queer horizon, 114
endurance, 135–139
Eng, David, 22; on assimilation, 134; on diaspora, 113
erotic, the: for Doyle, 16; for Foucault, 11–12; and funk, 11; for Horton-Stallings, 12; and the labia, 28; Latina labor and, 90; for Lorde, 63; and the photographs of *From Here I Saw What Happened and I Cried* (Weems), 114
excess: affective, 124, 159, 164; anality in relation to the maternal body as, 77; in Billie Holiday's voice, 1–2; that blackness produces (Scott), 82, 87; of a brown female body, 143; emotion, 123–24; flesh, 10; forms of embodiment, 3; and the gustatory, 70; of lack, 166; an open mouth suggesting, 1; ornamental, 128–29; parental affection, 133; of pleasure, 77; and the pornotrope, 9; productive, 24; responsiveness, 119, 125; sensation (jouissance), 13; the sensual as the space of, 16; sonic, 165; the spiritual and, 116; surface, 46–51; tears, 132; and the voice, 1–2, 115–16

family, 23; African American familial pathology, 139; fantasies of, 84–86; "reconfiguring the very notion of" (Johnson), 170; slavery's violation of the norms of the psychoanalytic, 108; values, 138
Fanon, Frantz, 22; on black masculinity, 142; on stereotype and phobia, 155; on subjectivity, 106; on white women's fantasies, 149–50
fantasy: and "excess flesh," 10; of home, 110; of mother (for Lorde), 174; rape, 149–50; of the surface, 51; and the "weepie," 132
feminine jouissance, 22, 73, 78–81, 87

feminine labor, 157–58
feminism: black, 32, 63; and *The Dinner Party* (Chicago), 186n1; feminist killjoys, 149; *Gut Feminism* (Wilson), 150; Hawk Swanson on, 69–70, 72; lesbian, 54–58, 61, 71, 75, 191n32, 193n22; orgasm and, 57–58; second wave, 56–57; and sexuality (Hollibaugh and Moraga), 71; white, 70–71, 92–93. *See also* womanism
femme, 150–53; and citation, 152; as "the queerest of queers" (Davis), 151. *See also* butch/femme dynamic
Ferguson, Roderick: on diversity, 25; on racialized labor, 7–8
fetishism: and black men, 155; and boundaries, 161; commodity (Marx), 156; and *Crush* (Catbagan), 25, 145, 153–56, 160–66; of desire, 166; and difference, 79; fetish videos, 153–55, 163–64; for Freud, 154; and ontological insecurity, 155; and the present, 124; racial (Amin), 200n32; and the "return" of the penis onto a woman's body, 80, 154; and surface, 51–52; and transparency, 48; and white feminine misery, 25, 160
fingering: and the lesbian phallus, 91; as "a technique of knowing in art and performance" (Bradley), 16; in *Untitled Fucking* (Hawk Swanson / Ibarra), 70
Firestone, Shulamith: on motherhood, 167–68
fisting: in *Mommy is Coming* (Dunye), 82–83
Fleetwood, Nicole: on opacity and "excess flesh," 10; on the visual manifestation of blackness, 97
flesh: excess, 10, 17; liquidity of, 29; location in space of, 38; mutability of, 14; regrowth of, 177; as the territory of the marginalized, 5; and time, 19; the transformation of black bodies into (Spillers), 5–6, 97

fleshiness: and the aesthetic, 16; of black bodies (and the materiality of the decorative), 50; and black femininity, 3; and brown jouissance, 3, 51; of chemistry, 44; of the instant, 18; of labor, 158–59; of materiality, 159; of the parental bond, 139; and pornotroping, 6–7, 9–12; and processes of objectification, 4, 7; and the production of selfhood, 4; and queer femininity, 178; of the surface, 55; and theorizing, 11; of the voice, 109, 115; Weems's, 115; and witnessing, 103
Foucault, Michel: "bodies and pleasures," 62; theorization of sexuality, 11–12, 23, 72–73, 178
Fraiman, Susan, 77
freedom: and fetishism, 155
Freeman, Elizabeth: on a fantasized original, 152; temporal drag, 55
Fresa y Chocolate (Gutiérrez Alea / Tabío), 24, 119, 122–25, 131–32, 141
Freud, Sigmund: on fetishism, 154, 156; and race, 22
friction: and the clitoris (tribbing), 57, 60–62; within feminism, 54–57; as a form of relationality and narcissism as a necessary form of self-creation, 22; frictional engagement and self-love, 64; and the vulva's materiality, 48
From Here I Saw What Happened and I Cried (Weems), 23–24, 95–118
funk: erotics of (Horton-Stallings), 11–12, 44, 50–51; and rhinestones, 50; and tribbing, 62

Galison, Peter: "machine ideal," 126
Garber, Linda: on the lesbian feminist, 56
gaze: and the black female body, 10, 46; male, 148; of the other, 34; scientific, 48
gentrification, 41
geopolitics, 38–39

Gerhard, Jane: on pleasure and liberation, 57–58; on the representation of Sojourner Truth in *The Dinner Party* (Chicago), 30; on the success of *The Dinner Party* (Chicago), 186n1
Getsy, David: on the sensuous relationship between artist, art, and viewer, 16–17
Gibson, Mel, 136
Gill, Lyndon: on the spiritual in the erotic, 197n58
Glissant, Édouard: on opacity, 14
God: Lacan's belief (?) in, 95; Seboulisa (goddess), 113; and spiritual excess, 117
Gopinath, Gayatri: on queer diaspora, 113–14
Gopnik, Blake: on the work of Kara Walker, 32–33, 44
grief: in *The Onion* (Abramovic), 137; and racialization, 23–24; and sexuality, 119–20
Griffin, Farah Jasmine: on Billie Holiday as a circulating public figure, 2; *If You Can't Be Free, Be a Mystery*, 10
Guattari, Félix: becoming-woman, 3
guilt: and black bodies in pain, 35–36; in *From Here I Saw What Happened and I Cried* (Weems), 97–99, 105; and misery, 149; white, 89, 98
Gumbs, Alexis P.: on mothering as queer, 114–15
Gutiérrez Alea, Tomás. See *Fresa y Chocolate* (Gutiérrez Alea / Tabío)

Halberstam, Jack: on tribbing and female masculinity, 60
Halperin, David: *How to Be Gay*, 150
Harkins, Gillian: on incest memoirs, 138; on incest vs. natality, 178
Harlow, Lil, 75. See also *Mommy is Coming* (Dunye)
Harris, Lyle Ashton: *Billie #21* (2002), 1–5, 9, 15, 18–19

Hart, Lynda: strap-on as "a real thing," 80
Hartman, Saidiya: on the fungibility of blackness, 107; on the lost mother, 170
Hawk Swanson, Amber: *Untitled Fucking* (2013), 22, 69–72, 88–94
Hayes, Allison: 145
Hayot, Eric: on the coolie stereotype, 135–36
Heath, Stephen: on femininity's relationship to artifice, 147
heels, high: in *Crush* (Catbagan), 24–25, 144, 152–55, 157, 165; in *Untitled Fucking* (Hawk Swanson / Ibarra), 70
Hemmings, Clare: on the lesbian feminist, 56
Hoang, Nyguen Tan: on bottoming, 83–84, 172
Holiday, Billie, 10, 15, 100; as signifier (in *Billie #21*), 4–5, 18–19; voice of, 1–2, 100–102, 109
Holland, Sharon Patricia: on the erotic, 197n58; on viscera and waste, 16
Hollibaugh, Amber, and Cherrie Moraga: on feminism and lesbianism, 71
Hong, Grace: on racial capital, 161; on workers of the global South, 162
Horton-Stallings, LaMonda: erotics of funk, 11–12; on sex work, 12
Hottentot Venus. *See* Baartman, Saartjie
Huffer, Lynne: on the catachrestic lips, 29; on motherhood, 167
hunger, 4–5, 9, 15, 40; as a form of brown jouissance, 18–19; and quiet, 106. *See also* appetite

"I": affectable, 13, 120, 158; as core of mother-father-child triangle, 55, 173; "as other to itself" (Jones), 2; stable (evacuated), 29; in the title of *From Here I Saw What Happened and I Cried* (Weems), 102–3
Ibarra, Xandra: and camp, 11; *Untitled Fucking* (2013), 22, 69–72, 88–94

iconicity: of Billie Holiday, 2, 18
I Know Why the Caged Bird Sings (Angelou), 138
imperialism, 89, 93, 160–61, 163
impermanence, 11
impossibility: of assimilation, 141; of a border between self and Other, 21, 29; and the coolie's body, 135–36; and fetishism, 154; of gendered and raced neutrality, 3; of grappling with blackness in tandem with gender and agency, 6; of individuality, 169; and intimacy (in the Bataillean sense), 18; of mother and father as positions for the enslaved, 108; of remaining only on the surface (Stockton), 52; of the singular subject, 28; of sovereign subjectivity, 9; the Thing as a space of, 13; of thinking Oedipality in relation to blackness and brownness, 174
incest, 73–74, 76, 138–39, 143, 174, 178. *See also* Oedipus complex
In Love (Chang), 23–24, 119–21, 133–43, 163
insatiability, 5, 19
instant, the, 18–19
interiority: and black intellectuals (for Spillers), 106; and drag, 147; and the labia, 28–29; and listening, 80; and opacity, 10, 13, 24, 102; restored, 108; and the subject, 120; and the surface, 49–53; and the voice, 95, 100–102, 106–7
intimacy, 7, 10, 18–19, 41–42, 68, 173; family, 77; and *Neapolitan* (Bustamante), 131; of the nose, 44
invisibility: and assimilation, 141; in *Crush* (Catbagan), 26, 145, 165–66; and femme identity, 151–52; and the mother, 167
Irigaray, Luce: and the denigration of the feminine, 39; on the feminist language of lips, 28–29, 37, 53; and the phallic economy, 38, 176; on spiritual excess, 117

Jagose, Annemarie: on Irigaray's lips essay, 28
Jardine, Alice: criticism of Deleuze, 185n9
jazz: Harris's series of self-portraits as (Deavere Smith), 3
Johnson, Barbara: on women and self-denial, 168
Johnson, E. Patrick: on "quare" vs. "queer," 176–77; on queer kinship, 170
Johnson, Jessica Marie: on Walker's Sugar Baby, 39–40
Johnson, Virginia. *See* Masters, William, and Virginia Johnson
Jones, Amelia: on performative self-portraits, 2
jouissance, 12–13; and anal sex, 72–73, 77; of being, 73–74, 87; beyond the word (Braunstein), 95; and the foreclosed mother, 87; and penetration, 77; of existing in the now, 127; and the voice (Barthes), 102, 116. *See* brown jouissance; feminine jouissance; phallic jouissance; "Spic Jouissance"

Keeling, Kara, 172
Keller, Yvonne: on lesbian pulp, 152
Kheshti, Roshanak: on listening as a loss of self, 79
Kim, Ju Yon: on Asian and Asian American performances of racialization, 135, 140
King, Tiffany Lethabo: on the relationship between slavery and white-settler colonialism, 8
kinship, 112–15, 173–74: and food, 138; and photography, 107–12
kissing: parents in *In Love* (Chang), 24, 119, 133, 141–43; and reading, 52–53
Klein, Melanie: on otherness and the infant, 168–69
knowledge: and the body, 11; new, 179; and possession, 59

Koedt, Anne: on sexuality and dissemination of physiological data, 57; on the vaginal orgasm, 58
Kristeva, Julia: on abjection, 87; on love for the mother and "the semiotic," 73–74, 76

LA riots, 135
labial, the: 28–29; and materiality, 29, 48; and proprioception, 38; and vulnerability, 21, 28–29, 37. *See also* lips; vulva
Lacan, Jacques, 78; and belief in God, 95; on invocatory drive, 107; jouissance, 12–13, 73, 95; as one-time owner of *The Origin of the World* (Courbet), 46
La Chica Boom. *See* Ibarra, Xandra
Landers, Sean, 53–54
latex gloves: in *Untitled Fucking* (Hawk Swanson / Ibarra), 22, 89, 91–92
laughter: and guilt, 35; as a result of accidental mother-fucking, 76, 78; and suffering, 34
Lee, Rachel: on Hayot's analysis of the coolie stereotype, 136
León, Christina: on the failure of some audiences to register Xandra Ibarra's performances as camp, 11
Likierman, Meira: on introjection and projection in children, 168
Lindsey, Treva B.: on Walker's Sugar Baby, 39–40
lips: in *Billie #21* (Harris), 2, 4; feminist language of (Irigaray), 28–29, 37, 53; meaning of, 187n7. *See also* labial, the
liquidity, 14, 109; and brown jouissance, 117; and the face, 105; the labia as a marker of flesh's, 29
listening: feminine jouissance as the jouissance of, 78–80; to photographs, 103, 114, 118; and topping, 22, 80, 89
loop, the, 24, 119, 121, 124–27, 137, 141–43
Lorde, Audre: on abuse, 34–35; on the erotic, 63, 66, 175; on kinship, 112–15,

173–74; and lesbian feminism, 55–56, 62, 176–77; on masturbation as a healing practice, 65; on political black lesbianism, 175; and womanism, 22, 53, 57; *Zami: A New Spelling of My Name*, 55, 112, 173–74, 177
Lowe, Lisa: on intimacy, 41–43
Luciano, Dana: on affect and sexuality, 23, 119–20; on sensation and the present, 124

MacKinnon, Catharine: on penetration, 73
Malone, Gloria: on patrons who posed with Walker's Sugar Baby in a sexually suggestive manner, 34
mammy, 170, 187n15, 188nn17–19, 189n20; Walker's Sugar Baby as, 31–33
Manalasan, Martin: on olfaction, 44
Mapplethorpe, Robert, 136
Marder, Elissa: maternal function, 109, 168, 201n4
Marriot, David: on fetishism, 154–55
Marx, Karl, 160, 165–66; commodity fetishism, 156
masochism: female, 137, 149–50; and masculinity, 136
masquerade, 146–49, 151, 154–55, 157
Masters, William, and Virginia Johnson, 57, 125–26
masturbation, 64–65; and Bustamante's *Neapolitan*, 132, 143; as a healing practice (Lorde), 65; recorded by Masters and Johnson, 125–26
McElya, Micki: on the mammy, 32; on the myth of the faithful slave, 188n16
McHugh, Kathleen: on femme identity, 152
McMillan, Uri, 14; "objecthood," 87–88
melancholy: of assimilation, 22, 134, 171; and gender incorporation (Butler), 147; and the maternal, 170–71; and misery, 147, 150

melodrama, 128, 131–32, 141, 198n36
melting: of the sugary blackamoors in Walker's *A Subtlety*, 42–45
Memmi, Albert, 22
MILF, 105, 193n23
mimesis, 145, 162–64; and brown jouissance, 25
Mintz, Sidney: on appetite as a driving force in colonialism, 40
misery: into aggression, 153; and melancholy, 147, 150; white feminine, 25, 149–50, 153, 160
model minority, 134–35, 160
Modleski, Tania: on melodrama's temporality, 132
Mommy Is Coming (Dunye), 22, 75–89
Moraga, Cherrie. *See* Hollibaugh, Amber, and Cherrie Moraga
Morgenson, Scott: settler sexuality, 8
Moten, Fred: on Billie Holiday's voice, 1–2, 100–102, 109; on the commodity, 165; on the material and the maternal, 166, 170, 172; on photographs bearing "phonic substance," 103, 172; on photography, 110, 114; on the resistance of the object, 171
mother, the, 167–79, 193n24: as absence, 170; "castrated," 154; desire for, 73; as impossible, 108; and jouissance, 87; maternal breast, 168; maternal/material, 110; 166; maternal function (Marder), 109, 168, 201n4; MILF, 105, 193n23; m/Other, 73–76, 79, 169, 172; mothering (in *From Here I Saw What Happened and I Cried* [Weems]), 24, 107–10, 114; motherland, 110; mother tongue, 102; photography as a silencing of the (Moten), 114; as a place, 172–73; and queer black sexuality, 55; and queer femininity, 167–68; and race, 170; "sodomitical maternity" (Nelson), 77; spatial relationship with (Lorde), 113. *See also* Oedipus complex

mourning: at the history of slavery and racism, 99; interrupted, 33; and the mother, 26, 109; *Neapolitan* (Bustamante) as Chicana, 121–22
mouth, the: in *Billie #21* (Harris), 1; and consumption, 28, of the mother (Lorde), 174; and the voice, 116, 109, 116. *See also* lips
Mulvey, Laura: on "weepies," 132
Muñoz, José Esteban, 114: on "brown feeling," 10, 119, 123; on brown paranoia, 122; "Latino camp," 128, 150; on Latinx affect, 124; melodrama in *Neapolitan* (Bustamante), 131; on queerness, 173; on subject/object oscillation, 127; whiteness as lack, 134
Murray, Yxta: on ownership and rights, 111–12

Nancy, Jean Luc: on feminine jouissance, 78; on listening, 80
narcissism: impersonal (Bersani and Phillips), 65–66; as self-creation, 22; the vulva's materiality and, 48
Nash, Jennifer: on the black female body as an injured site, 98; on ethnography and pornography, 59; on love within black feminist thought, 63–64
Neapolitan (Bustamante), 23–24, 119–32, 141–43
Nelson, Maggie: "sodomitical maternity," 77
Newton, Esther: on drag, 147, 199n6
Nixon, Angelique: on Lorde's exploration of her identity and home through the maternal line, 174
nostalgia: in Thomas's paintings, 53
Nyong'o, Tavia: on *A Subtlety* (Walker), 40–41, 43–44

Ochoa, Marcía: on viscera and waste, 16
Oedipus complex, 77, 171, 174: and the enslaved, 108; and the sovereign subject, 73; as a technology of domination, 8, 22–23
opacity, 10–16, 20–24, 29; and depression, 122; and excess surface, 46–51, 61; and the mother's body, 169; of otherness, 29, 79; perverse, 143; of perversion, 139; of the photographic form, 114; of the present, 141; of sound, 100; and topping, 22; and tribbing, 62; and vulnerability, 51; of Weems, 103; of white femininity, 155
Origin of the Universe 1 (Thomas), 21–22, 46–68
Origin of the Universe 2 (Thomas), 66–68
Origin of the World, The (Courbet), 21, 46–48, 54, 57, 63
ornamentation, 48–49
otherness: and feminine jouissance, 78; hovering around Holiday and Harris, 15; lips and, 29; and the maternal breast, 168; opacity of, 29, 79; physical and biological radical openness toward, 5
Our Bodies, Ourselves, 64–65

Page, Betty, 70
panopticon, 97
Parisi, Luciana: on sex in the age of cybernetics, 125
Parreñas, Rhacel Salazar: on Filipino women as "the quintessential service workers of globalization," 157–58
Parreñas Shimizu, Celine: on perversity and the bottoming of Annabel Chong, 134
part objects, 51
Pellegrini, Ann: on Riviere's patient, 149–50
Pérez, Hiram: on the performing brown body, 36
Pérez, Roy: on relation and sensuality, 16
perversion: in *In Love* (Chang), 119, 133–43; in *The Onion* (Abramovic), 137;

racialized perversity, 8, 24, 138; and segregation, 60
Pethes, Nicholas: on spirit photography, 118
phallic jouissance, 13, 22, 73, 78
phallocentrism, 38–39, 176, 178
phallus: lesbian, 81, 91; surrogate, 154. *See* strap-on
Phillips, Adam: impersonal narcissism, 65–66
photograph, the: as material instantiation of the instant, 18–19; spirit photography, 117–18; as a technology of embodiment (Jones), 2; as a technology of reproduction and mothering, 107–10; and violence, 97
pleasure: "bodies and pleasures" (Foucault), 62; body as an instrument of, 90; excess of, 77; of intimate familial power, 84–86; and jouissance, 13; and liberation, 57–58; and pain of black women, 2–3, 20; self-care and, 63; and slavery, 39, 85
Polaroid: as material instantiation of the instant, 18–19
pornography: as emphasizing antisociality and inauthentic feelings (Lorde), 56; and ethnography, 59; vs. fine art, 46–47
pornotroping, 5–13, 178; and abjection, 87; and femininity, 167; and grief, 23; and mothers/mothering, 170
possession: and desire, 7; and hunger, 15; of the Other, 79
power: in bed, 71, 90–91; and the female body, 158; through hot sauce, 70; and the individual (Schuller), 42; and penetration, 71–73
powerlessness: in being consumed, 37; and gender, 108; and pornotroping, 6
Powers, Nicholas: rage at the commodification of black pain, 33–34
prick. *See* phallus; punctum (Barthes)

proprioception, 27, 29–30, 36–38, 45
psychoanalysis: and gender, 108; and intersubjectivity, 23; and the maternal, 170–71; and race, 22. *See also* fetishism; Freud, Sigmund; Oedipus complex
Puar, Jasbir: on race and geopolitics, 38–39
pulp, 146, 163–64; lesbian, 152–53. *See also* camp
punctum (Barthes), 106
puncture: of Billie Holiday's head with a gardenia'd hatpin, 1; of masculinity in submission and penetration, 72; punctum (Barthes), 106

Quashie, Kevin: on quiet, 106
queer: diaspora, 113–14; femininity, 26, 167–68, 176–78; sex, 60–61, 69–72, 82–83; value, 164
quiet, 106–7
Quiroga, José: on *Fresa y Chocolate* (Gutiérrez Alea / Tabío), 131

Ramos, Iván: on *Untitled Fucking* (Hawk Swanson / Ibarra), 69–70, 90
reading: empathetic, 17–18; and kissing, 52–53
repetition: and camp, 150; comfort of, 143; and gender, 108; in the semiotic, 74; "of suffocated desire" in Billie Holiday's singing (Moten), 1; of violation of the black woman's body, 34. *See also* loop, the
reproduction: affective (Weems), 164; and photography, 107–10; self-replication, 109
residue: national, 132; of the past within the present, 200n32; or race/racialization, 56, 90, 133; of self-determination, 58; Thomas's emphasis on, 54–55, 61, 63
rhinestones: and funk, 50; as a record of a practice of self-love, 62; as vulvic embellishment, 21, 46–54, 190n12

Rich, Adrienne: de Lauretis on "Compulsory Heterosexuality and Lesbian Existence," 75
Riskin, Jessica: on the defecating duck, 120
Riviere, Joan: "Womanliness as Masquerade" (1929), 146–50, 157
Roach, Joseph: on acting and authenticity, 121
Roberts, Lacey Jane: on the queerness of crafting, 130
Rodríguez, Juana María: on queers and the erotic pleasure of intimate familial power, 84–86; on *Untitled Fucking* (Hawk Swanson / Ibarra), 69–70, 90
Rooney, Kara: on Walker's Sugar Baby and black feminism, 32
Rusert, Britt: on fugitive science, 178–79

sacrifice: in Harris's citation of Holiday, 4; and motherhood, 168
safer sex: as referenced in *Untitled Fucking* (Hawk Swanson / Ibarra), 91–92
San Pablo Burns, Lucy Mae: on mimesis and Filipinos, 162
Schuller, Kyla: on brown bodies as atavistic, 142; on power, 42; on women's "hyperimpressibility," 123
scissoring. *See* tribbing
Scott, Dareick: on abjection, 82, 85–86
scream, the, 165–66
Seboulisa, in "Dahomey" (Lorde), 113
Sedgwick, Eve: on anality and jouissance, 77
See, Sarita: on Filipino America, 160, 163
self-denial: and the mother, 168
selfhood: brown jouissance and the production of, 13; as collective and diasporic, 107; and consumption, 28; exceeding the "I," 172; and gender (for Harris), 3; and hunger, 5; matrilineal, 54–55; permeable, 28, 37; plural self, 2–3, 5, 15, 17; strategic possibilities of, 2
self-love, 62–68
semiotic, the: for Kristeva, 74; location of blackness in, 81
sensuality, 20–21: and the aesthetic, 16–17; ambiguities afforded by, 93; and *Billie #21* (Harris), 15; and blackness, 82, 87; and the captive body, 6, 9; and fleshiness, 178; and knowledge, 179; and the labial, 29; in Lorde's work, 174–75, 177; and the maternal/reproductive, 76–77, 169–78; and *Origin of the Universe 1* (Thomas), 55–57; outside of the penile and Oedipal, 91; and the paternal, 81; and perversion, 134; as political, 176; and relation, 16; sensual knowledge production, 65; of surface, 68; and Walker's Sugar Baby, 37–44
Shimikawa, Karen: on foreignness and assimilation, 140–41
shine: in *Billie #21* (Harris), 2–3; and the rhinestone, 48–50; the use of shine by black diasporic artists (Thompson), 50
Silver, Leigh: on the smell of the melting blackamoors in Walker's *A Subtlety*, 44
Silverman, Kaja: on the mother and female desire, 74; on photography, 18
simulacrum: fetishist as operating within the realm of the, 154; lesbian-dicks as the ultimate, 80
Sly and the Family Stone, 50
smell: in *A Subtlety* (Walker), 21, 44; Lorde's memory of, 173
Smith, Roberta: on Thomas's use of quotation, 47; on Walker's Sugar Baby as agential, 33
Society for Psychical Research (SPR), 118
Somerville, Siobhan: on large clitorises and deviance, 59
Sontag, Susan: on camp, 146, 150
spectatorship: and femininity, 148; and race, 23; and Walker's *A Subtlety* installation, 33–36

speech: and interiority (Spillers), 106–7; poetic, 74; and sex, 89; the voice as that which exceeds mere, 95. *See also* voice
spiciness: stereotype of the "hot 'n' spicy spic," 124; in *Untitled Fucking* (Hawk Swanson / Ibarra), 69–70
"Spic Jouissance" (Ibarra): Tapatía as, 93
Spillers, Hortense, 168: on (the failures of) *The Dinner Party* (Chicago), 30–31; on interiority and speech, 106–7; on the native, 8; on pornotroping, 5–6, 97, 108, 167, 170; on psychoanalysis, 23, 108
spiritual, the: and the Black Pentecostal Church (Crawley), 117; and the diasporic, 117; spirit photography, 117–18; and tears, 118; and the voice, 115–18
Spivak, Gayatri Chakravorty, 164; on the work of the infant as translation, 169
Stephens, Michelle: on desires to hear and be heard, 107
Stockton, Kathryn Bond: on kissing, 52–53
stomping: as an act of creation, 165–66; as a form of feminine agency, 151; as a rejection of domesticity, 152
strap-on: burrito in *Indigurrito* (Bustamente) as, 91; in *Mommy is Coming* (Dunye), 79; as "a real thing" (Hart), 80; Tapatío bottle in *Untitled Fucking* (Hawk Swanson / Ibarra) as, 22, 69, 89–93; as threatening (Butler), 81
subjectivity: and becoming flesh, 6; and desire, 23; and gender, 108; interiority as a balm against, 106; and masquerade, 148; sovereign, 5–6, 9, 12–15, 36–38, 45, 73; subject/object oscillation, 127, 142, 165
Subtlety, A (Walker), 21, 31–45, 146

Tabío, Juan Carlos. *See Fresa y Chocolate* (Gutiérrez Alea / Tabío)
Tadiar, Neferti X. M.: on mimesis and consumption, 164; on whiteness, 160–62

Takagi, Dana: on the visibility of racial identity, 38
Tapatía, 69; as "Spic Jouissance," 93
Tapatío bottle: as strap-on in *Untitled Fucking* (Hawk Swanson / Ibarra), 22, 69, 89–93
Tapert, Maggie, 75. See also *Mommy is Coming* (Dunye)
teeth: in *Billie #21* (Harris), 1–2
theory: and the body, 9, 11, 17, 176–77
Thingness: 13; and agency, 88; of black and brown flesh, 158–59; of Harris's flesh, 15; as a space of impossibility, 13; strap-on as "a real thing," 80–81; and surface, 49–50
Thomas, Mickalene: *Origin of the Universe 1* (2012), 21–22, 46–68; *Origin of the Universe 2* (2012), 66–68
Thompson, Krista: on the use of shine by black diasporic artists, 50
Thompson, Malik: on Walker's *A Subtlety* and becoming-spectacle, 35–36
Thompson, Nato: on Walker's *A Subtlety*, 40
time: being in, 19; and decay, 42–45; fetishization of the moment, 124; and melodrama, 132; reverse temporality in Chang's *In Love*, 138–43. *See also* loop, the
Tompkins, Kyla Wazana, 14; analysis of eating, 42; on "quare" and materiality, 177; on viscera and waste, 16
topping: as deep listening, 22, 80, 89; in *Untitled Fucking* (Hawk Swanson / Ibarra), 70, 72, 89–92. *See also* bottoming
toys: and noise, 165; and waste, 156, 162
translation, 38; the work of the infant as (Spivak), 169
Traub, Valerie: on tribbing, 60
tribbing, 60–62
trinkets, plastic: used in *Crush* (Catbagan), 156; used in *A Subtlety* (Walker), 42–43. *See also* toys

Truth, Sojourner: as represented in *The Dinner Party* (Chicago), 30

Ulysses (technologically enhanced dildo), 125–26
Untitled Fucking (Hawk Swanson / Ibarra), 22, 69–72, 88–94

Vaccaro, Jeanne: on crafting, 130
vagina: as void (in Courbet's *The Origin of the World*), 57
vajazzling, 190n12
value: queer, 164; violence and, 161
Venus Hottentot. *See* Baartman, Saartjie
vibrator, 125–28, 198n22; emotional, 124, 132
Viego, Antonio: on the untranslatability of traditional Latino maladies, 124
violence: individuality as the product of, 169; and photography, 97; and pornotroping, 6; and the self, 68; and sexuality, 7; and value, 161
virality: and brown jouissance, 25; and value, 164; viral videos, 163–64
visual: manifestation of blackness, 97; primacy of the, 38; quotation, 47
voice: of Billie Holiday, 1–2, 100–102, 109; excess and the, 1–2, 115–16; grain of the, 102, 109, 116; and interiority, 95, 100–102, 106–7; and the spiritual, 115–18
vulnerability: and anal sex, 83; and *Billie #21* (Harris), 5; of bodies within racist and patriarchal hierarchies, 61; and the breath, 166; emasculation, 81; and the labial, 21, 28–29, 37; and opacity, 51; as part of "a real life," 78; and the Polaroid, 19; and quiet, 106; and suffering, 136; the underside of fantasies of omnipotence, 169; and YouTube virality, 163–64
vulva: the black, 20–21, 27, 33, 46–48, 51; and *The Dinner Party*, 30; that eats / is eaten, 28; and tribbing, 61; of Walker's Sugar Baby, 33

Walker, Alice, 32, 58; *The Color Purple*, 139; on womanism, 55–56, 64, 68
Walker, Kara: *A Subtlety* (2014), 21, 31–45, 146
Wallis, Brian: on Weems's *From Here I Saw What Happened and I Cried*, 105
Walton, Jean: on Riviere's patient, 149–50
waste, 16; plastic as, 43, 156; production of, 161–62, 164–66
Watts, Stephanye: on being enraged by certain other attendees at Walker's *A Subtlety* installation, 33–34
Weeks, Kathi: on feminine labor, 157
Weems, Carrie Mae: *From Here I Saw What Happened and I Cried* (1995–1996), 23–24, 95–118
weeping: on cue, 121; from emotional impact, 34; in *In Love* (Chang), 110, 136–42; invoked by Weems's *From Here I Saw What Happened and I Cried*, 99; in *Neapolitan* (Bustamante), 110–28, 131–32; in *The Onion* (Abramovic), 137; as performance, 24, 121; and photography, 103; out of rage, 33; as referenced in the title of Weems's *From Here I Saw What Happened and I Cried*, 98–99, 103–5
Weheliye, Alex: on desire and pornotropic enfleshment, 7; on hunger, 4–5, 40; on violence and the pornotrope, 9
Wesling, Meg: on "queer value," 164
Westbrook, Lindsey: on *Neapolitan* (Bustamante) as Chicana mourning, 121–23
white femininity, 25, 144–66
white supremacy: and the production of blackness and brownness, 8; and the production of flesh, 6
Williams, Linda: on tribbing, 60; on visibility and female sexuality, 46–47

Wilson, Elizabeth: on feminine aggression, 150
Wilson, Jackie Napolean: *Hidden Witness*, 96, 102
Wilson Bryan, Julia: on craft, 130
Wittig, Monique: on lesbians vs. women, 58
womanism, 22, 53–68
"Womanliness as Masquerade" (Riviere), 146–50, 157
Woodward, Vincent: on cannibalism in slave culture in the United States, 36
World's Biggest Gangbang, The, 134, 137

Worley, Jennifer: on lesbian pulp, 152
woundedness, 23–24, spectacularization of,
Wright, Michelle: on Lorde's deployment of diaspora, 113

"yes, and": and Afropessimism, 9
"you": devoured through the mouth (in Lorde's "Meet"), 175; use of in Weems's *From Here I Saw What Happened and I Cried*, 99–100, 108

Zami: A New Spelling of My Name (Lorde), 55, 112, 173–74, 177

ABOUT THE AUTHOR

Amber Jamilla Musser is Associate Professor of American Studies at George Washington University and the author of *Sensational Flesh: Race, Power, and Masochism*, also published by New York University Press.

www.ingramcontent.com/pod-product-compliance
Lightning Source LLC
Chambersburg PA
CBHW020404080526
44584CB00014B/1170